MW01701979

The Admiral

By *Albert Gleaves, USN*

Also by Albert Gleaves

James Lawrence, United States Navy, Commander of the "Chesapeake"

A History of the Transport Service

The Life of an American Sailor: Rear Admiral William Hensley Emore, United States Navy, From His Letters and Memoirs

Life and Letters of Rear Admiral Stephen B. Luce, U.S. Navy, Founder of the Naval War College

DECORATIONS AND AWARDS

Distinguished Service Medal
By the U.S. President

Distinguished Service Medal
By the U.S. War Department

War Cross with Lime Tree Leaves
By President, Republic Czechoslovak

Order of the Striped Tiger (Wen Hu), First Class
By President, China

Grand Cordon of the Sacred Treasury
By Japanese Government

Commander of the Legion of Honor
By French Government

The Admiral

The Memoirs of
Albert Gleaves, USN

Foreword by James D. Watkins, *Admiral, USN*

Preface by William P. Lawrence
Vice Admiral, USN

HOPE
Publishing House

Pasadena,

California

Presented to
Evelina Porter Gleaves Cohen
on her 90th birthday,
May 26, 1985,
by her family

Manuscript editor: Faith Annette Sand

Cover design: Mary McCormick

Art director: Harold Burch

Cover: Facsimile of letter written by
Admiral Gleaves to his daughter, Anne.

Library of Congress Cataloging in Publication Data

Gleaves, Albert, 1858-1937
The Admiral: the memoirs of Albert Gleaves,
Admiral, USN.

Includes index,
1. Gleaves, Albert, 1858-1937. 2. Admirals—United
States—Biography. 3. United States. Navy-Biography.
I. Title.
V63.G54A33 1985 359'.0092'4 [B] 85-8419
ISBN 0-932727-02-6

To

Evelina Heap Gleaves

and our children

Anne Heap Gleaves VanMetre

and

Evelina Porter Gleaves Cohen

and their children

1934

The Admiral

Contents

Foreword

This memoir by Admiral Albert Gleaves, which discusses a rich seagoing career that extended over almost five decades, will be read, enjoyed and cherished by all who are interested in our nation's naval heritage of going down to the sea in ships.

When Albert Gleaves first entered the fleet after graduating from the U.S. Naval Academy in 1877, he served in a navy largely inherited from the Civil War. He vividly describes his experiences in the old navy which was giving way to a modern fleet of steel and steam; he served in several warship classes that emerged in the last two decades of the 19th century. Admiral Gleaves' colorful accounts of his cruises to the South Atlantic, the Mediterranean and the Western Pacific during his early years in the fleet demonstrate our navy's long tradition of representing the United States throughout the world.

In 1897, Admiral Gleaves assumed his first command, USS *Cushing,* the navy's first modern torpedo boat and progenitor of the 20th century destroyer. Although Admiral Gleaves later commanded larger vessels, his special interest in the development of the navy's destroyer forces was evident throughout the rest of his career.

When the United States entered World War I, Albert Gleaves, then a rear admiral, was Commander Destroyers Atlantic Fleet. The critical role played by those vessels in defending the North Atlantic sea lanes from German submarines rested on the preparations made by Albert Gleaves and his fellow destroyer pioneers. But, as the conflict unfolded, the admiral received new orders as Comander Cruisers and Transport Force. That organization ferried approximately one million American soldiers to France. Remarkably, not a single soldier lost his life at sea during this demonstration of American sea power. Their unique story is a classic example of naval power projection.

Albert Gleaves concludes his stirring reminiscences with a fascinating discussion of his activities as Commander in Chief, Asiatic Fleet between 1919 and 1921. In addition to operating off the coast of China, the Asiatic Fleet carried out the complex task of supporting U.S. policy in Siberia, where civil conflict raged between communist and non-communist Russian forces. Admiral Gleaves also describes his frequent contacts with Japanese officials at a time when tension was growing between the United States and Japan.

Although Admiral Gleaves concentrates his memoirs on his experiences as a seagoing officer, readers should bear in mind that the admiral also was a prolific naval writer. Before and after his retirmenet in 1922, he published biographies of three notable naval officers (James Lawrence, William H. Emory and Stephen B. Luce), a history of the Cruiser and Transport Force, and many articles on professional subjects. Considering this literary background, the professional quality of the admiral's memoirs is hardly surprising.

This fine work, from the able pen of an officer who served his country with great distinction, is a welcome addition to the published literature about our navy. This book's appearance serves as a reminder that our naval service's traditions and legends were laid by Admiral Albert Gleaves and other gifted leaders. These helped shape the United States Navy in a very exciting and dynamic time. We who serve today owe them a debt of thanks.

James D. Watkins
Admiral, U.S. Navy

Preface

As a boy growing up in Nashville, Tennessee, I used to play with my friends in Centennial Park near my family home. The principal landmark of Centennial Park—developed in the 1890s to celebrate the 100th anniversary of Tennessee's becoming a state in 1797—was the full-scale copy of the Parthenon in Athens, Greece. This magnificent structure plus the presence of a large number of schools and universities in Nashville has caused our city to be referred to as the "Athens of the South".

However, the structure in the park that most appealed to me was the concrete replica of the bow of a navy ship from the World War I era. As young boys are wont to do, my pals and I spent endless hours climbing over this structure imagining ourselves engaged in fierce naval battles.

This activity stimulated an early interest on my part in the navy. I remember listening raptly as my father talked of the illustrious naval hero and fellow Nashvillian, Admiral Albert Gleaves, who was famed for his position on top leadership in the navy during World War I and for his success at brilliantly and safely transporting a million American troops to and from Europe while serving as the commander of the transport forces.

Our country honored Admiral Gleaves for his achievements with its highest decorations; Nashville honored him by placing his bust in the capitol. I recall proudly viewing this when I visited our statehouse.

These early influences stimulated my interest as a teenager to attend the Naval Academy. There I was pleased to encounter another bust of my fellow Nashvillian on display in the Naval Academy's Memorial Hall where our most famous naval heroes are honored. I proudly pointed this out to my fellow midshipmen. I also studied extensively as a midshipman about Admiral Gleaves' exploits during World War I and how he developed convoy tactics that have been employed with great success by the navy in subsequent conflicts.

In 1978 when I returned to the Academy as superintendent, I was pleased to find a portrait of Admiral Gleaves hanging in the Naval Academy Museum. I asked the museum director to move this portrait to my office so I could display it to the many prominent guests who visited me there. As I daily viewed the admiral's distinguished countenance, I was inspired to measure up to the high standards he maintained during his career and also reminded of the lofty traditions of our "Volunteer State".

I am extremely pleased that the family of Admiral Gleaves has consented to publish his memoirs. This work will be an immensely valuable contribution to naval history and serve as a wonderful tribute to one of our greatest naval leaders.

William P. Lawrence
Vice Admiral, U.S. Navy

Introduction

Trevelyan says, "The most devout believers in the doctrine of the transmission of family qualities will be content with tracing back descent through four generations". Four generations is all of which I have knowledge, but it is sufficient.

I know little of the family of my father, Henry Albert Gleaves. His forebears came to Tennessee from Virginia before Tennessee was a state. His father and grandfather, Thomas and Michael, were farmers. The latter fought in the battle of Kings Mountain, presumably under Shelby.

His maternal grandfather, Henry Bowyer, was a lieutenant of the First Continental Dragoons—"Light Horse" Harry Lee's regiment—and later a member of the Cincinnati. After my marriage I found I was related through the Bowyers to my wife, but the interval of a century or more made our happy union quite legal.

Michael Gleaves prospered, and for his services received from the government a grant of 700 acres of land in Jones Bend not far from the Hermitage. During World War I the DuPont Company bought this property and established the "Old Hickory Powder Mills" there.

My mother's great grandfather, John Tannehill, came to this country from Scotland and settled near Pittsburgh in the early part of the 17th Century. He had seven sons all of whom are said to have served in the Revolutionary army, but the names of only two appear in Hammersley's Register—Adamson and Josiah. The former, a captain of the line, rose to rank of brigadier general, and the latter, an ensign in the 9th Virginia during the Revolution, afterwards transferred to the Paymaster's Department. Both served with Washington at Valley Forge and after the war lived in Pittsburgh. There they became prominent in civil affairs and both were members of the Pennsylvania House of Burgesses. General Tannehill also served in Congress (1811-13).

Josiah Tannehill was my grandfather's father. He married Maria Wilkins, the sister of Judge William Wilkins, who held various important offices—U.S. Senator, Secretary of War, Member of Congress and Minister to Russia. Another brother, John Wilkins, was quartermaster general of the army during the War of 1812.

My grandfather, Wilkins Tannehill, married Eliza Dewees, a direct descendant of William Rittenhouse who built the old paper mill on the Wissahickon Creek in Philadelphia's Fairmont Park. It is a strange coincidence that I am now (1935) living on the Old Lancaster Road where my great-grandmother Dewees passed over 150 years ago in a covered wagon with her family, including a newborn baby, on her way to Lexington, Kentucky. That journey lasted some 90 days. The baby was my grandmother, Elizabeth.

I know little of my grandfather's early life, except that as a young man Judge Wilkins sent him to Nashville, Tennessee, to establish a trading post with the Indians. He lived there from 1808 until his death in 1858. He was a literateur and wrote several books that are in the Library of Congress.

As Dominie Sampson said of an Indian colonel, he was "a man of great erudition considering his limited opportunities". Wilkins Tannehill became a leading Mason and attained the 32nd or 33rd degree. For many years he and Andrew Jackson, a close friend, alternated in the office of past master of the Tennessee Lodges. He authored a manual of Free Masonry which for 50 years after his death was used as a textbook in the Lodges of Tennessee.

He also wrote *A History of Roman Literature from the Earliest Times to the End of the 15th Century.* The latter, long out of print, occupies only a small niche in the Temple of Literature. In the preface he modestly writes of this

> attempt by a "backwoodsman" without any opportunity for consulting extensive libraries, to condense and comprise within narrow compass the most promising and interesting events, connected with the progress of literary and scientific improvement, from the earliest period through a long succession of ages, and amidst a great variety of circumstances.

Mr. Tannehill was one of the orators at the laying of the cornerstone of the state capitol on July 4, 1845, and he welcomed to Nashville such personages as Lafayette, Monroe and Jackson. He was also editor of the Nashville *Whig* and the *Herald.*

When General Lafayette came to America to lay the cornerstone of the monument at Bunker Hill in 1825 he visited Nashville. Mr. Tannehill was then mayor and received the general at the boat landing. At the banquet which was given by the city to the general, and at which Governor Campbell presided, the marquis was escorted to his place on the dais by General Jackson and my grandfather. At the reception and banquet given to Lafayette by the Masons, Mr. Tannehill presided.

The W. T. Berry & Co. Book Store in Nashville was owned by the three sons-in-law of Wilkins Tannehill—Berry, Gleaves and Bayless. Until the Civil War it was probably the most prosperous in the South. Like the old Corner Book Store in Boston, it was more like a club than a place of business. As a lad I recall often seeing there Generals Kirby Smith, Bushrod Johnson and Ewell. The latter with his wooden leg especially excited my attention.

Old "Major" Harris, as he was called in Nashville, who really was a pay director in the navy on the retired list, was a frequent visitor and gave me no end of advice when I received my appointment to the Naval Academy. "Keep your own accounts," he said, "and be careful how you eat fruit in the tropics."

Our pastor said, "Remember, a wise head holds a still tongue". Alas, I fear I have not always followed his advice!

1 At the Naval Academy

From earliest boyhood the navy had a strong fascination for me, which was strange for I was an inland lad with no sea affiliations or traditions except for my cousin Albert Gleaves Berry who graduated from the Naval Academy with honors in 1869. I was born in Nashville, Tennessee on January 1, 1858, and can just remember certain excitements in connection with the early part of the Civil War.

My vague recollections of that time are the review of the Rock City Guards by General Beauregard in 1862, which I witnessed from our nursery window, and the "panic of Nashville" when the Union gunboats came up the Cumberland River to assist the army. I distinctly remember the booming of the guns when Thomas drove back Hood in the Brentwood Hills between Nashville and Franklin where the battles were fought in 1864. But even clearer, I recall the salutes fired from the batteries on Capitol Hill (at the foot of which was our home) to celebrate the surrender of Lee at Appomattox. Then after that I remember the hundreds of paroled Confederate soldiers in front of General Thomas' headquarters on High Street.

When news came of the assassination of Lincoln, one of the young officers on General Thomas' staff advised my mother to put the proper mourning draperies on our home. She had not thought of doing this as she did not realize that we were directly on the line of the march of the Federal troops.

When I was 15 years old, Horace Maynard, Congressman at Large from Tennessee, appointed me to the Naval Academy as cadet midshipman at the request of my uncle, W. T. Berry, a strong Union man. Years later, in 1881, when Mr. Maynard was Minister to Constantinople, I was serving in the *Nipsic* in the Mediterranean. Unfortunately, he left Turkey just before the ship arrived so I missed meeting him, to my deep regret. He was a man of distinction who had served his state and country well. One of his sons, Commander Washburne Maynard, was presented with a sword by the citizens of Nashville for his services in the Spanish War.

It was arranged that a friend of my father's who lived in Philadelphia should take me to the Naval Academy, but this plan fell through and I took the trip alone. On a bright afternoon in June 1873

I arrived at the old station on Main Street in Annapolis and had set out for the Maryland Hotel when another boy, walking along the street, overtook me. He was about my own age.

"Are you going to the Naval Academy?"

"Yes."

"Ever been here before?"

"No."

"Well, you'll probably bilge. Nearly everyone does the first time. I did last September, but your congressman will probably reappoint you. They usually do."

"What do you mean by 'bilge'?" I asked.

"Fail in the examinations. They are very difficult."

It had never occurred to me that there was any doubt of my passing the examination.

At supper shortly afterwards, my newfound friend said to one of the Negro waiters, "How are the examinations this year? Many bilging?"

"Yes sir, they say it's pretty hard. Nearly all the boys are bilging this year."

This destroyed what little appetite I may have had for the supper of thin fried beefsteak and baked potatoes.

My friend told me his name was Constant and he was from Indiana. He advised me to consult a Mr. Thompson the next day who made a business of coaching boys for the Academy, and in the meantime to buy a few books—a geography, arithmetic and grammar—and begin to study.

I bought the books without delay. Returning to the large room which Constant and I had taken together, I began in a bewildered sort of way to brush up. Naturally under the circumstances I accomplished nothing and was in despair when Constant came in, bringing with him another boy whom he introduced as "Mr. Wakenshaw from New Jersey."

Constant was a breezy sort of chap and immediately proposed a game of cards. Both boys lighted cigars and neither seemed disturbed by any thought of the impending examination. Having been brought up in the austere principles of the conservative Presbyterian families of that day, I confess the sight of the cards was rather alarming since card playing was held among the cardinal sins. So, although I had occasionally smoked, I declined the cigars and went to bed.

On my leaving home my father had given me a generous check, which I had cashed in Philadelphia. I had in addition a smaller sum for incidentals. The first amount was intended to pay for my outfit at the academy and had to be kept intact.

My new companions paid no further attention to me, but I lay awake for a long time, my thoughts confused and uncomfortable, and not at all certain that I had acted wisely in sharing a room with strangers who smoked and played cards. However, I finally fell asleep, clutching my money tightly in one hand and my little silver watch in the other.

The next morning before attempting to see the coach I decided to go down to the Naval Academy grounds and have a look around. It was a beautiful place, a park surrounded by handsome brick buildings—the quarters of the officers and midshipmen—facing the Severn River where the river flows into Chesapeake Bay. On that brilliant summer morning it seemed to me as the magic cave must have appeared to Aladdin.

Presently I saw two officers in uniform strolling with a lady and a boy of my own age. The officers were Admiral Worden, superintendent of the Academy, and Captain Carter, the commandant. Both had long beards and wore gold-laced coats which made them look very formidable. As I had a letter to Captain Carter from a former shipmate, I presented it then and there. He was very kindly and introduced me to Admiral Worden, who said, "He is a good-looking boy for a Tennessean!"

The lady was Mrs. Dent, a relative of President Grant, and the boy was her son. He entered the Naval Academy in my class. Captain Carter advised me to take Mr. Maynard's letter to the secretary of the academy immediately and begin my examinations without delay, "thus saving expense and suspense," he added.

My two companions who shared my room had arranged to study under Mr. Thompson and they did not enter the Academy until several days later.

In those days the physical examination preceded the mental. The latter examination seemed very difficult and lasted several days. When it was over, as I suspected, I was recalled for oral questioning in arithmetic. This ordeal was called "Going before the Battery" and frequently ended in the candidate's failure. The "Battery" in my case was composed of Commander Schley, Professor Richard Smith and Professor Hendrickson. To my young eyes Hendrickson's brassbound coat, black eyes and black whiskers were terrifying. I was not detained long and was told to wait outside.

While the "Battery" was deciding my fate and I was mentally composing a telegram to my father informing him of failure, a trim young lieutenant in uniform came out of the boardroom, slapping his leg with his cap. Observing my doleful countenance he stopped and said kindly, "Keep a stiff upper lip, youngster!" This was my first meeting with Willard Brownson who became a lifelong friend.

In a few minutes the door opened and Commander Schley handed me a sealed envelope to deliver to Mr. Chase, the secretary of the Naval Academy. That 200 yards from the old recreation hall to the superintendent's office was a long walk for me. At the head of the narrow stairway leading to the offices stood a boy with his father. He had sat next to me at the hotel table and had started his examination just before I did. Now the picture of woe, he told me he had failed.

I handed my envelope to the secretary who tore it open, glanced at it, and said, "I am happy to inform you, Mr. Gleaves, that you have passed."

After that I took the oath of allegiance, answered a few more questions and was enrolled in the navy, June 12, 1873 as a Cadet Midshipman.

Those who entered the academy at that time were known as June plebes and were quartered on board the old wooden frigate, *Santee* lying at the academy wharf. Here we learned to "lash and carry", and to sleep in hammocks. We were taught how to pull an oar, knot and splice, and handle sail on board the sloop, *Dale.*

My station was on the main royal yard of the *Dale*. I soon learned to climb shroud and mast, but never stood on the main truck—as did my classmate Tommy Dodd, like the captain's son in the poem of "Old Ironsides".

Valentine Nelson of Knoxville entered the academy at the same time I did and was in my class. We became firm friends. His father, Judge T. A. R. Nelson, had been Evarts' assistant in the impeachment trial of Andrew Johnson and was an intimate friend of Captain Carter.

The letter I had presented to Captain Carter was from Mr. A. D. Wharton of Nashville, who had graduated high in the Naval Academy class of 1860 and had served with Carter in the *Seminole,* but had resigned and gone in with the South. Carter had begged him to stay with the flag, but ties of family and the entreaties of friends were too strong. Wharton served with distinction on the Mississippi River in the Confederate ram *Arkansas,* and with Admiral Buchanan and Captain J. D. Johnston in the *Tennessee* at the battle of Mobile Bay.

One Sunday morning that summer on the *Santee,* Nelson and I were invited to luncheon by Captain Carter. It was rather an awe-inspiring occasion for us. The guests, as I remember, were Admiral Worden (about to be relieved of duty at the Academy and ordered to the Mediterranean), Commodore Fairfax, Captain K. R. Breese—the new commandant of midshipmen—and Mrs. Breese, daughter of Governor Curtin, the War Governor of Pennsylvania. When the sherry was served both Nelson and I declined, and the question arose as to whether it was proper to offer wine to midshipmen when they were visiting in officers' quarters. Admiral Worden said it was proper to offer them wine, but that it was also proper for them to decline, which put Nelson and me quite at our ease.

Commodore Fairfax, a lineal descendant of Lord Fairfax, was an officer of note and distinction. Not only had he fought pirates in Sumatra, but was on board the *Missouri* under Captain Paulding when she was destroyed by fire at Gibraltar and had served with Biddle in Japan. Later he had effected the surrender of the filibuster Walker at Greytown and was executive officer of the *San Jacinto* under Wilkes. He also had directed the taking of the Confederate commissioners Mason and Slidell from the British steamer *Trent* and was on Admiral Farragut's staff when the remains of George Peabody were landed from the British ironclad *Monarch* at Portland, Maine, in 1870.

Nearly all of the officers on duty at the Academy in 1873 had fought in the Civil War. Their *aurae* excited our admiration and aroused our aspirations. There were Admiral Worden, the hero of the *Monitor,* and his gallant first lieutenant, Dana Greene, "dashing Breese", who led the landing party at Fort Fisher, Lieutenant Brownson, who had fought river pirates in Central America, and Carter, transferred temporarily to the army who won his spurs at the battle of Mills' Springs and commanded a successful cavalry raid into East Tennessee—for which he was recommended for promotion to brigadier general (proving that a sailor may do well on horseback). Also there was Lieutenant Commander John Schouler, the beau ideal of a naval officer—young and very handsome, an accomplished linguist and a skillful artist—who had just been commended by the navy department for saving a merchant steamer, in which he was a passenger, from wreck on the coast of Florida. Rear Admiral Worden was succeeded as superintendent by Rear Admiral C. R. P. Rodgers, a veteran of several wars, known for his distinguished courtesy and handsome presence.

As I look back upon it, it seems to me the officers were especially selected for their duty. They were very hospitable to the young midshipmen and among my closest friends were Jewell, Derby, Emory, Silas Terry and "You may fire when you're ready" Gridley". All these, and many more, were among the officers who had made their reputations under fire and been sent to the Naval Academy to set an example of "virtue, honor, and patriotism" to the midshipmen.

At the beginning of the academic year, in September 1873, my class mustered about 125, including two Japanese students, and about a dozen "turn backs" dropped from the preceding class of 1876. There were boys from various parts of the country. Although only eight years after the Civil War, many were from the South, among whom I made my special friends.

My roommate was Tom Green from Texas. His father, General Green of the Confederate army, had been killed in an engagement with Admiral Porter's gunboats in the Red River Expedition. After Tom Green left the Academy, Orchard of Missouri and I decided to room together after the practice cruise in the *Constellation.* This we did for three years. He was a high-toned fellow, one of the most brilliant men in the class. He retired when a Commodore.

My other classmates included Oliver, a Georgian; Frank Heath, of the District of Columbia—grandson of John Y. Mason, once Secretary of the Navy; Hodges, of Mississippi—who closed his life comparatively early after terrible suffering and the loss of both legs; Billy Bronaugh, of Kentucky; Philip Lansdale, of the District of Columbia—son of Admiral Farragut's fleet surgeon, and who was killed in Samoan jungle fighting; "Q" Parker, of North Carolina; and Benson, of Georgia—who during the World War held the distinguished position of chief of operations and principal advisor to the secretary of the navy.

Fullam, of New York, led the class; Dunn, of Rhode Island, was the inventor of the anchor that bears his name; Bostwick, of Wisconsin, was the author of a book of clever poems depicting Japanese life; O. G. Dodge, of Kansas, transferred from the line and became a professor of mathematics in the navy. Then there was Tom

Brumby, of Georgia, Dewey's flag lieutenant who hauled down the Spanish flag at Manila.

After more than threescore years, eleven of the class are still alive and borne on the Navy Register, but, of course, all are retired. Of those who started with my class only 43 were graduated in June 1877. President Hayes delivered our diplomas and the secretary of the navy, R. W. Thompson, of Indiana, made the address. The day was bright and very hot, even for Annapolis, and one of the class fainted in the ranks.

The annual ball was given to the graduating class by the succeeding first class and was perhaps the greatest event of the year to the graduates. The night before the paymaster of the old *Powhatan,* anchored in the river, invited all the class of '77 to be his guests at a dinner in town. To many of us that was disastrous as there had been a class luncheon previously.

2 To the South Atlantic *in the Hartford*

In August 1877, I received orders to the *Hartford* being fitted out at Norfolk for a cruise to the Brazils. I found her in dry dock and anything more forlorn or more calculated to promote homesickness would be difficult to imagine. The crew were on the receiving ship, or guardo. Most of the officers were on leave; those who were not lived ashore. The executive officer was Lieutenant Commander Harrington who at all times kept the midshipmen (an even dozen of us) busy aloft or in the boats, getting in stores by day, and standing a strict "heel and toe" watch at night. It was our introduction to the service, and we accepted the conditions as matter of course.

Once for a few days we were sent to the *Franklin,* the guardo, to relieve the midshipmen there. There I committed a dreadful breach of tact. During our official call on the captain I asked him whether the court-martial had acquitted him for the loss of the *Saranac.* I was perfectly innocent of intentionally saying the wrong thing and only wanted to help along a dragging conversation, but fully realized my mistake when he replied sarcastically, "If I had not been acquitted I do not suppose I would be in command of this ship!" The delight of the executive officer, old Felix McCurley, at my naive question was obvious, for there was enmity between him and the captain.

The fact that my first ship had been Farragut's flagship at New Orleans and Mobile Bay made no particular impression on me at the time. It is now nearly 60 years since then and, as I write, only one senior officer of those then in the *Hartford* is living.*

The summer heat was oppressive, but the monotony of the navy yard was enlivened by the attractions of society in Norfolk, just then beginning to be friendly toward federal officers. There were many trips to Old Point where the charming home of the De Busseys, just outside the fort, was a gathering place for the young people of both army and navy.

In those days the old Hygeia Hotel was in full swing and a popular resort for the heat-driven Washingtonians. Old Sweeney at the bar made the most wonderful mint juleps, and in the evening the

*Admiral Harrington, who has died since this was written.

ballroom overlooking the bay was crowded with dancers. In Norfolk the Blows, Leighs, Blairs, Spotswoods, Walkers and others kept open house, and I have never ceased to remember that first summer after my release from the Naval Academy with a pleasure that no subsequent experience afforded. When we sailed, more than one susceptible heart was left behind.

In September the *Hartford* was ready to receive Commodore E. T. Nichols, who was to command the South Atlantic Station. On the 17th he broke his broad pennant at the main truck, made a brief speech to the officers and men assembled on the quarterdeck in which he spoke of his pride in having Farragut's old flagship as his own, and concluded by inviting the officers to his cabin for a glass of champagne.

On October 13th we sailed for the Brazils, via Madeira. Thus my first sea duty was under sail. Our practice cruises, of which there had been two in the *Constellation,* were of course under sail. The *Hartford* had steam, but only as auxiliary power, and it was many years before I served in a vessel of all steam. I saw the sailing period expire, and how hard it died! The old officers tried to hold on to sails, as shown in Admiral Porter's famous order, when practically Secretary of the Navy, directing that *all* naval vessels as far as possible should be full ship-rigged.

A quarter of a century later when the so-called "New Navy" was authorized, the first four vessels were sparred and rigged with sails. As late as the mid-'90s we drilled at boarding and repelling boarders using Chinese gongs, rattles, cutlasses and boarding pikes—the same implements used in the Revolutionary War and in 1812, and now seen only in the naval museums.

In this connection an anecdote, told me by Admiral Dewey not long before his death, of one of the early steam frigates may be permissible. The engineer had done his best to reconcile the crew to the "damn kettles" and, for their convenience in getting hot water for scrubbing, had rigged a steam pipe to the deck with a short piece of hose attached to heat the water in a bucket.

One day Dewey saw an old-timer go to the pipe with a bucket of water (probably fresh and stolen from the scuttlebutt), insert the end of the hose in it and turn the valve as he had been shown to do. There happened to be a vacuum in the pipe and the whole bucketful siphoned away. The old shellback looked at his empty bucket a moment, then put the end of the hose to his mouth like a speaking tube and shouted down it, "You send back that water, you G . . . d . . . scientific son of a . . . ."

To my astonishment, a midshipman who had graduated the year before told me it would probably be two months before the *Hartford* arrived at her station. He was right. The ship had a two-bladed propeller which, when not in use, was triced up clear of the water.

How well I remember the boatswain's call, "All hands hoist the propeller," which was accomplished by the use of a viol block large enough to take an eight-inch hawser led to the capstan on the quarterdeck. This rendered the ship to all intents and purposes a sailing ship.

We arrived at Rio December 17th and anchored outside the harbor, as yellow fever was raging in the city. In those days we kept a storehouse there, and at that time it was in charge of Paymaster Gillette. He came on board to call on the commodore, and we sailed as soon as possible after some necessary overhaul. Shortly after our arrival at Montevideo we heard of the death of the paymaster, his wife and a daughter, of the plague.

At Montevideo we fired the customary salute of 21 guns, but received no reply. In the afternoon a delegation of Uruguayan officers came off to the ship, three miles out, and begged for some saluting powder in order to return our salute!

The voyage to the River Plate took the best part of three months, and in this time the midshipmen had cut their eyeteeth, if not their wisdom teeth. We had learned many things not in the books. The greatest of these was that no one can be a good officer who does not know how to handle those under his orders, or does not sympathize with them, and that tact, judgment and fair play are the foundations of a successful sea career.

Our crew for the most part were good stock, but there were elements of insubordination and discontent among them making for mutiny. It was said that many of them were leftovers from a bad lot that had come into the navy during a threat of war with Spain three years before over the *Virginius* affair.

Until we left Madeira our Captain H. A. Adams was at the helm, so to speak; but when a painful disease forced him to give up the active command and go on the sick list, Lieutenant Commander Harrington became king. Soon afterward trouble broke out. Topsail halyards were wracked, shots were taken out of the racks and rolled along the deck, marlinspikes were dropped from aloft, gun sights and truck washers were thrown overboard. The bearing of some of the men became more and more insolent and summary court-martials were frequent. It was evident that unless there was a radical change in the discipline, conditions would become even more serious.

Finally one morning when it was found that the battery had been disabled during the night by cutting the breechings and removing the linchpins from the gun trucks, the first lieutenant—as he was called in those days—decided to take action. All hands were called to muster on the quarterdeck. The boatswain's mates piped their whistles and their cheery calls rang through the ship, "All hands to muster!" followed by the warning cries: "Lay aft there, everybody!"

The scene made a deep impression on me. The wind was fresh and the sun shining brightly in a cloudless sky. The commodore on the horse block was a silent observer, the audacious trade wind flirting with his long white side-whiskers. The officers in gold-laced frock coats were assembled on the weather side of the quarterdeck, while the 400-plus men of the crew were crowded together on the lee side facing them. Lieutenant Commander Harrington, "Blue Book" in hand, stood at the capstan in the center of the quarterdeck, waiting for the reports of the midshipmen and mates of the lower decks.

When the decks were reported clear and all hands up and aft, Mr. Harrington began his speech. It was all the more effective for its Homeric simplicity. After rehearsing their mutinous actions, he said, "Congress has thought this crime so serious as to make it punishable by death." Then opening the "Blue Book" at the articles of war he read in stirring tones, "Anybody who shall maliciously injure any part of a vessel, tackle, armament or equipment, shall be punished by death or such other punishment as a court-martial shall adjudge."

Closing the book with a bang and tossing it on the capstan he shouted, "If I can find the man or men who did this thing, I'll do my best to bring each one to the yardarm!" With a dramatic gesture he pointed to the main yard where "Big Ben" was tugging at the main tack in the freshening breeze. It was thrilling! Turning toward the fife rail around the mainmast where the boatswain's mates were assembled, he said, "I don't know who the guilty man is, but he is standing somewhere before me, and when I look at my old friend David Clark or some other man whom I respect equally, I say to myself, 'My God, is this the man?' "

Clark was the chief boatswain's mate and the leading petty officer in the ship. A short fat man who wore a full beard, he was a great favorite with everybody. The distinction of being thus singled out at "all hands" pleased him greatly. For many days after that he held himself more than ever aloof from the crew, wore his cap pulled down further over his eyes, chewed his tobacco more vigorously as if in profound thought, and passed the calls in a deeper and more resonant voice.

A short time after we reached Montevideo, in January 1878, our handsome captain died. His disease had baffled the surgeons. One day he would be out on the half deck, then for a week no one would see him and we were told that he was suffering intense pain in his head.

On the forenoon of the day that he died I was midshipman of the quarterdeck. The orderly told me that the captain wanted to see me. He was lying on his bed, fully dressed in uniform. He said, "The men are caulking right outside the cabin and are driving me almost crazy. Have it stopped at once."

I never saw him alive again. He died that night, and my thoughts were all of the "old man" whose fate it had been to die so far from home. A post-mortem aboard ship showed that he had a tumor on the brain.

I was on the quarterdeck when his death was announced. It happened to be just at the routine time for "shooting Charley Noble". I have never been so startled as I was by the report of that pistol. In those days Charley Noble was the galley smoke pipe and once a week the ship's cook cleaned it out by firing a pistol through it filled with rice.

The next day his body was rowed ashore and buried from the U.S. Legation, with the naval honors of his rank. He was only 42 years old and had made a creditable record in the Civil War, as well as in China at the Barrier Forts in 1856. The long line of our own boats was joined by those French and Brazilian men-of-war then in port—all with boat flags at half-mast making an impressive array—the casket being in the launch in the lead.

My time in the *Hartford* was divided between Rio and Montevideo, with a few days at Maldonado at the mouth of the La Plata where we had target practice—so called—firing at half-barrels lashed together to form a pyramid, surmounted by a pole with a reg flag. This crude practice continued in the navy for many years until Captain Scott, of the English Navy, raised great gun target practice to a science and Admiral Sims, of our own navy, had the energy, foresight and initiative to interest President Theodore Roosevelt in the system, who ordered its adoption in our ships.

After the death of Captain Adams, Mr. Harrington remained in command for several months. When we returned to Rio, in the summer of 1878, Captain W. K. Mayo was ordered to the command. The South Atlantic Station was unpopular and the Department had trouble in finding anyone willing to go there. Captain Mayo was known as a martinet and his coming was looked upon by all of us with considerable apprehension. Great was the relief in the midshipmen's mess when we found that the new captain's disciplinary attentions were devoted chiefly to wardroom officers.

In appearance he resembled somewhat a clergyman and his benevolent bearing was attractive. He was apparently very religious, which the midshipmen thought a bad omen. Once when I was calling on him and his wife at the Hotel des Etrangeres in Rio, I bemoaned having come into the world too late to take part in the Civil War. The captain took a Bible from the table, opened it at Revelations and read a verse or two about the Four Horseman. Closing the book he said, "As long as those words are true of the Red Horsemen you will have your chance."

We midshipmen soon discovered that he was not only friendly towards us, but was "the sailor's friend", which foreboded evil. Only those who have served at sea know what this means and what possibilities of disorganization lie in the phrase.

The crew of the *Hartford* was a heterogeneous collection of various nationalities. This was usual at that period. Few Americans enlisted in the navy, and those who did were invariably beachcombers and the like. Often they were deserters from other ships who reenlisted under different names. North countrymen, Swedes and Norwegians, predominated. They were known as "square heads"—stolid, heavy and dumb—but faithful and, as a rule, excellent seamen. Portugal furnished a large percentage of the stewards, while Norfolk and its vicinity contributed more than half of the colored servants.

The worst elements in the ship's company were the degenerate Englishmen, for the most part deserters from their own navy or merchant service. They were known as "limeys", and were not liked either forward or aft. The best element beside the few old-timers was perhaps Irish—splendid sailors, hard-drinking and hard-fighting, but ready at all times to reef a topsail in a gale of wind, join a landing party or man a cutter in a rugged sea.

Although conditions before the mast in a man-of-war were constantly improving, yet—as Captain Parker said of the service when he entered the navy in 1842—it "was pretty much as it was in Marryatt's time." Admiral Luce bears the same testimony. There was no cold storage, no electric light, no heat and no fresh water except in the casks. The navy rations consisted of coffee, tea, "salt horse", hardtack, rice, flour, pickles, desiccated potatoes, pork and beans.

The officers' mess, of course, carried canned food. Eggs packed in sawdust did not become actually inedible for several weeks. The crew ate from "mess cloths" of black painted canvas spread out on the decks. Swinging mess-tables were not introduced until much later. The water from the casks in the hold was often unpalatable. It was tough going and the food even in the admiral's quarters was not luxurious.

I have heard a great deal of the seagoing of the Old Navy, but as a matter of fact we did not have a great deal of it in the *Hartford,* barring the voyage out and the return, and a cruise to the Falkland Islands. That was after I had been detached.

My own experiences on the Brazilian Station were confined to Montevideo and Rio and the short passages under sail between. It was a dreary cruise. At Montevideo, owing to the shallow water, we lay three miles from shore. There were neither steam launches nor motors, but there were five cutters and several big sailing launches. It was a wonderful school, however, and midshipmen learned what many of us had not learned at the Naval Academy—that is, how to handle a boat under sail and in all weathers.

At Maldonado I wrote my first and only verse, which consisted of four lines:

'Twas in the sparkling month of May
The frigate *Hartford* sailed away
For exercise in the Lower Bay
At Maldonado.

This was two lines more than the poet-boatswain Captain Parker tells of who wrote:

Far o'er the billow the moonlight is streaming
Dispelling the vapour and gloom of the night.

Like the boatswain, my Maldonado doggerel was as far as I ever got.

In those days Rio was very different from what I am told it is today with all the modern improvements. The *Rua de Ouvidor,* the principal shopping street, was a narrow thoroughfare lined with jewelry shops on either side. At the water end was Jimmy Graham's drinking saloon. "Jimmy" had served most of his life as a sailorman, but for some years had given up the sea and taken to mixing drinks for a living. He had a long list of American drinks, with corresponding prices, painted on the saloon wall. It was a curious catalog—"morning glory, stone fence, whiskey cocktail, mint julep and gin sling". Jimmy's place was always well patronized.

The *Alcazar,* which was the opera comique, and the Grand Opera were the other principal amusements. The latter was especially fine and there I heard Campanini for the first time. The repertoire included nearly all of Verdi's operas, and I heard *Aida, Les Huguenots,* and *L'Africaine.*

We made excursions to Tijuca and to Corcovada, walking and climbing from Santa Teresa to the summit. We planned a scaling expedition of Sugar Loaf but never got there. Once or twice we went over to Nictheroy, across the bay.

The naval storehouse had been maintained by the Navy Department for many years, but was abandoned during our visit in the harbor and all serviceable stores were sent to the United States in the *Old Guard.* Many thousand dollars worth of hawsers and other ship stores had been destroyed by white ants. Hundreds of boxes of spools of thread, apparently intact, crumbled to dust when touched. The storehouse was situated on Rat Island, in the upper harbor, which was the scene of desperate fighting between the Revolutionists and the Nationals a few years later.

The *Hartford's* crew was a memorable lot. There were old David Clark, the chief boatswain's mate, and James Robinson, the mainmast man—a fine-looking specimen of an American bluejacket whose white beard flowed over his breast. Also there were apprentices—one named Greer, was a handsome, clean-cut lad who died of tuberculosis, and another named Injes was an artist in the making who tattooed my forearm with the coat of arms of my own state. There were many more whose faces I remember distinctly but whose names have gone.

I never saw David Clark after I left the ship, but remember his telling me once that Mr. Harrington kept everybody in the ship on the "quiv-quiv". The wardroom steward was a Frenchman. One morning going ashore in the market boat he told me he had been a Catholic priest, but had been unfrocked for misconduct. We began talking about religion and I said I could never understand the Trinity—how three could be one. He said, "Look at your thumb. It consists of flesh, bone and nail—three parts in one." I have never fogotten the simile.

Another member of the crew was an Irishman, Daniel Conway, the ship's bugler—a fine fellow when sober but a devil in liquor. He claimed to be a survivor of the Charge of the Six Hundred at Balaklava and told me he was a bugler and saw Lord Lucan hand the order from Lord Raglan to Lord Cardigan to charge! One day after visiting the British man-o'-war *Volage* with a liberty party, he returned to the *Hartford* raving drunk and cleared the gun deck with a battle-ax before he was put in irons.

Admiral Nichols will always stand out in my mind as the beau ideal of a sailor officer. We all knew that in the River Fight he had commanded the *Winona,* that he had received the surrender of New Orleans, and that he was one of Farragut's trusted lieutenants, but what was more to the point, he never lost an opportunity of being pleasant to us youngsters.

The first Christmas at sea, early in the morning, he sent our mess a big basket filled with all sorts of good things from his own stores. The card attached was inscribed, "With the compliments of Santa Claus." His steward had been seen crawling around under the hammocks and the evidence was conclusive. In reply to our thanks he said, "I know no one on board ship poorer than a midshipman's mess and I always try to remember the poor on Christmas."

At Montevideo the ship's cook fell ill and begged for a priest. It was blowing a pampero, but a cutter was lowered and sent ashore in charge of Cadet Midshipman Witzel. There was no difficulty in obtaining a priest, and I have never forgotten that man's nerve. On the return to the ship, three miles from shore, the sails were reefed down, the boat plunged and rolled in the heavy seas, while the wind threatened to dismast her. It was a fierce experience for a landsman and every now and then he would say in broken English to the midshipman: "Zee ne-ces-si-ti of zee oc-cas-ion geeves us zee courage."

Owing to the dicontent among the crew, the *Hartford* on the passage to the Brazils crossed the equator without the usual ceremonies so dear to the sailor. The crossing occurred at midnight. It was in the middle watch when the messenger came down into the steerage and woke us all up, saying that the officer of the deck wanted all midshipmen on deck at once, with sidearms. Owing to the repeated difficulties with the crew we thought that the long-expected mutiny had finally broken out and we were not long in getting on deck, only to be greeted by the officer of the deck (whom we all disliked) saying, "Gentlemen, I congratulate you on crossing the Line."

I recall the calm night, the moon shining on the white sails, the sleeping watch on the deck, and the wrath in our hearts, as growling and cursing, we tumbled down the ladders back to our hammocks, Hiero Taylor even going so far as to shout and rattle his sword as he stamped his way into the steerage. Of course, the noise awakened the wardroom, and the executive officer, probably also thinking the time had come to settle things with the crew, rushed out of his room in his nightshirt, revolver in hand, to quell the disturbance. What he said to the officer of the deck the next morning we never knew, but our imaginations ran wild!

One Sunday morning while at anchor in Rio harbor I was midshipman of the quarterdeck. Just after quarters for inspection, a boat came alongside from an American ship anchored off Sugar Loaf and a man came on board. I met him at the port gangway. He was a good-looking, strongly built seaman, but his eyes were bloodshot, his face red under the tan, and he was evidently controlling himself with an effort.

He said, "My name's Hodges. I am master of that American schooner down there under Sugar Loaf and I've come on board for assistance. I've killed my first mate and my crew has mutinied."

This was really exciting and when Mr. Harrington came on deck to hear the story he told Lieutenant W. P. Day, who had the deck, to take an armed boat's crew with the midshipman of the watch, together with Captain Hodges, and investigate the trouble.

It looked like a real party to me and always "seeking some advantage" like the Knight in the White Company, I thought my opportunity had come. But I was mistaken. The schooner was the *Maggie E. Grey* of Baltimore. The crew had mutinied and the captain had killed the mate, but when we pulled alongside there was no evidence of anything unusual and the crew appeared perfectly harmless and subdued. We returned to the *Hartford* with the Master and one man, whom the former said was the worst of the crew. As we pulled away one of the men leaned over the rail of the schooner and said, "That's the man, Captain, who has made all the trouble."

The matter was referred to the consul general, Mr. Adamson, who finally decided to send the schooner home in tow of an American steamer, the *Bald Eagle*. Captain Hodges was subsequently tried in the federal courts at Baltimore for murder, but I do not remember the result.

As I look back over 60 years to my first cruise, there are not many bright spots. I was glad of its end, although it was caused prematurely by sorrow. I had little thought of the future at that time and when off duty my hours were usually given to excursions on shore.

One day there came a shock. The mail, three weeks old, brought the news of the death of my youngest sister. My father had died the preceding December after a long illness, and knowing that I was more needed at home than on board ship, the admiral allowed me to return to the United States in October 1878.

I can never forget the kindness and sympathy shown me by the admiral, Captain Mayo and all the officers when I left the ship to take passage on the then new *City of Rio de Janeiro*. On this, her first voyage, she carried 43,000 sacks of coffee. Among her passengers were Dr. and Mrs. Richardson of New Orleans, and their nephew, Morgan Whitney, whom I met years afterwards at the Mardi Gras in 1895, as well as a Mr. Beecher, nephew of Henry Ward Beecher, who was my constant companion on board, although I never saw or heard of him after we landed.

We arrived in New York three weeks later in biting cold weather. I went at once to Philadelphia to join my mother and sisters who had not the slightest idea that I was within 5,000 miles of them. Looking through the windows of the drawing room, and seeing the family gathered there, I felt as I imagine Enoch Arden did on his unexpected return from sea.

3 A Cruise in the *Plymouth*

From October 1878 until March 1879 I was on leave. It was during this period at home that I made a request which, had it been granted, might possibly have added an important and interesting chapter to these memoirs. More probably, it would have prevented them from ever being written. This was the reply to my letter.

Ebbitt House

Washington, D.C.
February 25th, 1879

Cadet Midshipman
Albert Gleaves
U.S. Navy
West End, Nashville, Tennessee

My dear Sir,

Yours of Feb. 18th is received. In reply I would say that the number of officers for the Arctic Expedition will probably be limited to five—a lieutenant, a master, a surgeon, an engineer and myself.

Though I see no chance of your being detailed, an application to the Department will at all events place you on record as having been desirous to go to the Arctic Ocean.

Respectfully,

George W. De Long
Lieutenant
U.S. Navy

I have always regarded my return home at this time as an error of judgment, at least from a selfish standpoint. I could do no good there and lost six precious months of my sea service—and, incidentally, a cruise either to the Falkland Islands or to the Cape of Good Hope. After I left the ship, the *Hartford* visited Port Stanley and at the same time a number of midshipmen were transferred to the *Essex* to relieve her midshipmen returning to the Academy for examination for promotion. The *Essex* cruised to Cape Town and St. Helena, so I missed either one of the two interesting voyages.

My shore leave in Nashville was entirely uneventful, and I was glad to get orders to the *Plymouth* at the suggestion of my classmate, H. M. Dombaugh, who wrote that he was the only midshipman on board. The ship was about to sail from Boston on an extended cruise in the West Indies. My application for duty in her was granted, and on a cold snowy day in early March I arrived in Boston and went to the Tremont House until I could get my bearings.

I found the *Plymouth* in dry dock and not ready to sail for several weeks. In the preceding November, while in the West Indies she had had yellow fever on board. The outbreak occurred just after I had seen her in St. Thomas on my way home in the *City of Rio.* I had gone on board to visit two friends, Midshipmen Rollins and Mallory (Class of '76). Shortly afterwards both died of the fever and the ship was ordered home.

It was decided to strip her, fumigate her, then dock her and freeze out the germs. It was not then known that no germ can be destroyed by cold. A winter in Boston is cold enough ordinarily to satisfy an Eskimo, but when the cold is intensified by being in a stone dry dock, and the thermometer is low enough to kill anything that can be destroyed by cold—it was thought that the yellow fever germs could be exterminated.

Dombaugh told me that he was living at the Crawford House in Charlestown, as were several other officers, and advised me to move over from the expensive Tremont. My pay was only $75 per month and it was necessary to economize.

The captain of the *Plymouth* was David B. Harmony who was as much of a martinet as Lieutenant Commander Harrington. He was a tall, fine-looking man, with long reddish side-whiskers on a very red face. The executive officer was Francis A. Cook, a genial, efficient officer, well liked by everyone. Lieutenant C. H. Stockton was the navigator. Silent and scholarly, he kept much to himself. Among the watch officers was Lieutenant Swift, also decorated with "siders" of extraordinary length which in bad weather he tied under his chin in a square knot and in fair weather let flow wing and wing like a schooner's sails before the wind.

As there were only four of us in the midshipmen's mess, which included an assistant surgeon and the pay clerk, we boarded during the cruise with the wardroom, but had our meals in the steerage. It was not a satisfactory arrangement for us, because we never by any chance got the first cuts or the breast of a fowl.

My first meeting with Mr. Swift was in the steerage country the day I reported for duty. He was tall and slim and wore a long, fur-trimmed overcoat and a fur cap. He called to me asking, "Is this Mr. Gleaves?" When I admitted the fact, he said, "I am the caterer of the wardroom mess. Let my have $30 for your mess bill."

In the course of time the medical experts pronounced it safe to undock the ship, and we were hauled alongside the seawall and began taking in stores. Sails were bent, light yards sent up and fires started in the donkey boiler for heating purposes. The crew moved on board from the guardo and officers returned to their quarters.

It was a time for hustling, for everyone was anxious to escape the ice, cold and snow of Boston. When we were ready for sea, a board from Washington came on board for final inspection. They reported against the ship's return to the West Indies, venturing the opinion that if she did go, yellow fever would break out again, for certain members held that yellow fever germs could not be killed by any known freezing mixture. But the report was disapproved and orders were issued to get to sea at once.

As we set to sail one afternoon, Lieutenant Commander Cook called from the bridge to Dombaugh, who was on the poop, "Is everything clear aft?" Dombaugh, taking it for granted that everything was clear, without looking over the stern answered, "All clear, Sir." That was his mistake. A six-inch line was hanging over the taffrail and when the propeller began to revolve it just naturally wrapped the line around itself.

The captain was furious. The ship was tied up to the dock again and the propeller was not cleared for several hours. Dombaugh was put under arrest. The next morning I was sent to the commandant's office on an errand and there heard an old white-haired officer ask why the *Plymouth* had not sailed. The reply was, "Oh, one of the damned midshipmen let a line get foul of the propeller."

After a delay of 24 hours we cast off from the dock again and steamed out of the harbor, making sail as usual outside after hoisting the propeller. Our first port, according to schedule, was to be Guadeloupe. Scarcely had we struck hot weather when, as predicted by the Washington Medical Board, yellow fever made its appearance. The captain decided to return north immediately. Not having coal enough to make port in case of head winds, and with no time to be lost, we headed for Bermuda.

This prompt retreat from the tropics prevented the spread of the disease. Only two men came down with it—old Peter Eagan, a boatswain's mate and veteran of the Civil War, and the engineer's yeoman who recovered. When Eagan was taken to the sick bay, Dr. Wolverton directed that he be given a nightshirt, to make the old man as comfortable as possible. Eagan protested, saying that he had never heard of a sailor in a nightshirt who got well. So to humor him, he was allowed to retain his blue shirt.

When the ship arrived off Georgetown, Bermuda, we signaled for a pilot, who promptly boarded us. As soon as he did so, and not till then, was the yellow flag displayed. We anchored in the outer harbor and when the health officer came out to us we were placed in strict quarantine. The case was reported to the governor who was at first not inclined to allow us to coal. He finally consented but urged us to sail at the earliest practicable moment.

One hundred tons of coal were purchased at $12 per ton. We were forbidden, however, to land the pilot—a negro and about the most impudent of his race. We took him north and at Portsmouth turned him over to the British Consul at Portland who, I presume, eventually returned him home.

After leaving Bermuda we ran into a storm of cyclonic proportions. It was during a lull in this gale that old Eagan died and was buried. The barometer fell to 29.03 and the wind blew with hurricane force from N.W. It was a grand funeral with the fierce wind of the North Atlantic howling through the rigging, louder than the pipes of the organ of St. Peter's. The snow was blinding, lying thick on the weather shrouds, from which the violent motion of the ship would shake it off to the deck below. The sea was running high, and occasionally a wave tumbled on board to dash itself around on deck until drained off through the scruppers and freeing-ports.

We were under short sail, lying to under steam and mizzen storm stay sail and mizzen stay sail. When the grey dawn broke the ship was rolling through an arc of 59° in a heavy sea. At 11 a.m. came the call. "All hands bury the dead."

The weather was clearing a little, but the sea was still wild. The funeral was held under the break of the forecastle, where all the crew and officers were crowded together. Mr. Cook read the Episcopal service, but his voice could be heard only by those closest to him, for the voices of wind and sea drowned his words.

The body, sewed up in a hammock and covered by the flag, was taken aft on a board, the bearers staggering along to the lee gangway hardly able to keep on their feet. The end of the board was placed in the gangway. Then watching for a smooth time, at the words, "We commit his body to the deep," the inboard end was raised, and the body slid into the water dragged down by an eleven-inch shot attached to the foot of the hammock.

Turning to Mr. Manning, the boatswain, Mr. Cook said, "Pipe down, Sir." The men went forward and lighted their pipes at the oil lanterns that hung from the beams near the galley and the daily routine was taken up.

I have often regretted that I never asked Eagan to tell me of his young days in the service. I saw him every day and was fond of him. He was the first captain of the eleven—inch pivot of which I was the midshipman. At the time of his death he must have been well over 60. He had served with men who had been in the War of 1812, and perhaps knew old Ben Treferthen who was in the *Chesapeake* when she fought the *Shannon,* and who at that time was still alive and living in Boston. But I was young in those days, looking forward not backward.

We made Portsmouth, New Hampshire, and were quarantined off Whale Rock where the ship was fumigated—an unpleasant task done by sealing up the decks and burning sulphur which was, incidentally, disastrous to gold lace! Our mail and fresh provisions were brought daily by a steam launch from the Kittery Navy Yard and delivered to our big sailing launch anchored 500 yards from the ship.

The weather was cold and stormy, blowing a gale nearly all the time. One morning at daybreak a schooner which had come in during the night was seen to be anchored close on shore not far from us—a lee shore on which the sea was breaking in a heavy surf. It was evident that the schooner was dragging. The matter was reported to our skipper who consented to allow Mr. Cook to send Boatswain Manning to her to find out if there were any trouble on board.

The boatswain returned reporting that the crew was demoralized, the captain having been knocked overboard by the jibbing of the spanker boom and drowned the night before. Unless aid was rendered soon to the drifting vessel, it would be in the surf. He asked to be allowed to take our sheet anchor, plant it to windward of the schooner and haul the vessel out to a safe berth.

For some reason the captain refused and ordered our own boat to be hoisted in. By noon the schooner was striking heavily. Her crew abandoned her and we could see them scampering up the beach. It was not long before she was in the breakers and being dashed to pieces. The next morning at daybreak there was not a vestige of her left.

We all thought the matter would be reported to the navy department, but so far as I ever heard nothing came of it. The New York *Herald* had a brief account of the loss of the schooner, and that was all.

Captain Harmony was a forceful man and stands out as a landmark in my experience. He had served with Farragut in the *Mississippi* in the battles resulting in the surrender of New Orleans and later was at the bombardment of Fort Fisher. A high liver, the captain was something of an anglo-maniac, and in manner and pronunciation rather affected the English. He was a law unto himself and did pretty much as he pleased.

Like most sailors he was inclined towards the church and was correspondingly profane. One Sunday at sea we were at divine service. The paymaster always read the service and the captain made the responses in a loud voice, the rest of us joining in feebly. In the tropics, service was held on the gun deck under the open main hatch.

On this particular occasion a group of sailors had gathered around the main fife rail by the hatchway on deck. Forgetting that the church pennant was up, they were laughing and talking and disturbing the service. Suddenly the captain called out, "Stop, Paymaster."

With his kid-gloved finger in his prayer book, he stepped up the ladder until his head was above the spar deck. In the most wonderful, profane and picturesque sea language he told the lounging sailors just what he thought of their lack of respect for the observance of Sunday and then ordered them all forward. Resuming his chair and reopening the prayer book, he said, "You may go ahead with the service, Paymaster."

Sometimes on deck he wore colored glasses to protect his eyes, but only when in certain humors, which justified the quartermaster's saying, "When the Old Man has four eyes keep clear of him." I remember one afternoon when, equipped with goggles, he appeared on the poop. Observing the quartermaster at the standard watching him, he sang out to him, "Keep your damned old eyes on the compass." And so it went.

He belied his name and was a typical skipper of the Marryatt school. At times he was a veritable old storm-a-long, so Dombaugh and I tried to keep out of his sight. One night going aft to heave the log, I ventured on the weather side of the poop deck. In the darkness I did not see the Old Man until I collided with him. I tried to escape under the spanker boom to leeward, but was too late.

"Who is that?" he shouted. "What are you doing on the weather side of the poop? Don't you know better than to come aft on the weather side? How long have you been in the service?"

These questions were fired rapidly and explosively and ended with a peremptory order to get to leeward, out of his way! Even to my immature mind it seemed wholly unnecessary to make me cross the deck at the mizzenmast only to recross at the taffrail, because the log had to be hove from the weather side.

The day Dombaugh was suspended, before we had sailed from Boston, he asked me to go ashore and made a purchase. "The Old Man," he said, "has ordered me several times to buy a sextant and I have never done it. Now he will be sure to ask if I have obeyed his order, and unless I can say I have, he will probably court-martial me."

"Dummy" told me of a pawnshop in Charlestown, not far from the navy yard, where there was a "pig-yoke" which he thought could be bought for $5 which would be sufficient to answer the captain's requirement. I secured the instrument and for the rest of our short cruise it was in daily use. At first Dombaugh could only handle meridian altitudes, but later he was able to take time sights as accurately as the navigator with his standard sextant.

Years afterwards when Dombaugh was at the War College and I was at the Torpedo Station, he presented me with this ancient astronomical tool. I presented it to the museum at the Torpedo Station. From there it was sent to the museum at the Naval Academy, where it is now. As a matter of fact Captain Harmony never asked Dummy again about the sextant!

As soon as we were released from quarantine Dombaugh and I were detached and ordered to the Naval Academy for examination for promotion.

We stopped in Boston and there I saw *Pinafore* at the old Boston Museum. It was never better put on the stage. Barnaby was the Admiral; Whitney, Captain Corcoran; and Marie Wainwright was Little Buttercup. The crew of the *Pinafore* were borrowed from the receiving ship, *Wabash*. All the technical details were perfect. There was not a defect to mar the harmony. The yards were manned in shipshape style, the side tended and Sir Joseph Porter came on board to a gun salute which couldn't have been better fired by the flagship! Dick Dead Eye was superb, but I don't remember who took the part. At all events he has had no successor in this country.

4 On the *Nipsic* in European Waters

My class ('77) assembled at Annapolis from all parts of the world in the summer of 1879 to be examined for promotion from cadet midshipmen (the classification at that time) to midshipmen. All were present except three or four belated in the South Atlantic.

The examinations were unusually difficult and the final marking made many radical changes in the class standing. Several who had starred at the Academy dropped to the bottom, and conversely, some "wooden" men made phenomenal rises. When all was over we were ordered to our homes to await orders for our next cruise.

In July 1879, I was appointed a midshipman. The following October I received orders to the *Nipsic,* a small 1500-ton ship fitting out at Norfolk for the European Squadron—always the most desirable of the sea stations. It was good to be in Norfolk again, renewing the old associations which had been broken off two years before. There were not many changes in society, except that the people were even kinder and more hospitable because the Civil War time animosities were slowly dying out.

The captain of the *Nipsic* was as gallant and fine a man as ever breathed salt air or walked a quarterdeck. He was beloved by everyone on board and I have always considered him the most just officer I have ever known—without exception. This was Commander C. M. Schoonmaker, of a distinguished New York family. I never knew a man with a higher sense of duty, but his efficiency was somewhat impaired by a diffidence that at times was painful.

Death found him on duty in the hurricane in Samoa in 1889. He had a fine Civil War record and had distinguished himself particularly at Mobile Bay when executive officer of the *Manhattan* in the fight with the *Tennessee.* My old friend John Gibbons wrote me an excellent account of that heroic disaster. Schoonmaker once told me that he was ambitious to own a Jurgensen watch and bought one at Copenhagen when the ship went north. I have often wondered if this watch was lost with him at Apia.

Lieutenant Commander John Stark Newell was the executive—a big, handsome man who handled the ship like a pilot boat—she was not much bigger. He was a man of strong personality and dominated wherever he happened to be—wherever he sat was the head of the table! Extremely smart in appearance, punctilious in every point of service etiquette, firm and exacting, he was not always as affable as the youngsters would have liked.

The navigator was Lieutenant L., the son of an eminent Presbyterian divine. Without doubt, he was the most impatient man I ever knew. Once when L. was officer of the deck, I heard him call to the marine orderly in the gangway, "Corporal of the Guard! Corporal of the Guard! Corporal of the Guard! Why in hell don't you answer me?"—all in one breath—the last words reaching the marine about the same time as the first.

The watch officers were J. O. J. Kelley, Nathan Hale Barnes, A V. Wadhams, and C. I. Norton—all lieutenants—and that gentle and most lovable of gentlemen, Master Charles E. Fox. Fox was a grandson of the famous Charles Morris—the executive of the *Constitution* in her fights with the *Guerriere* and the *Java.* On the staff side of the wardroom were Mr. David Smith, the chief engineer, and a prince of a good fellow plus shipmates—Paymaster Jonathan Quincy Barton; gentle old Dr. Coles; Davy Jones, the jovial past assistant engineer; and Jesup Nicholson, the marine officer.

The midshipmen's mess was the best in the service. They were McCartney, '75, Henderson and Griffin, '76, and several assistant engineers who joined later in the cruise. Mike Dunning, assistant engineer, was one of the most popular men I have ever been associated with. We had only two warrant officers—one of whom was John Brown, the boatswain, a typical sailorman of the period, possessed with a keen sense of humor.

The outstanding junior officer was Richard Henderson of North Carolina, of whom there were as many stories told as of Captain John Percival (Mad Jack Percival of the Old Navy) or of Lucien Young of the New. Henderson was a natural born sailorman—built for going to sea—whose life was crowded with adventures. He was renowned for his most original sayings. While they were unconventional and would not pass a censor, yet they were decidedly humorous and to the point. Henderson was popular with officers and crew—the latter adored him—and was a natural leader of men, devoted to the service. However, he belonged to a school of officers that no longer exists, and could not exist under present conditions and remain in the service. He retired in 1905 as a commander and died just before the World War. Scoot Henderson looms large in my recollections—a tall, slim, fair-haired man whose good-looking, bony face and blue eyes framed by square, firm jaws denoted his strong character.

The *Nipsic* had been rebuilt at Washington Navy Yard. It was called "repaired" on the books, but, as remarked by Lucien Young of whom more anon, "The Bureau built a new ship around the old hawse-pipe."

It was so in those days. Usually one ship was kept "under repairs" at a navy yard for years and appropriations for her furnished ready funds for other purposes. Once when the old monitor *Monadnock* was at the Mare Island Yard, someone asked the chief engineer of the yard, "When are you going to finish the *Monadnock*?"

He replied, "Don't say a word—she is our nest-egg!"—a loose remark for which he had to account later before a court of inquiry.

All things come to an end, and the reconditioning—in modern language—of the *Nipsic* was finished at last and she was assigned to the Mediterranean Squadron. Before sailing, however, orders came to investigate an alleged outrage to an American citizen engaged in the alfalfa business in Venezuela. The *Nipsic* was commissioned at Norfolk and shortly afterwards sailed for La Guayra to look into the reported insult to the Flag. The cruise to Venezuela was uneventful but pleasant, and we found that, as usual, there had been no insult to the American Flag and that the American citizen who had made the complaint was a naturalized American.

At this time our senior watch officer was Jimmy Kelley, a sort of unofficial attache of the New York *Herald*—a man with a facile pen and nimble wit whose friends said had not been 2000 miles from the Washington Monument since his first cruise out of the Naval Academy. The outraged citizen was described by Kelley in the *Herald* as the "customary exile from Austrian Dungeons, with a capital *D*, who had given up throne-tumbling for the ancillary pursuit of rope-making." This contribution to contemporary history brought Kelley a mild reproof from the department.

We returned to Norfolk in a few weeks and completed arrangements for our foreign cruise. Kelley left us before we sailed for Europe and went, I believe, on the admiral's staff on the home station. In later years we were shipmates again.

The *Nipsic* sailed for Gibraltar, via Madeira, in January 1880, and did not return to the United States until February 1883. During this time the ship's company, both officers and men, remained practically intact, a thing unheard of nowadays. We changed skippers in

October of 1881 because Captain Schoonmaker's cruise expired then. There were some minor changes among the junior officers, but that was all. We did have a few deaths and accidents, but no epidemics. The only accidental death that I recall was that of a lad who fell to the quarterdeck from the main topmast crosstrees. I was standing a few feet away, heard the unmistakable thud of crushed flesh, and saw the white bones of his elbow sticking in the oak deck.

On our first visit to Gibraltar, Captain Schoonmaker took me as his aide when he called on the governor, Lord Napier of Magdala. The sailors and soldiers called him General *Napeer*. Our consul, Mr. Horatio Sprague, went with the captain, of course, and the occasion was a red letter day for me.

Mr. Sprague said the last person to whom he said good-bye in the United States was Daniel Webster. He had been retained at Gibraltar through various administrations for his great services during the Civil War, including the prevention of coaling by Confederate cruisers. His son succeeded him and was there until his comparatively recent death after many years of service.

Lord Napier's distinguished appearance and courtly and gracious manners made a strong impression on me. He asked Captain Schoonmaker if he was married. When the captain said he was, the governor replied, "Our naval officers as a rule are bachelors, but I have rarely met an American officer who was." Then turning to me he said with a smile, "But I am sure you are not married."

As we passed out of the Government House, Mr. Sprague said, "That's the man who, like the King of France, went up a hill—and then came down again."

I did not understand the allusion, but did not ask for enlightenment. Afterwards on reading the history of the Abyssinian War of 1868 in which Lord Napier won his title and a pension, I understood.

Soon after arriving in the Mediterranean, the ship was sent to Constantinople, at the request of Mr. Gwynne Harris Heap, our consul general, because of missionary troubles with Turkish officials in Armenia. About this time, General Longstreet arrived as minister to Turkey relieving Horace Maynard. He established his residence at the famous Myssiri Hotel, at that time the only hotel in Pera for English or American travellers. Mr. Serdamore, in his delightful *Sheaf of Memories,* calls it "the most dismal caravanserai in Eastern Europe." Myssiri himself at this time was a figurehead living in the hotel, but had been Kinglake's interpreter throughout the Crimean War and was now an advertisement to attract tourists.

It was my day's duty to be sent ashore with the captain's compliments to the new minister and ask when it would be convenient for him to receive Captain Schoonmaker. Never in all my life had I been so impressed by anyone. His dignified bearing and gracious reception—for he received me standing—were beyond description. At that time he was just 60 years old, tall, erect and massive, his hair and beard white, his voice still husky from the wound in his throat received at Spotsylvania. To my young eyes he looked the embodiment of a war god!

Mr. Heap, a diplomat of the old school, made all arrangements for the presentation of General Longstreet and the officers from the *Nipsic*. We assembled at the legation and from there were driven to the Doma Batche Palace on the European side of the Bosphorus. At the palace we were received by the officers in waiting and the famous Osman Pasha, the hero of Plevna.

At that time the Ottoman Empire was crumbling to its foundations. The Sultan Abdul Hamid was a weak, unattractive looking man with a restless, unsteady eye. During the audience he appeared nervous. Not impressive.

Mr. Heap told us that in former times coffee was served in gold-lined cups encrusted with diamonds, and that the custom was to present each visitor with the cup he used. Osman Pasha gave me a cigarette, which I kept for many years as a souvenir of a very distinguished soldier.

The next evening there was a state dinner at the admiralty. We were received in the handsome council chamber, celebrated as the scene of the debates of the Constantinople Conference. General Longstreet proposed a toast to the sultan, "the center figure of the Ottoman Empire," with the hope that he might "always rest serene on his pillow." Longstreet made a marvelous impression on the Turkish officers. The wound in his throat especially excited their admiration, for the Turks love a soldier.

Naturally, as a midshipman I did not come in social contact with our admiral. He was something too great and splendid to be approached by the lowly. Rear Admiral John C. Howell was in command of the European Station when the *Nipsic* joined it. He was tall, fine-looking and very distinguished with his white hair and closely cropped mustache. The gold lace of his uniform was as free from tarnish as if made of pure gold and he carried himself with commanding dignity.

The day he inspected the *Nipsic* I saw him at close quarters, and he was just as grand as when viewed from a distance! His inspection of the ship did not please him. Our captain was much chagrined by the copy of the report, the original having been sent to Washington. The admiral began with unfavorable comments on Captain Schoonmaker's uniform—tarnished lace, etc., and a special reference to his chapeau. We did not know of this for a long time—at least the part which criticized our captain—but a short time afterwards noticed his appearance at general inspection absolutely resplendent in Starkey's best gold lace, a new cocked hat and a Starkey sword—which in those days was the last word in naval adornment.

Even as Captain Schoonmaker took note of the admiral's criticism of his personal appearance, so did the executive put the screws on officers and crew. Our drills were excessive for those days—gun drills, sail drills, exercises with spars, boats and carrying out anchors. There was not much shore going until after three o'clock. The result was that Mr. Newell got himself disliked, at least by the midshipmen who thought it a hardship not to get ashore immediately after morning drills. As the ship did very well at the next admiral's inspection, we were partly reconciled and the restrictions were eased.

In due course Admiral Howell was relieved by one of the strictest martinets of the navy—J. W. A. Nicholson. His sobriquet, "War-horse," was won not in action but from a slip when he was a young officer by his translation of *hors de combat,* more in accordance with the phonetic sound than with the French meaning, by which he was very much out of the running.

Nicholson was rather a small, slender man with a long, full beard usually buttoned inside his overcoat in stormy weather. In after years I knew his family and their devotion to him proved that he must have had a lovable side. Looking back and recalling some of his actions and orders as commander-in-chief, I cannot square his treatment of subordinates by any necessary rule of conduct. Essentially he was a type of sea officer common enough in the days of Marryatt, but which went out of fashion with spars and sails. He came of a distinguished New York naval family. According to Cooper, his grandfather, Samuel Nicholson, was the first officer to give an order on the deck of the old *Constitution.* Nicholson had the highest ideals of the service, had served with distinction in the Civil War and was a favorite—on shore.

One night on board the *Lancaster* at Nice he sent for Mr. Goodrich, the executive officer. "Mr. Goodrich is on leave," Captain Gherardi told him. Whereupon Admiral Nicholson shouted, "Every time I want an officer I am told he is on leave. Telegraph at once for all officers on leave to return to their ships."

That same night in Paris, a midshipman on sick leave from the *Nipsic* was at a private musicale where the lovely Miss Lippincott (whose stage name was Bianca) sang. In the party were her mother and Grace Greenwood, along with the American artist, Edwin Lord Weeks. The next day, Sunday, was to be Varnishing Day at the Salon, and Mr. Weeks invited the midshipman as his guest, arranging to meet him at the Champs Elysees entrance at nine the next morning.

At seven the midshipman was awakened by the concierge with a blue telegram, signed by Captain Seeley: "Return to the ship at once." At nine o'clock, instead of being at the door of the Salon, he was on the express bound for the Cote d'Azur, imagining another urgent call for the ship to aid missionaries in distress in the Near East. On arriving at Villefranche he was astonished to find the ship lying idly in the harbor with no signs of preparing for sea. Thus I missed the only chance I had of attending the opening of the Paris Salon.

On one occasion the squadron was tied up to the mole at Leghorn, with orders to get under way at daylight. Just before casting off our lines, the captain sent me on board the flagship with a message to the admiral. Having delivered it to the officer on the half deck, I was starting up the ladder to the quarterdeck, when I heard a gruff voice sing out, "Send that midshipman here."

I turned and faced the War-horse for the first and only time in my life. He had his beard buttoned up in his sea cape.

"Who are you and where do you come from?"

"I am the midshipman from the *Nipsic,* sir."

"Can you take a message straight?"

"Yes, sir."

"Well, tell Captain Seeley that he will be prepared to separate from the squadron on signal when we get clear of the breakwater. Have you got it? Now repeat it. That's right."

I was glad to get out of the ship. When I returned to the *Nipsic* and gave the admiral's message to the captain, I informed him that the admiral had cut off his beard! This was unbelievable, but I insisted that I was not mistaken.

Mr. Newell then remarked, "He probably had it tucked inside his cape."

I do not think I fell in with the War-horse again, but from time to time heard of him, and the news was always the same. He never reformed! Many years afterwards it so happened that I married a cousin of Mrs. Nicholson's.

Speaking of admirals, I have served with many, but never until I went into the cabin was I brought into close contact with any of them. Before then I served under E. T. Nichols, J. C. Howell, J. W. A. Nicholson, John Lee Davis, Gherardi, Sicard, Sampson and Schley. When I came into command I had close-ups of Admirals Barker, Dewey, Coghlan, Walker, Bradford and Schroeder—under the immediate command of each of whom I served from time to time.

All of them—except Bradford and Schroeder, who were later products—were men who had been tried in battle and had served under Farragut and Porter in the Civil War. Without exception they were typical of what is expected of the American sea officers. Even if not always correct in their judgments or methods, they were a fine lot of American gentlemen devoted to their profession, and not one who did not in himself set an example of honor, loyalty and patriotism. All were prime seamen too, adhering perhaps a little too much to the ideas of the sail period, which was natural, but boldly assuming the care and handling of the modern steel ships, whether singly or in squadron.

Of course, all these men were not of the same type of mind. Some were prosaic and cautious, strict in interpretation of the regulations, seeing nothing but the letter of the law and following it to the death. Others were a law unto themselves, believing the naval regulations to be intended as a guide for those who carried no light of their own, and more honored in the breach than in the observance. These used their own discretion, never requested instructions, acted on their own and let it go at that. The latter were the better all-around officers, and made the better leaders. There was still another type; but I never had the ill fortune to serve under what sailors despise most—the "psalm-singer". This rare species, not uncommon in my early days, has now, fortunately, entirely disappeared.

I remember hearing the story once of an old sailor whose unparliamentary language clearly defines this type. "When you are with Captain A," he said, "one day you are a gentleman and the next day you are a son-of-a—, but with Captain B you are a son-of-a— all the time, and you know where you stand."

I told that story once to a high government official who said, "That's not a nice story, Mr. Gleaves. No man is a son-of-a—."

On January 1, 1881, my birthday, I was commissioned an ensign.

At the time I served in European waters it was the custom to send the ships in turn to cruise in the North Sea and Baltic during the summer. The *Nipsic's* turn came in the summer of 1881. When I went to London on a few days leave, Griffin and I had the fortune to meet a member of Parliament, who took us into the Speaker's Gallery. He pointed out the celebrities on the floor.

I was deeply impressed and those brief glimpses of Gladstone, John Manners, Salisbury, Parnell and Justin McCarthy stand out in my memory today, as clear as photographs. I heard Mr. Gladstone make a few remarks, and saw him then sit down, smiling and rubbing his chin.

My host said, "Note the young man who is now speaking. Some day, if he lives, you will hear of him. His name is Arthur Balfour."

Pointing out John Bright, he said to me, "What do they think in America of him?"

I recall my inane but perfectly safe reply: "We think he is a great man."

"Sir," said the MP, "he is the greatest man."

I was sorry I had not been more enthusiastic, but at that time John Bright was little more than a name to me. I was only 23.

What I enjoyed most in London was "Dickens' London". I had read with interest a short time before in the old *Scribner's Monthly* an article on that subject and wanted to see that part of London. On my arrival in, I had gone to our despatch agent, the celebrated Mr. B. F. Stevens, at No. 4 Trafalgar Square, and found him most congenial and sympathetic.

When I told him I had only a few days leave from the ship, then at Gravesend, he said, "Well, let us see what you should see." After enumerating the usual sights of the tourist, he said, "You must eat a whitebait dinner at Greenwich and you should by all means go to the Fish Market at Billingsgate."

Then he turned me over to Mr. Petherick, his aide, and Petherick did the rest—as he had for many years for naval officers, their wives and friends. A man of the widest knowledge of London and the greatest accommodation, Petherick was the one to consult when in doubt, the column upon which hundreds of us have leaned, the oracle to whom we have appealed. It was Petherick who showed me how to get to the Old Curiosity Shop, to Lincoln's Inn fields, and who showed me the house where Mr. Tulkinghorn was murdered. He also directed me to the shop of the little wooden midshipman, in Threadneedle Street I believe, where so far as I know he still stands with his sextant at his eye.

I bought a pamphlet on seamanship in the shop, and as I stood there tried to imagine old Sol Gill and Captain Cuttle in the back room. The very polite clerk of the shop told me that only a week before an American had offered a large sum for the midshipman, but the owner had refused to sell. I went to Fountain Court where Ruth used to meet Tom Pinch. I never found the trail of Pickwick himself in London, but I did at Gad's Hill—near which at that time the Leather Bottle Inn still existed and was an object of interest. I recall that in the grounds at Gad's Hill there was a children's party going on, which I viewed from outside the palings.

It was Mr. Petherick also who told me how to get to Miss Pinkerton's Academy in Hampstead, and to the house where Amelia Sedley lived in Russell Square.

In June 1882 the *Nipsic* had just arrived at Venice from Trieste, and was at anchor off the Public Gardens. One night our usual party was ashore when someone told us that news had just been received of the "massacre" at Alexandria. We did not know at first that about 400 Europeans had been murdered.

It was exciting news and we rushed on board ship to inform Captain Seeley, who said he would sail at daylight, stopping at Corfu and Zante for the latest cable news. Unfortunately he remained so long in both places that we missed the bombardment on the first day, although the cable news stated Admiral Seymour in command of the English fleet at Alexandria would begin the bombardment without delay. Even then we might have arrived in time if the captain had not decided to sail instead of steaming. We anchored in the outer harbor early on July 12. The fight with the forts had begun the preceding day, so we missed the show.

About noon our admiral, War-horse Nicholson, signaled to his ships, "Disregard movements of flagship."

In the afternoon he got underway in his flagship, *Lancaster*, steamed along the lines of the British ships and was loudly cheered by the British sailors. Just why he did this was never explained, but he was bitterly assailed in the press at home for his action and abused for "playing favorites" and siding aginst the "underdogs".

The days following the bombardment were full of excitement for all of us. Before the bombardment the French squadron, to show they were not in it, had gone to sea. Admiral Seymour's operations stirred up all the European chancelleries. It was entirely a political move to clinch England's hold on Egypt. The story is told in interesting detail in Wilfred Blunt's *Secret Diplomacy in Egypt.*

Shortly after the last gun was fired from the British fleet, the Arabs set fire to the city. Dense volumes of smoke arose and at night the flames made a brilliant picture of palaces, mosques and minarets. To save the city from total destruction and preserve order, Admiral Seymour landed a force of bluejackets and marines and invited the foreign naval commanders to take part in saving the consulates of their own nations.

Admiral Nicholson promptly responded and directed Captain Gherardi to organize a landing party under Lieutenant Commander C. F. Goodrich, the executive of the *Lancaster*. Commander Charles Beresford, who had just leaped into fame by his fine handling of the *Condor* during the bombardment, was placed in charge of the entire landing force as chief of police, and the foreign contingents were requested to report to him for assignment.

Order was soon restored by summarily shooting all looters and firebugs. Every man caught red-handed in crime was given a trial, such as it was, and if found guilty was shot and buried *sans ceremonie.*

On the following Sunday afternoon I obtained permission to go ashore. We visited the lighthouse fort which had been knocked to pieces and its guns dismounted by the fire from the ships. One heavy gun had been upended by a shell exploding underneath it, burying most of its crew under the carriage. Its muzzle was pointing up in the air at an angle of about 45°.

The city, or at least a large portion of it, was a smoldering ruin. The public square was destroyed. Starving cats and dogs slunk about in the hot sun among the debris.

At the consulate I saw Captain Gherardi and met Colonel du Chaillu-Long, the African explorer who was acting at that time as correspondent for the New York *Herald.* I remember that Captain Gherardi said to Long—I can repeat his words almost exactly—"When Admiral Seymour asked me to protect the American consulate, I said I would like to establish the American consultate at the Ramleh Gate, as it was believed that Arabi would enter the city there, if he attacked it. 'But, my dear sir,' the admiral said, 'that would be belligerency.' I replied, 'Yes, I know that, but the lawyers could settle that afterwards.' "

Gherardi also said that when the Russian sailors landed, the officer in command reported to Lietuenant Commander Goodrich who told him that he could not receive the report as he was not in charge. Lord Beresford was the one to receive it. The Russian said his orders were to report only to an American officer, and if the report was not accepted to return to his ship. This he did.

A drumhead court-martial, composed of three British naval officers, was in session in Mehemet Ali Square in front of the American consulate. Nearby was a working party of English sailors digging graves. A number of looters were to be shot at five o'clock, which was the time we were ordered to be on board. I asked Mr. Newell if we could remain until justice had been administered and was told that we could not!

It was a week or more before the army transports arrived and then the sailors returned to their ships. There was a great deal of feeling between the two services on account of the delay. At the club a British naval officer said to me, "It is always like this. We clear the way, land, restore order, and then the army comes, gets all the kudos, and we go back on board and are forgotten."

I am sorry to say that whatever feeling the British army had against their own navy, at least one of the army officers showed but scant courtesy to the Americans. It was in this way: Our consular representative in Alexandria was one Menasci, a cosmopolite. He was very rich and his father had built a palace in the heart of the city, which the mob wrecked on the eleventh of June. When the storm was seen to be inevitable Menasci *pere* fled to Europe, leaving his son in charge of the consulate.

After the massacre, General C. P. Stone, at the request of young Menasci, moved into his residence and brought his family down from Cairo to occupy it. One day after the occupation of the city by the British under General Allison, Menasci invited Captain Seeley to bring two officers with him for a drive along the canal. The captain asked Mr. Newell and myself to go.

At the first outpost the carriage was stopped by a sergeant who informed us we could go no further, pointing to an abatis across the road. Menasci said that our party consisted of the American consul and the captain and officers from an American man-of-war in the harbor.

The sergeant saluted, left us for a moment and crossed the road. After some conversation with a British officer, evidently the officer of the day—who did not take the trouble to come over to us and who appeared to be very angry—he returned with a message that we could not go through. The officer's manner was so discourteous that Captain Seeley reported the affair to General Allison who expressed his regrets and promised to investigate the incident. That was all!

After the bombardment young Menasci turned his palace over to the wife of Stone Pasha and her daughters who had come from Cairo. In a few days they got rid of the debris, and as far as might be, put things to rights. Here the officers of the *Nipsic* spent much of their time on shore.

General C. P. Stone, who had been formerly in the United States Army, was the chief of staff of the khedive's army. When the English troops arrived he knew his days as such were numbered. One day on his way home from the Ras-el-Tin Palace he found the town posted with a proclamation signed by the minister of war that the Egyptian army had been disbanded. Nothing had been said to him, but he went at once to a clothing shop, doffed his uniform which he had worn for many years, and went on home. It was the first time his daughters had ever seen him out of uniform and they burst into tears, realizing that something unforeseen had happened.

The next day the khedive sent for him. He found the khedive at his palace with his ministers and General Allison. As Stone entered the chamber the khedive said to Raghab Pasha, "See how quickly General Stone obeys orders."

Stone replied, "You have disbanded the army and I am one of the army."

"Oh," said the khedive, "that order was not intended for you."

I believe that several years afterwards the khedive, or the Egyptian government, granted a generous pension to Stone, which was continued to his widow when he died in New York in 1887. At that time he was the engineer in charge of the erection of the Statue of Liberty.

Arabi retreated to Kaffredouer, a few miles outside of Alexandria, and after maintaining for several days a threatening position retired to the interior. He was defeated at the battle of Tel-el-Kebir by the British in the course of a few weeks and exiled to Ceylon. While he was in his fortifications opposite Ramleh, I obtained permission from Sir Evelyn Wood in person, then in command, to go to the front. While waiting at the little railroad station, I got into conversation with an English sergeant, waiting there for the mail. "You English are here now and you will never leave."

"Oh, no," he replied. "H'England don't want h'Egypt. She's got too many h'irons in the fire now. She can 'ot 'em h'all, but she can't 'ammer 'em h'all h'out."

One day Ensign Griffin returned from shore and said he had been under fire. Arabi's shells had passed over Mr. Moberly Bell's residence while he was there. We all knew Mr. Bell—the huge and cordial correspondent of the London *Times,* afterwards its manager. I posted to his temporary quarters, and when several shells had passed overhead, felt my mission accomplished. Returning to the city, I informed my shipmates that I too had been under fire. Griffin was a fine character in every way: one of the few men I have known who always lived up to the duties of a Christian gentleman. He was a true example of the Red Cross knight in armor.

On our way home when the cruise was over the ship was to stop at Lisbon and take on board the body of Midshipman Sparhawk, recently deceased. We had already stowed on the poop deck the bodies of the late fleet surgeon, Dr. Gibbs, and a child of Lieutenant Wadham's. At Gibraltar we had taken on 2000 pounds of guncotton brought down from London in a British merchant ship for transportation to the United States. It was the first guncotton every taken in quantity on board an American man-of-war.

We also had an American state prisoner, picked up at Smyrna to be turned over to the federal authorities in New York for a life term at Sing Sing. He had killed a man at Alexandria and received a life sentence from the mixed tribunal. I have forgotten his name, but remember that he was taken out of his cell on Sundays and made to attend divine service, always conducted on the berth deck by Mr. Newell, who never failed to read with emphasis that portion of the service for "prisoners and captives". It seemed to me that this was rubbing it in—meet and proper perhaps for an ordained minister, but unnecessary in a service read by a layman.

On entering the Tagus River we ran ashore in a thick mist, and broke the crankshaft. While hard and fast ashore we signaled for a tug. I remember the international signal—P. N. (which means "want a tug"). It was a point to be remembered when later the tug company claimed £1000 salvage on the ground that we had hoisted a distress signal. It was easy to prove that our signal had been an ordinary request for a tug and not a distress signal, and moreover that by the time the tug came out and gave us a towline, the ship was afloat.

The chief engineer, David Smith, was sent to London with blueprints to rush the manufacture of a new shaft and we settled down for a six-week stay in one of the most delightful and hospitable ports of Europe.

Before we finally broke the homeward-bound pennant, "Professor" Wiggins had published his warning of a cyclone that would sweep over the North Atlantic and destroy all ships at sea. This tempest was to occur just as the *Nipsic* was expected to be in mid-ocean. Of course, nothing happened but old Owen Brett, the ship's cook, was gloomy and wont to proclaim daily at the galley that being loaded down with court-martial prisoners, corpses, jailbirds and guncotton, we were sure to run into Wiggins' storm, and he never expected to see the Bowery again.

But he did—too much of it in fact. He went ashore when discharged and was promptly relieved of $1500, his savings for three years, by the sharks in Sand Street. My old quarter-gunner, who swore he'd never go to sea again, lost $700 the first night he was out of the ship, and as soon as he was sober enlisted again for another three years.

Although we were all disappointed to be held up just as the cruise was ended, we had a good time. It was January and society and the opera were in full swing. Almost every night on which I was off duty I went to the opera—which was very fine, the spectacular effects gorgeous and the price of the tickets within my means.

The king and queen were usually in the royal box, while opposite sat the king's father, Don Fernando, and his American wife, who had been an opera singer—and strangely enough, named Fanny Essler. I do not know whether she was any relation to the famous one of that name so closely associated with the Duke of Reichstadt.

One night in the foyer I met Major Serpo Pinto, just returned from his last expedition to Africa. He was a small, dark man, undistinguished in appearance.

Our special friends in Lisbon were an American-English family, the Winns. Mrs. Winn was a Georgian who had married her husband in the United States. They had moved to California and subsequently to Lisbon, where Mr. Winn was manager of his sister's estates in

Portugal. Their hospitable home was the rendezvous of the *Nipsic's* officers, old and young, and one of the young ladies decided to return to America as the wife of the young marine officer in the flagship, Lieutenant Waller—afterwards a Major General in the Marine Corps.

We reached New York in due course. The weather was very cold and the hills on Staten Island and around the Bay Ridge looked bare and bleak. My last recollection of the pay clerk and Henderson, as we approached Sandy Hook, is of them standing in the gangway betting whether the pilot would step on the deck with his right or left foot. I also remember that I had to pay $72 duties for the "illegal transportation of private goods in a public vessel" which was dear for the few curios that I had picked up in Europe for my family—and not "for sale or traffic".

When the *Nipsic* was paid off in New York in February 1883, she had been in commission 42 months and had cruised 45,000 miles under sail and steam. With the exception of the captain, two or three officers and a few men, her personnel was the same as when she was fitted out at Norfolk in 1879.

Looking back over the years, I have always regarded the cruise in the *Nipsic* as the happiest I ever made—perhaps because I was at the most impressionable age. To quote William Rothenstein: "Those were the days of vital friendships when our faith and trust in one another were as yet undimmed."

5 First Cruise to China

After six months on leave at my home in Nashville I succumbed to sea fever and applied to the navy department for orders to the *Trenton,* then fitting out at New York for the Asiatic Station.

There was no trouble in getting orders, for the navy was absolutely stagnant and there were more officers than the department could profitably employ. Millions had been wasted by unscrupulous politicians on so-called repairs to worthless ships which had no fighting power and were scarcely seaworthy. Some officers were on leave in Europe, others found duty under the treasury department in the coast survey and lighthouse districts, and some were with the geological survey.

A few engaged in business until Congress forbade officers, even when retired, to accept positions with any firm having contracts with the government to supply war material—they were required either to give up their jobs in civil life or resign outright from the navy. Most of them resigned and their services were thus lost to the government. It was not a wise law.

During these discouraging years there was one man who pointed the way to better things. The story, or legend, of Admiral Luce has been told elsewhere, and is not likely to be forgotten—at least by the navy. He was the father of the training system and founder of the War College. Having seen the light ahead, he never despaired of making others see it. He knew that Doubting Castle was not to be won without a fight with Giant Despair. I have often thought it would be appropriate to carve in the arch over the entrance to the War College, "luce et labore".

The days of wooden ships were numbered, and the *Trenton,* the latest creation in wood and canvas, was the last of her kind. She was launched in 1876, made a cruise in the Mediterranean, then returned to the United States for refitting. It was at this time that I was ordered to her, and joined at New York in the fall of 1883.

The *Trenton* was fitting out for the Asiatic Station, and as she was to take out the Korean envoys—at that time in this country on a diplomatic mission—was to go via the Suez Canal and India. The cruise promised to be pleasant and interesting. The captain was R. L.

Phythian and the executive officer, Lieutenant Commander Royal Bird Bradford—an extremely strict man. Among the officers was my own cousin, Albert Gleaves Berry, the second watch officer and esteemed an exceptionally fine sailorman.

The *Trenton* was fitted with incandescent lighting, the first warship of any country to be lighted electrically. Her experience with the plant was of great benefit subsequently in installing electricity in other ships.

In December 1883 we went to Newport for our outfit of torpedoes, which at that time consisted of the spar torpedo—the same type as used by Cushing to destory the *Albemarle* 20 years before—although the Whitehead torpedo had already passed out of the experimental stage and was in use abroad.

At Newport I was invited to a reception at Halidon Hill to meet Matthew Arnold, who was then lecturing in this country. He was, as I recall him, a tall, spare man, not especially prepossessing in appearance. I had some conversation with him. He was making lots of money on the lecture platform, but this did not prevent his severe criticism of Americans and their manners on his return to England. He thought Americans devoid of "culture", ignorant and vulgar—principally perhaps because he didn't meet anyone who knew of Obermann. If only then I had known something of his friend Arthur Clough, and had casually referred to "Quam Corsum Ventus" as one of my favorite poems, he might perhaps have tempered his opinions!

We returned to New York from Newport, picked up Min Yon Ik and his colleagues of the Korean Mission and, after participating in the ceremonies of Evacuation Day, sailed for the Straits December 1, 1883.

Stopping for coal at the Azores, we were entertained by the Dabneys, who had represented the United States there for three generations. The Dabneys at the Azores, the Spragues at Gibralter, and the Heaps at Tunis and Constantinople had held these consulates for so many years, that, as was said of old Commodore Tingey, commandant of the Washington Navy Yard for 29 years, they might have willed them to their sons. The Dabneys and Heaps have passed, but a Sprague still remains at Gibraltar.

During the voyage across the Atlantic we met a succession of heavy gales and sail was reduced to treble reefed topsails, storm mizzen and mizzen storm staysail. On the third day, the gale broke and all plain sail was made to royals. Thereafter the weather was pleasant and on the 28th of December the Rock of Gibraltar was sighted.

I was one of Mr. Bradford's aides and was thrown with him constantly. In port my duty was to weigh the coal as it was put in the lighters ashore when we coaled ship—the dirtiest and most disagreeable job I ever had, and one that should not have been assigned to a commissioned officer. It had cost the government $20,000 to educate me, and it seemed to me that this was a high price to pay for weighing coal!

At Gibraltar the Duke of Edinburgh came on board to return the captain's call and to look at our electric plant. He was in command of the Channel Squadron, flying his flag in the *Agincourt.* Captain Phythian invited the officers to his cabin to drink a glass of champagne with the duke, who was affable and very pleasant. His aide, a naval lieutenant, startled our electrical officers for a moment by asking, "What is your margin in volts?" which was proper technique, but an American would have put it differently.

The Koreans messed in the cabin with the captain and had their quarters in the admiral's cabin, otherwise unoccupied. From Marseilles they went to Paris, accompanied by Lieutenant Swinburne and their special escort, Ensign George Foulke—an expert in the Japanese language and customs, a brilliant young officer who soon became the United States minister at Seoul, an unprecedented assignment for such inferior rank.

While at Marseilles the ship was moored to the breakwater, stern-to of course, and while there it came on to blow so hard that it was necessary to get out additional securing lines. It was hard work, for the sea was short and heavy and the ship was surging on the stern line already out. A line was at last got ashore by Ensign Tillman, who did it so well that Mr. Bradford sang out to him from the ship, "Good boy!" After the ship was secured, the captain sent for him and said that in view of his conduct he would not make the report he had intended to send to the commander in chief when we arrived on the China Station, for Tillman had been reported by the executive as insubordinate at Gibraltar—arising from trouble he had with his hammock-boy.

One day Albert Berry invited me to lunch with him at a smart cafe in the Rue Cannibierre and introduced me to bouillabaisse. It was the first time I had eaten the dish made famous by Thackeray. As we ate the Provencal fish soup and drank the "Yellow Sealed Chambertin", Berry quoted the poem. I thought it was a red-letter occasion. I have forgotten many important events in the last 50 years, but somehow that luncheon remains very clear in my mind.

We next went to Naples to give our diplomatic passengers an opportunity to visit Rome. While exercising spars and sails, our main topgallant mast was sprung. Showing the difference between then and now, the stick for a new spar was obtained at once on shore, towed to the ship, hewn into shape and fitted by our own carpenters, assisted by the carpenter's gang from the *Kearsarge,* which happened to be in port. By the next afternoon it was in place and rigged! Nowadays it would be difficult, if not impossible, to get the wood for a spar in the first place, and then there would be no one on board to make a mast of it!

Our last port in the Mediterranean was Port Said. While there, the practice was inaugurated in our navy of standing at attention in salute when passing another man-of-war while the national airs were played. It happened in this way: On entering the Canal we passed close to a British man-of-war tied up at the docks. Each ship played the national air of the other while her men and officers lined up along the rails and stood at attention. Our men paid no attention until the order was given from the bridge.

This is now an international custom, as is also standing at attention and saluting when colors are made, or at any other time when the national anthem is played either afloat or ashore. So far as I know the *Trenton* was the first ship of our navy to observe this ceremony. It is navy regulations now.

At Ismailia, at the hotel, I fell in with an old friend I had known when at Alexandria in the *Nipsic.* He told me that another friend, Maurice Bey, had been wiped out—as he expressed it—while serving with Hicks in the Sudan a few months before. It was at the tragic affair at el-Teb.

Major Maurice Bey was a retired British marine officer serving in the Egyptian army, while his brother Maurice Pasha, a retired post captain in the Royal Navy, was the captain of the port at Alexandria. Both men seemed proud of their kinship with our own Captain Farquhar, afterwards Rear Admiral U.S. Navy. At the battle of el-Teb Maurice Bey was last seen alive on a gun carriage, waving his sword.

It was at his house, after a delightful dinner party, that I first heard the expression "doch-an-darach"—only I thought our host said "Dock and Dorris". Of course, I knew, from the way he put it that it meant a parting drink—a stirrup cup. A tall, fine-looking Arab in a white gown came in with a shining brass tray on which were brandy and soda.

"Before you go," said the major, "we'll have a doch-an-darach."

I looked many years before I found the words, but at last ran them down in one of William Black's novels. Similarly I had once looked for "Louis XIX" and also the legend referred to in Kipling's allusion to Judas in the "Last Chantey". I succeeded in finding both, thanks to my friend Mrs. Charles A. Post of New York and to my classmate J. B. Gilder.

On the way down the Red Sea we were signaled by a small sail boat that wished to communicate. It proved to contain two English officers who requested the captain to put them ashore at Suakin, but in view of the fact that a war was on and they were belligerents, the "old man" declined to do so.

Aden—the hottest place in the world—and Bombay—the most interesting—were our next stops. Then we came to Ceylon without especially noticing the spicy breezes or that man was unusually vile. But I did make the opportunity of seeing Arabi Pasha, then a prisoner of the British government, in the cinnamon groves of that beautiful island.

Two messmates joined me in a party to call on the exile and, without announcement or permission, we presented ourselves at Arabi's villa. Perhaps it was an impertinent thing to do, but I was anxious to see *en face* the man whose name two years before had run round the world. His son came out on the vine-covered veranda to meet us, and in a few minutes Arabi himself appeared.

He was not enthusiastic, but polite. A fine specimen of manhood with a kindly countenance, he had a flowing white beard and an easy, affable manner. We told him that we belonged to the United States ship *Trenton,* then at Colombo, and had come out to pay our respects. When I volunteered the rather tactless information that I had been at the bombardment of Alexandria, his manner distinctly chilled.

"What were you doing there?" he asked sharply.

"I was in the American squadron of observation," I replied.

"It was no concern of the United States!" he said, and this concluded our morning call.

Somehow we felt that we had been there long enough, and so—as Jane Eyre might have said—we politely but firmly withdrew. However, I had made another knot on my string of celebrities.

At Hong Kong I was transferred to the old side-wheel, two-masted steamer, *Monocacy,* built at the close of the Civil War and sent out to China in 1867. Our consul at Hong Kong was the famous Colonel John S. Mosby. He politely invited me to tiffin to meet our minister to China, John Russel Young, and the new commander in chief of the station, Acting Rear Admiral John Lee Davis. There were twelve or 14 at the table that Sunday morning, but Admiral Davis and Mr. Young did most of the talking.

The admiral was a fine-looking man who had a distinguished Civil War record and a reputation for severity. He was what is known as a sundowner. I remember he said among other things, "My father told me when I entered the navy not to marry before I was a lieutenant, or before I was 30." It seemed to me good advice and I decided to follow it. Mr. Young talked a great deal of his experiences with General Grant on the latter's voyage around the world.

It was the first time I had met the admiral of whom I had heard much. In immaculate white linen uniform and with neatly trimmed white beard setting off his firm, square chin, he was an impressive figure. He was accounted one of the best in the navy, and I soon learned that he decried the approaching age of sailless ships. He and the minister were worth listening to, but the "I's" swarmed like wasps around the table.

It was rumored that Admiral Davis had received his orders to the station on condition of strictly enforcing the Secretary's obnoxious order that officers should not allow their wives to follow them when on sea duty. A word or two about the "wife order"—as it was called. When it was first issued, an officer wrote officially to the admiral that he had ordered his wife to go home and she refused to obey. He requested instructions! The wives of other officers followed their husbands from one port to another until the officers were detached from their vessels, and, so to speak, dropped on the beach wherever the ship might happen to be, thereby losing sea pay. They remained ashore until the administration changed and the order was rescinded by Mr. Whitney.

The admiral was somewhat of the school of Smollett's Commodore Trunnion. He thought the navy was headed for hell, and one day said to his flag lieutenant that he didn't know what would become of the service when he and his contemporaries were dead. He remarked to Consul Wingate at Foochow that there wasn't a sailor in the squadron, nor an officer, who knew the difference between a topgallant sheet and a topsail reef tackle!

Colonel Mosby was a remarkable character. Somewhat below average height, he was slender, clean shaven, with close-cropped hair and an eye like a hawk. He usually dressed in white flannels and wore a low crowned, soft wool hat of cardinal red. He offended many officers by asking them where they were from and, if they came from north of the Mason-Dixon line, ending the acquaintance so far as the colonel was concerned.

Once when I was talking to him in his office I picked up a book on the flyleaf of which he had written these lines from Moore:

"Rebellion"

How many a spirit born to bless
Hath sunk beneath thy withering name,
Whom but a day's, an hour's success
Had wafted to eternal fame!

It gave me an opportunity to ask him about his experiences in the Civil War. He replied it was something he never talked about and wanted to forget. War was only a recollection of dead and wounded men and agony and distress, he said, and although he was in the midst of it for four years he had never been wounded, "not even scratched."

When the Democrats came into power Mosby, of course, was recalled. Before leaving China, Li-Hung-chang offered him command of the Chinese armies. He told me this in a cutter going ashore from the *Monocacy* in Hong Kong Harbor. I recall his expression, his flat red hat pulled down almost to the bridge of his nose, as he added, "I declined and wrote him that I was no damned soldier of fortune."

I met him afterwards several times in Washington. He died in 1916.

My cruise in China was uneventful and, except for the months in North China, uninteresting. The admiral would not allow the ship to go to Japan and we passed months in the Chinese rivers, mostly at Canton. We were at Foochow when the French squadron under Admiral Courbet destroyed the Chinese squadron at the Pagoda Anchorage, nine miles from the city.

The captain of the *Monocacy* was Commander F. J. Higginson, at times a very difficile man, and life on board was not especially pleasant. But I was his white-haired boy and, as Jo says in *Bleak House,* "He was wery good to me, he wos".

During the unsettled conditions ashore he sent me to our consultate in Foochow to act as signal officer. The consulate was on a high hill overlooking the river anchorage and in clear view of the ship. The consul was Mr. Wingate, a very agreeable person.

On 16 August 1884 Admiral Courbet had arrived at the Pagoda Anchorage with a squadron of modern ships which had been at Formosa awaiting eventualities. He chose the birthday of the empress for his move, entered the river and ran past the forts with his ships dressed with the Chinese Yellow Dragon Flag at the mastheads in honor of the day, and anchored his ships *above* the Chinese vessels!

On the morning of the 23rd of August I was sent by Captain Higginson to the consulate with a message from Admiral Davis, who had transferred his flag temporarily to the *Monocacy* from the *Juaniata,* which remained at the Pagoda Anchorage. Mr. Wingate showed me a cable just received from Minister Young at Peking, and also from the British consul at Foochow, to the effect that Admiral Courbet "would begin reprisals in the river Min at one p.m." that afternoon.

For two days a typhoon had been blowing at sea and at Foochow there were strong winds and heavy rains. Sharp at one o'clock, when all the ships at the anchorage, Chinese and French, had swung to the ebb tide—the most favorable position for the French—a pistol shot was fired from the *Volta.* This was the preconcerted signal for the French to open fire.

In less than a quarter hour the Chinese squadron was destroyed and upwards of 2,000 Chinamen killed and drowned. The French loss was six men, all of whom were on the bridge of the *Volta* with the admiral and the pilot, Mr. Thomas, an Englishman. The admiral was the only one who escaped the shell that swept the bridge. Thomas was decapitated by it. Soon after the action the French left the anchorage and steamed down the river, taking the forts in reverse. They then returned to Formosa.

Shortly after this Admiral Courbet died "mysteriously" on board the *Bayard* while blockading off Ma-Kung Roads. Readers of Pierre Loti will recall his beautiful tribute to the admiral in his, "Propos d'Exile," in which it is hinted that he died of dysentery. But an officer of the *Triomphante,* in which Loti was serving at the time, told one of our officers that Courbet committed suicide when he received the cable from Paris to relinquish the blockade.

The dispatch was handed to him one evening while walking the quarterdeck with the officer of the deck. He read the message, then said aloud, "This disgraces the service and disgraces me." He then went to his cabin and shot himself. If this story be true, Loti's beautiful tribute to his chief may be more clearly understood.

I recall Admiral Courbet's appearance distinctly—a short, compact figure with white hair. He came on board the *Monocacy* at Shanghai to return Captain Higginson's call. I was officer of the deck at the time and had the duty of piping him over the side.

At Shanghai one of the sailors in the *Monocacy* committed suicide and I was sent ashore to arrange the details of his funeral. The Reverend Mr. Partridge, a missionary clergyman at Jessfield, consented to read the special service used in the Episcopal church. At its conclusion he departed from the ritual to say a few words to the sailors of the escort, in the course of which he said, "The sailor has his vagaries, but he is the tenderest-hearted creature God ever breathed the breath of life into."

The men were so pleased with this that a few days afterwards the chief boatswain's mate, Troy, asked me on behalf of the crew to request Mr. Partridge to come on board the following Sunday and preach to them, saying that he would guarantee a big attendance. In all my experience I think this the most unusual. I afterwards met Mr. Partridge in New York, when he was Bishop of Kansas.

The *Monocacy* remained many tiresome weeks at Foochow. I used to wonder whether the ship would ever go anywhere else. Canton, Foochow and Shanghai seemed to be our patrol. At last Admiral Davis gave us respite and ordered the ship to Tientsin for the winter.

We arrived off the Taku Forts before the close of navigation of the Peiko River by the ice. This was an interesting, historic spot celebrated in our naval history by Commodore Tattnal's famous phrase, "Blood is thicker than water." The forts on either side of the river, known as the Mud Forts, were heavily armed and have been the scene of much fighting, both before and after that time. On the way up the river to Tientsin we passed a vessel coming down with Li Hung-chang on board. He was on deck. We must have saluted, although I do not recall it.

The social life of Tientsin was most attractive. The American consul, "Uncle George" Bromley, was active in his efforts to make it pleasant for the people on board ship, and was a winning card wherever he went. The weather was very cold and dust storms were frequent. One day the French gunboat painted ship—man-o'-war white—and that night and the following day dust storms literally plastered the ship from truck to waterline with Mongolian sand.

Navigation was closed in the Peiko, the river was frozen over and the long dock front deserted. Our surgeon, Clem Biddle, dug out of a storehouse an old ice boat and rigged it completely. He and I had the exciting diversion of ice sailing, which we varied with bicycling on the old-fashioned high front wheel bikes.

The *Monocacy,* of course, had no heating plant or electricity. She was heated by red-hot bricks in buckets of sand, brought in from the fireroom. Candles and oil lamps supplied our light.

During the winter I was invited by Colonel Denby, our minister to China, to visit the legation. There were no railroads in those days and the journey of 80 miles had to be made either on ponies or in carts. Ensign Talcott, my companion, and I started in Chinese carts for Peking early one morning—he in one cart, I in another. A third was loaded with our bedding, food and luggage.

We arrived at the gates of Peking early in the afternoon of the third day. Colonel Denby met us on horseback and rode with us to the legation in the "Legation City", a distance of five miles. I can never cease to be grateful for the kindness and hospitality of Colonel and Mrs. Denby during the days I was under their rooftree.

In later years I saw much of the colonel in Washington. The diplomatic service has had few such able and representative men. He was our minister in China for 15 years. Of unusual physique and extremely handsome, he had affable and courteous manners—those of someone accustomed to court and camp. In the Civil War he had commanded an Indiana regiment with distinction and subsequently filled many important positions—his last, I believe, on the Philippine Commission with Dean Worcester. Frequently he came to our quarters at the Navy Yard in Washington where he was a most entertaining guest, telling us it was a pleasure to go where he was not asked to do things for people!

The weather was very cold, but there was not much snow. Dust storms were frequent. Mr. F. D. Cheshire, the first secretary of the legation, turned his pony over to me, and Mr. W. W. Rockhill, the second secretary, rode with me nearly every day. I saw the sights and learned a lot about Chinese life and customs from him, for he was familiar with the intricacies both of the streets and Chinese methods.

Rockhill was an interesting man who at that time was preparing himself for his journey to Tibet. A direct descendant of Oliver Cromwell, he owned a piece of silver marked with the protector's monogram. He was of a prominent Philadelphia family, had been educated at Saint-Cyr-l'Ecole and had served as a lieutenant in the French army for a brief period in Algeria. While in Paris he took up the study of Oriental languages and before going to China had translated into English a Sanscrit work on medicine. His wife said she had suggested that he print as a foreword the lines from Samantha Ann in Josiah Allen's book, "I wonder who'll read what I have wrote?"

Every night during our visit there were dinners and receptions at the various legations. Society was confined to the diplomatic set and, of course, during the winter remained unchanged—which must have been a bit trying owing to the strict observance of the rules of precedence. The wife of an American attache remarked to me, "I have been taken in to every dinner but one this winter by Dr. Williams!" (He was the famous author of *The Middle Kingdom*.)

We visited the Great Wall, going to the Nankow Pass on ponies. I find from my diary that we left Peking December 9, 1885. I remember that the weather was bright, clear and cold, the carts had no springs and the ruts in the frozen ground were very deep.

The outstanding memory of this visit was my surreptitious visit to the Temple of Heaven. It was as taboo to foreigners as the Forbidden City. I was anxious to get inside and, having borrowed Mr. Cheshire's pony and his "mafoo" as guide, I decided to make the effort. At breakfast Colonel Denby warned me not to try it. I only said that I didn't expect to get inside the temple, but there would at least be some satisfaction in being near it—seeing the walls of the enclosure at close range.

About nine o'clock one morning in December, 1885, the mafoo and I left the legation, and in a short time covered the five miles to the Temple of Heaven, not expecting to go inside. When we got to the West Gate there were no soldiers in sight and where the outer wall was broken down we rode over it, going full speed around to the East Gate of the inner wall.

There we found two Chinamen, and after much talk succeeded in persuading them to help us over the wall for the sum of $2.50—which was all the money in my pockets. One of them produced two ropes, by which we scaled the wall, leaving the ponies with the other man outside at the sentry box. Inside we visited the Temple Altar and the Well of Purity. On the way out I looked through the gate at the South Altar but could not get in as there were people there and the gates were closed. I am very proud of this exploit as I was the first foreigner who succeeded in getting in for several years.

At tiffin the colonel said, "Well, did you go to the Temple of Heaven?"

"Yes."

"You didn't see anything?"

"I went inside."

He was astonished and incredulous, and only remarked "I hope you will not speak of this to anyone. It might cause trouble."

A short time after this a student interpreter of the British legation asked me if it were true that I had got into the temple. He and several other students had made the attempt, but had been detected, arrested and threatened with death. They only escaped punishment by insisting on communicating promptly with their minister. This student was named Wilkinson and he has described his adventure in a book published under the title, *Where Chinese Drive.**

As several others spoke to me of it, I told the minister that I had not mentioned the affair to anyone whatever. Mrs. Denby, who was present, said, "I was the one who told it to everyone who was here at the tea yesterday. I did it because I was proud that it had been accomplished by an American. You know, Mr. Denby, if it had been a British naval officer who got into the temple, Lady Hart would have spread the news over the city."

I was much gratified several weeks later when, on being introduced to Gen. James Harrison Wilson on board the *Monocacy* at Tientsin, he asked, "Are you the officer who got into the Temple of Heaven?"

Forty years afterwards, when commander in chief of the Asiatic Fleet, I went to Peking as the guest of the Chinese government. My daughter, Evelina, was among those who met me at the railway station and the first thing she said was, "I have flown over the Temple of Heaven!" My children had often heard the story which I have thought worth telling here.

General Wilson was then traveling in China in the interests of an American railroad syndicate, with special regard to improving the

*So called from a line in Milton. North China, until the day of the automobile, was the only part of China where the Chinese used horses.

banks of the Yellow River—which as nature made them cannot retain the annual floods that sweep down from the mountains in the spring, destroying life and property. One day in the wardroom of the *Monocacy* (this was in 1886) he said, "Why don't some of you young fellows write the history of the navy? I have a young friend in New York who has just written *The War of 1812*. His name is Theodore Roosevelt. He isn't 30 years old, knows nothing of the navy except what he has read, yet his book is said to be the best account of our fight with England on the ocean."

The winter of 1886 was a gay one in Peking—dinners every evening, receptions in the afternoon and lively skating parties at the lake. When the winter was ended and the Peiko opened again to navigation, the *Monocacy* sailed for Shanghai, thence to Hong Kong. Upon the arrival of the *Trenton* at Hong Kong, I was transferred to her for passage to the United States.

Before Admiral Davis came out, the *Monacacy* had lain in Yokohama for months on end and her people had acquired a gay reputation—to such a degree that the new admiral swore by all the gods of decency that she should never go to a Japanese port as long as he commanded the station! Although when I joined her shortly afterwards not an officer on board had been in her during the former regime, the curse hung over the ship and her cruising was confined to Chinese ports and Hong Kong.

It was a fearful sentence to pronounce on innocent men. Tropical China is a horror in summer: moist and oppressive heat, rain without a breath of wind, with stagnant calms or hurricanes. A fine rain falls continuously and drips off the awnings to the decks. The atmosphere is so damp that luxuriant vegetation grows on your shoes!

I can never forget those nine consecutive months at Canton. In fall and winter the conditions were not unpleasant: Shanghai and Chefoo were delightful in season and Peking was a dream city in winter. Thus my cruise in Chinese waters was finished. I returned home without seeing Japan and became known on the station as the man who made a full cruise to Asia without getting to Japan.

The *Trenton* returned to the United States via the Mediterranean, stopping at Gibraltar and the Azores. I recall that the night after sailing from Fayal there was a dead calm. The ship drifted and swung with the currents, and headed on every point of the compass between sunset and sunrise. Finally a favorable breeze sprang up and she was brought to her course. Although the *Trenton* had engines, the Department forbade the use of steam except in emergencies.

When the ship in the course of four months reached Hampton Roads, Captain Phythian asked the commandant of the navy yard for a tug to tow us up to the yard. The reply was, "No tug available. Come up under sail."

This would be paralyzing in these days of steam, but Phythian was a sailor of the old school. He carried out the order to the letter and I never saw a better piece of seamanship than when he laid that big ship alongside the seawall at the Portsmouth Navy Yard under topsails, "without cracking an egg-shell".

Those days of ship handling are over. When the old *Constitution* was recently fitted out again as she was in 1812, it was publicly announced that there were no officers or men to man her as a sailing ship, so the old vessel was towed from port to port to show our people with what ships and weapons our navy won its imperishable fame.

I recall also that once when the *Constellation* was towed to her summer berth at the training station she was moored with her head upstream. When Admiral Luce observed this he said to the captain, "Thomas, if she cannot go to sea, why don't you wind her and at least let the old girl look at it?"

The *Trenton* went out of commission at Norfolk three years to the day from the date the flag was hoisted. To me the cruise had few bright spots and I was glad when I received my detachment and was ordered home and granted six months leave of absence.

This seems a good place to insert something more about Captain Higginson who was from Boston, of course, and had a brilliant Civil War record. He had served with Farragut in the Mississippi, with Porter at Fort Fisher and had taken part in the famous, but futile, powder boat expedition there. Although a man of eccentricities, he was nevertheless a brave and gallant seaman.

In the *Monocacy* he had an orderly who, in a manner of speaking, was "not all there". One morning after making the eight o'clock reports to the captain, he said to me, "The captain ordered me to get out of his cabin and said I was a damn fool because I could not remember all of the message you gave me." Then with some animation he added, "I am no damn fool, Sir. I was orderly for General Pope in the army for 13 years, and I can read the *fer*ometer, the *ber*ometer and the *ker*ometer, but I can't remember figgers." A week later this man was in a straitjacket.

I remember the captain invariably wore white gloves when he went to the mast to investigate reports in the conduct book if he were not in a good humor! The white glove was a danger signal, of which the men soon learned to beware. The safest answer to his questions was, "I have nothing to say."

"The cruise to Asia without going to Japan" had not been without compensation. During nine months at Canton I paddled many miles through the network of canals in the vicinity, sometimes with Dr. Biddle, often alone. There was a good library at the club and I read, among other books, Milman's *Holy Roman Empire,* Malthus, Macaulay and old numbers of the *Edinburgh Review*. In one of those old numbers there was a brief review, not altogether favorable, of Longfellow's poems, just published in England. The writer sneered at the name: "*Longfellow*! Phoebus, what a name!"

There was a fine library also in the English Club at Shanghai and big comfortable leather chairs where I spent many hours when the afternoons were rainy. I tried to get interested in the *History of Melancholy* but without success. Fortunately there were hundreds of the famous three-decker novels which Kipling has celebrated in a poem.

I especially devoted much time to ordnance literature obtained from the despatch agent in London. Dr. Biddle also took me through a course of quantitative analysis. He was learned in chemistry, a charming, cultivated fellow, and I was very fond of him. There was a spare room in the *Monocacy* which we used as our laboratory and we passed many hours there in the rainy season. Years afterwards I saw him often when I was governor of the naval home in Philadelphia.

6 On the *Dolphin* and the *Boston*

When I graduated I had made up my mind not to accept shore duty until I had been at least eight years at sea. This term of self-appointed probation was now over and I was assigned duty under the bureau of ordnance, first at the navy yard in Washington for a few months, and then at the proving grounds near Annapolis.

When I reported for duty at Washington, Comdr. Rush Wallace, the commandant, said, "I have orders for you to report in person to the chief of ordnance."

My bosom swelled with pride in anticipation of some special preferment. I thought he might have heard of my interest and studies in ordnance when in China. I floated on air—in the old horse cars—to the navy department and sent my name in to Comdr. Montgomery Sicard. I had to wait so long before gaining admission to his office that my chest was considerably deflated. At last I was told that the chief would see me.

I had often heard of him and his very marked drawl. He looked at me and said, "Well?"

It was very embarrassing. I told him that Commodore Wallace said that he wanted to see me.

"Did I?" he drawled. "Well, what did I want to see you about?"

I left his presence very crestfallen.

On May 26th, 1887, I was promoted to lieutenant, junior grade.

My shore duty lasted three years and was full of interest as the navy had just begun to build steel guns, make armor plates and brown powder and was, in fact, in a state of transition. All the tests were made at the Proving Ground in charge of Lt. A. M. Knight—an indefatigable and resourceful worker.

Just before my shore duty expired came the best fortune of my life. On June 12, 1889, I was married to Miss Evelina Heap, the daughter of Maj. David Porter Heap, a nephew of Comdr. David Porter of *Essex* fame.

Having served on the South Atlantic, European and Asiatic stations, I decided to remain, if possible, in the home squadron, and accordingly hoped for orders, when time to get to sea, to the despatch boat, *Dolphin.* She had the distinction of being the first ship of the "new" navy, and was also—according to the enemies of the administration—"the ship that broke John Roach's heart".

The story of the *Dolphin* is a part of the history of the Navy. The idea was to discredit the new navy as laid down by the old administration. The *Dolphin,* being the first of the first group completed, bore the brunt of it. She was ordered on a shakedown cruise, first under the redoubtable Capt. Dick Meade who reported her a "crazy quilt".

Two boards in succession then solemnly passed judgment—one praised, the other condemned. Finally the department ordered her to make a cruise around the world, which she accomplished with much credit to her designers and builders. She continued in active service until 1921, when she was sold.

I joined the *Dolphin* at Norfolk in November 1889 after the ship was ordered to report for duty to Rear Adm. J. G. Walker. Adm. Walker commanded a division of ships when Admiral Bancroft Gherardi was in command of the North Atlantic Fleet and was one of the most efficient officers produced by the Civil War. As a young man he had command, under Farragut, of several ships in Porter's squadrons on the Mississippi, and had always acquitted himself with distinction.

After the war he was a marked man in the service and his subsequent record was enviable. He became chief of the bureau of navigation in 1881—at that time the most powerful and influential duty under the department. This position he held for eight years, during which time he instituted many reforms in the service. He had a wide acquaintance with the prominent men of the day and generally used his influence wisely for the benefit of the navy. As an administrator and organizer of the first rank, he was perhaps not always just, but a man of his position and influence is bound to make enemies as well as friends.

At the end of his service as chief of navigation he became commander of the European Squadron, which he had organized before he went to sea. It was composed of the newest and most powerful ships of the navy at that time, although they would be poor compared with the ships of the fleet today. The *Chicago,* of 4,500 tons, wore his flag, and the *Boston, Atlanta* and *Dolphin* completed the squadron—the so-called "White Squadron of Evolution".

I had occasion to go to him with my request for sea duty the day before he left the department. His office was filled with officers whom he had selected for his staff. Everyone seemed animated and in great good humor. To me he said, "Get your request in at once as I am leaving tomorrow, and after me the deluge!"

That was the first time I had heard the famous words of Louis XV—or was it Madame de Pompadour? At all events as camouflage, I requested duty on board the *Charleston* in the Pacific, but this was turned down by Walker's successor, Commodore Ramsay, and I was sent to the *Dolphin* on the home station.

At that time the *Dolphin* was commanded by Comdr. Charles O'Neil, a survivor of the *Cumberland.* I have always regretted that I did not hear from him the story of the famous battle with the *Merrimac.* O'Neil became chief of ordnance and was the first officer promoted from enlisted men to reach the grade of flag rank.

It was my orders to the *Dolphin* that first brought me in contact with Commodore Ramsay, then the leading officer of the navy, and my relations with him thereafter were very pleasant.

Our first cruise in the *Dolphin* was to pick up at Porto Rico Frederick Douglass, the new minister to Hayti, and take him on a tour of inspection around the island. It had been a subject of discussion in the press as to what ship would take him. The captain of the first ship ordered was summarily detached and put onshore when he asked the department who would pay the minister's mess bill. This started the newspapers guessing what the next captain would do.

Captain Robley Evans in the *Ossipee,* I believe, was asked what he would do if ordered on the duty. He replied, "Obey the order, of course. I consider Mr. Douglass the foremost man of his race and that is more than I can say of any White man I know."

The *Dolphin* was detained for two weeks at the New York navy yard for repairs. In casting off from the dock we had rammed the seawall and smashed the new hawse pipe. Then a tug came out and pointed us down the East River. The skipper was very angry. The weather was very cold.

After crossing the Gulf Stream we were soon in warm weather and wearing whites. The trip around Hayti and Santo Domingo was uneventful, except for an unpleasant experience at Gonave when nearly everyone in the wardroom who had eaten what the caterer had promised to the mess as a "delicate suckling pig" thought they were in for trichinosis! For a time it really looked serious, as microscopic examination showed that the pig was not "delicate" but impregnated with trichinae spiralis. A day or so afterward the bumboatman who had sold the pig came alongside for more trade. The corporal of the gangway sang out to him, "You can't come on board this ship. You sold a bad pig to the wardroom."

"Any of 'em dead yet?" he asked.

When we took Mr. Douglass on board at Porto Rico he had his White wife and his secretary with him. The entire party messed in the cabin with Captain O'Neil. They gave no trouble but I think it was a relief to all hands when they were safely returned to Porto Rico a week or so later.

One day during the morning watch, while lying off Gonave, Mr. Douglass was talking to me on the quarterdeck about the future of the islands and said, "As long as the natives have only to get their breakfast off the trees they will never work."

Frederick Douglass was a most interesting person. He had belonged to Col. Edward Lloyd of the eastern shore of Maryland. When he was at the New York yard, waiting for the man-o'-war which was to take him to Hayti, it was said the Colonel Lloyd's son, an ensign in another ship at the yard, called on his father's former slave and that Douglass said of this visit, he had received many honors in his life, but none had touched him so deeply as this attention shown by the son of his old master.

After leaving Hayti, the *Dolphin* visited Kingston, Port Royal and Key West, then preceeded north to join Admiral Gherardi's squadron. Shortly after this the secretary's yacht, so-called, the *Despatch,* was lost near Chincoteague Inlet and the *Dolphin* was detailed to replace her. My brother-in-law, Paymaster Lawrence Heap, was on board the *Despatch* at the time.

At the same time I was transferred to the U.S.S. *Boston,* 3,000 tons—another vessel of the new navy. She was commanded by Capt. G. C. Wiltse and among her officers was Lt. Lucien Young, almost forgotten now, but then and for many years one of the outstanding characters of the service.

During the summer of 1890 the *Boston* took part in the maneuvers of the combined squadrons of Admirals Gherardi and J. G. Walker off the New England coast, the principal feature of which was a review by the secretary of the navy. It was a strange collection of ships of all classes.

Mr. Tracy had invited the foreign naval attaches to be his guests on board the *Dolphin* to witness the show. It was a sorry affair: no two turning circles alike, scarcely any two vessels of the same class and all of different characteristics. It must have been amusing to the foreigners.

Years afterwards at a dinner at the Union League Club Mr. Tracy told me that the two events in his administration that had pleased him most were the originating of annual fleet reviews and the sale of the tract of land lying between the navy yard and the Brooklyn Naval Hospital. There were others who thought differently!

Late in the summer the ships dispersed and the *Boston* went to the navy yard at New York. Shortly after that the trouble with Chile regarding the riots of our sailors in Valparaiso became serious. The *Boston* was detached from the home squadron and ordered there to join the *Yorktown,* commanded by Comdr. Robley D. Evans.

We sailed from New York October 24, 1890, and after a short visit at Saint Lucia, proceeded to Bahia. Saint Lucia, one of the fortified islands of the West Indies, was especially interesting on account of Rodney's victory in the adjacent waters. I went with Captain Wiltse as his aide when he dined with Governor Goldsborough, who was proud of his distinguished relatives in the United States Navy and knew much of their history and achievements.

On November 18th we reached Bahia and after coaling and making the usual official calls, continued on to Montevideo. The weather was getting very warm, the sea and sky were giving indications of a gale and the barometer was down to 29.58. On Thanksgiving Day we had a fine dinner beginning with terrapin soup and ending with plum pudding. Before the dinner was over the gale was upon us and the ship was rolling violently through an arc of 84° in a heavy cross sea. The ship was slowed to 30 revolutions and with sail taken off was run off until she was more comfortable, but the forecastle was under water most of the time.

At noon on Thanksgiving we passed directly under the sun and crossed the Tropic of Capricorn, our run the previous 24 hours being only 127 miles. There was a remarkable electric display and for the only time in my experience I saw St. Elmo's fire at the mastheads.

At this time our course was not far off the Brazilian coast and hundreds of gulls followed the ship. During the day we passed a large bark running before the wind under foresail and topsails and also sighted a vessel hull down on our lee beam, lying to on the starboard tack. Bad weather continued until we arrived at Montevideo on December 3rd, when it came on to blow a violent pampero which made our anchorage precarious in the shallow water of the harbor.

These few days of storm were the only bad weather in the run of 6,096 miles from New York to Montevideo, which was made in 30 steaming days. This was not bad, considering the bad condition of the engines which, as someone said, were held together only by rope yarns.

At Montevideo I met General Manney, a fellow townsman, who was charge d'affaires. Manney had been a Confederate brigadier from Tennessee. After the war, like many others, he decided that the grass was greener in Republican pastures than in the Democratic fields, so went over and became "reconstructed".

Montevideo had improved much since my first visit there, 14 years before. The shops and walks about the town had put on a Parisian attractiveness.

We heard here that the "Squadron of Evolution" had been ordered to Peru, indicating that our relations with Chile were not improving. When Captain Wiltse received a cable from the department that Gherardi's squadron was ordered to Valparaiso, we thought that war would soon be on.

Sailing from Montevideo in the afternoon of December 11th, we squared away down the coast for the Strait of Magellan. The engines gave much trouble and were constantly breaking down—not encouraging for going to war! Our speed, which was supposed to be maintained at 12 knots, was reduced to less than 180 miles per day, often even less.

The nights were bright with moonlight and the fair northwesterly wind gave the captain his opportunity for making sail. About 8:30, after sunset one day, a remarkable-looking cloud rose from the southern horizon—camelback in shape and gray in color, subtending an angle of about 135°. As it rose over the ship reaching to zenith, the wind shifted to SSW and all sails were taken in. Then we waited for the wind.

Nothing happened, although the *Yorktown* a few weeks before had run into a severe electric storm in about the same latitude which had seriously damaged her masts. The sea continued to increase and a fresh southerly wind sent the thermometer down rapidly. It continued cloudly, overcast and threatening until we entered the strait, when the weather cleared and that was the last bad weather we had for many weeks.

The scenery in the Strait of Magellan is bleak, but grand. It deserves all that Darwin says in praise of it in the *Voyage of the*

Beagle. While coaling at Sandy Point, a number of us went ashore for a closer look at this southernmost settlement in the Western Hemisphere and bought some guanaco furs for $11 each in American gold. It was just 8:30 and sunset when we got to the cemetery where were buried the British officers and sailors blown up in H.M.S. *Doterel* just a short while before. When we got on board at 9:10 it was not yet dark.

The passage through the strait from Sandy Point to Glacier Bay occupied about 14 hours. On the south side were magnificent glaciers and heavy snowstorms. The north side was clear but barren, without a sign of life. At 10 a.m., December 19th, we passed Cape Pillar, three miles off, and for six hours rolled deeply in the swell that sailors say rolls around the world three times before it strikes anything.

Outside the main islands are numberless scattered rocks on which the long swell of the open ocean incessantly rages. We passed out between the East and West Furies. A littler farther south there are so many breakers that the sea is called the Milky Way. As the *Voyage of the Beagle* said, one sight of such a coast is enough to make a landsman dream for a week about shipwrecks, perils and death.

Albatross and cape hens followed us in numbers. By resorting to the old trick of paying out thread from the stern to entangle their feet we succeeded in catching one albatross—a magnificent fellow—but he became so seasick when landed on deck that we let him go. We ran north in a smooth sea, our bird companions dropped out of sight astern and the day before Christmas the *Boston* anchored in the Bay of Valparaiso.

We found the *Yorktown* at anchor and Captain Evans came on board at once to report to our captain. From the officers of the *Yorktown* we heard all the latest "war" news. There was nothing definite, but relations were strained and threatening. The Chilean fleet of some six fine-looking ships commanded by Captain Vial, half Englishman, were at buoys moored in line ahead seaward.

Numerous American visitors came aboard, among them Frederick May of Washington who said if we had war with Chile he wanted to enlist in the *Boston.* Our consul, who was nicknamed "Quatro Dedos" on account of being shy one finger, came down in the wardroom full of fight and ready to do a bit of trading with the officers for U.S. gold in exchange for Chilean money.

After dinner several of us went ashore to the municipal park, which was brilliantly lighted. The inhabitants appeared to be peaceful and having a good time enjoying the holiday. When we went down to the marina to return to the ship we found Captain Evans and several officers from the *Yorktown*. They had been to a reception at the residence of an American but had not had a cordial greeting. The Americans were showing plainly their disapproval of the attitude of the United States Navy in the quarrel which was daily assuming more serious proportions.

The next afternoon Lieutenant Rush and I were ashore, and as we walked through the streets we planned a personal campaign against the Chilean Navy in the event of war—provided we could get a tug! On returning to the ship we heard the astonishing news that our ship was ordered to San Francisco. As a matter of fact, although it was so given out, we were ordered to Callao, looking in at Iquique en route to observe if any defenses of the harbor were under construction.

It was now plain that the United States was in earnest in the demand for an apology and reparation. We heard that Admiral Gherardi's ships were also ordered to the South Atlantic and, as Captain Glass put it, the bow of every ship in the navy was headed for Valparaiso.

There was a slight diversion from the monotony of ship life on New Year's Eve when the boldest of the sailors, with horns, drums and rattles, paraded through the wardroom shouting Happy New Year, and double eight bells were struck. It was irregular, but neither the captain nor Mr. Swinburne seemed to mind it.

Every day rumors floated to us from north and south that war was inevitable. One day Captain Wiltse said to me, "Rumors of war do not amount to anything. When you have been in the service as long as I have, you'll pay no attention to them until you hear the first crack of a gun."

I never forgot this. It is generally true.

While we were waiting at Callao for eventualities sightseeing, the clubs and bullfights served to while away the time. I made a trip to Chiclayo on the Aroya road in the Andes—13,000 feet above sea level, as far as the railroad was open at that time. On the 16th of January 1891 we were presented to the president of Peru at the Palace Casa Verde. Two weeks later the *Yorktown* arrived from Valparaiso.

At the same time the papers published the United States' ultimatum to Chile demanding an unreserved withdrawal of Premier Mattas' threatening note, an indemnity for the murder of the *Baltimore*'s men and, lastly, a salute to the United States' flag—the reply to be made in not more than two days. The Chileans accepted the terms by a graceful backdown and the quarrel ended without bloodshed. Our ship was now really ordered north to San Francisco.

Before we sailed, the British flagship with Admiral Hotham and Capt. Hedworth Lambton came in. It was a pleasant break, for cordial relations were soon established between the two ships. On February 22nd we had sports on board to celebrate the day, in which the Englishmen took part.

Our captain at this time was about 55 years of age. The English admiral was just the age of Lieutenant Laird, our second watch officer. Captain Lambton was my age. There had been practically no flow of promotion in the American navy since the Civil War. Promotion was as stagnant as the material was out of date!

At Callao I met an interesting retired officer of the Peruvian navy. He had fought the turret guns of the *Huascar* in her battle with the *Shah* in 1878 when a shell entered through the gun port and exploded, killing several of the crew.

One day I went on board the *Naiad,* store ship of the P.S.N.C., to look her over as a marine curiosity. She had been one of Nelson's favorite frigates at Trafalgar, and at that time was new, having been launched in 1797. She was 149 feet long, with a beam of 29 feet. Her tonnage was 1,014. At Trafalgar she was commanded by Capt. Thomas Dundas. It was thrilling to walk her decks, but the only relics of Trafalgar on board were the capstan and an enormous brass speaking trumpet. Rush and I tried to buy the trumpet from the ship keeper but had no luck.

As we left the harbor on the 27th of February, the engines broke down for the nth time since leaving New York. About 10 p.m. we crossed the Equator and four days later arrived at Panama where we stopped several days. Some of us crossed the isthmus on the train to Aspinwall (Colon). The railroad track lay through a thick jungle and from the car windows we saw the rusty remains of locomotives and machinery abandoned by the French company.

From Panama we went to Corinto (Nicaragua) and thence to Libertad (El Salvador) where we received President Ezeta on board with the usual honors of salutes, manning yards and champagne.

At San Jose in Guatemala, our next port, Mr. Gosling, the British charge d'affaires, and the United States minister came on board with Major Macomb, Lieutenant Rieber and Lieutenant Rowan of the United States Army, who were connected with the international survey contemplating a through railroad line to Sandy Point in the straits. I accepted Mr. Gosling's invitation to dine with him when I reached Guatemala City.

The wife of the charge was Swedish. I noticed on the wall of the drawing room an engraving of Count Axel von Fersen. When I asked about it, she said that he was a forebear of hers and told me the story of the iron ring. As is well known, Count von Fersen was in love with Marie Antoinette and the queen sent him an iron ring in which was engraved, "Faint heart he who forsakes her". She told Count Esterhazy she had had the ring made to fit one of her own fingers and it had been worn by her for two days before she sent it, so that the chill of iron might bear with it the warmth of her own blood.

Mrs. Gosling's mother was the last of the Fersens. While writing to her daughter in Budapest: "Though we are in January and the thermometer is at . . ." the letter ended here abruptly. Hearing a noise at that point she had risen to see what it was. In some way her dress caught fire from the lamp and she was burned to death.

My hostess continued, "There is an old Swedish custom when the last of the family dies to paint the coat of arms on porcelain and a representative of the king breaks the plate at the grave. This was done."

There is a well authenticated story of Count von Fersen in America when he was serving with Count Rochambeau in Rhode Island. It is said that he was sent out of France on account of his love affair with the queen. While in Newport he met Miss Anna Hunter who gave him and Count de Ternay lessons in English while they taught her French. He wrote home that his attentions to Miss Hunter were not an *affaire de coeur*. The present Miss Anna Hunter of Newport now has photographs of miniatures of Count von Fersen and her great-great aunt which they had exchanged when Miss Hunter sailed for England. She married Count Jean Louis Falconet.

I shall never get on with this yarn if I do not cut out some of these digressions. We went on to Acapulco and there found orders to search the Socorro Islands, 250 miles off the coast, for shipwrecked Americans from the *Tahiti,* a brig of evil reputation—a blackbirder loaded with 400 slaves from the Gilbert Islands for the coffee plantations of Guatemala. This vessel had been found floating bottom up in that vicinity.

The captain put me, accompanied by Ens. C. F. Hughes, in charge of a party of sailors and two cutters. We made a thorough search under a blazing sun, cutting our way through thick cacti with machetes but, with the exception of an old oar washed up on the beach, there was no sign of human life—past or present. While we were ashore the navigator with the *Boston* made a running survey of the islands. In the adjacent waters were shoals of thresher whales which seemed to be having a good time judging from their splashing.

From the islands we went to Mazatlan and thence to San Diego for coal. At the club in San Diego I met Mr. Charles Nordhoff who told me he had been a powder monkey on board the *Columbus,* Comdr. Biddle's flagship in the voyage to Japan, which preceded by two years that of Commodore M. C. Perry.

The *Boston* went to San Francisco in May 1892 for refit. While there, news came of the threatening political situation in Hawaii, and orders soon came for us to go to Honolulu. Before we sailed, however, we lost several of our crew by a powder explosion at the naval magazine at Mare Island. A working party from the *Boston,* in charge of the gunner, had been sent from the ship to load shell. It was never known what caused the explosion, but 16 men, including the gunner, were killed. The officers and crew erected a monument to their memory in the naval cemetery. Lieutenant Young delivered the funeral oration.

On the 11th of August the *Boston* left the navy yard and after stopping at Santa Cruz sailed for Honolulu on the 14th. The run to the islands was uneventful, save for the death of Kehoe, a young apprentice who fell backward from a ladder while going from the gun deck to the spar deck. Fate is mysterious: This boy fell vertically only a few feet, but fractured his skull. I have seen men fall from aloft without serious injury. He died in a few days.

The burial service was impressive as it always is at sea. Captain Wiltse stood at the head of the stretcher, the marine guard fired three volleys, the boatswain's mates piped down, sail was made and the engines started ahead. It was a different mise-en-scene from that when we buried old Peter Eagan off the bleak New England coast during a snowstorm in a heavy gale. At Kehoe's funeral the sun was shining in a clear summer sky and the genial northeast trades were breaking the blue sea into small white caps.

Our refit at Mare Island was not notably successful as our enginesa broke down again on the passage to Honolulu. We wondered if they would hold together long enough to get us back home. The captain was a monument of patience. Two years before, on 23 tons of coal per day, the *Boston* easily made ten knots. Now we burned just twice the amount and could scarcely make nine knots. However, the wind was fair and the sails eased the engines to a certain extent, but the topsails and topgallant sails caught the smoke from the funnels and drove the cinders over the white decks. As we went south we ran into numerous rainsqualls and the wind drew to the eastward.

On the 24th of August we arrived at Honolulu and moored inside the reef. The *San Francisco,* flagship of Adm. George Brown, was in port awaiting our arrival, and went to sea that afternoon. The admiral was very popular in the islands and had made several cruises there. He had brought the body of the late King Kalakaua back to Honolulu after his death in San Francisco. They were close friends and among the many presents given him by the king was a handsome diamond ring which the Prince of Wales, afterwards Edward VII, had given Kalakaua when the latter visited London on his tour around the world.

When we had been in Honolulu for several days we were presented to Queen Liliuokalani at the palace. She was coldly polite and did not appear to be overjoyed to see either our minister, Mr. Stevens, or Captain Wiltse. The queen, a pureblooded native, had traveled in Europe and the United States and was a woman of the world. Evidently she sensed the approaching political storm which was inevitable and which was to blow her off her tinsel throne.

Our stay in the islands was delightful: boating parties, moonlight bathing at Waikiki, bicycle riding through a beautiful country—all combined with a charming society—absorbed the time of the young officers.

Once the ship went over to Hilo giving us the opportunity of visiting Mauna Loa, the largest active volcano in the world. Its crater, nine miles in circumference, is filled with an ever boiling incandescent sea of lava. Shortly before our visit, there had been an eruption which sent rivers of lava down to the sea. Never can I forget my impressions of standing at night on the edge of that crater watching the fascinating boiling of the molten lava below.

The Sandwich, or Hawaiian, Islands, as they are now called, are strategically the most important outpost of the United States. For years they were a tempting prize to the nations of the world, but all feared to take them. Every European nation knew that the rape of those islands would mean immediate restitution, or war with the United States.

In 1842 Lord George Paulet sailed into Honolulu Harbor, hoisted the British flag over the city and then reported the fact to his admiral, Thomas, then at Valparaiso. There were no cables or steamers to speak of in those days, so it was a long time before the admiral could announce his disapproval to Kamehameha III, then sitting uneasily on the throne of his ancestors. In gratitude to Admiral Thomas the king named the public square in his honor and it bears his name to this day.

In October the minister received news of the wreck of the *William A. Campbell* off the west coast of Mexico and the *Boston* went out to search for traces of her. We just missed one of her open boats which had sailed 2,100 miles across the Pacific and finally landed in the surf at Hilo. This was the only boat from the *Campbell* to reach land, the others having been dismasted and swamped on the Mexican coast.

We found that the rumors of disturbed politics in the islands had not been exaggerated. The Royalists were favored by the English, while our minister, Mr. Stevens, headed the opposite party—which included the Judds, Carters and the Wilders. The Americans enthusiastically welcomed Captain Wiltse who easily fell into their way of thinking. Just how far they admitted him into their confidence, of course, we did not know, but he was evidently sympathetic.

The son of Mr. Woodhouse, the British minister, was supposed to be engaged to the Princess Kaiuolani, then at school in England and not expected to return to Honolulu for a year. The prime minister was Sam Parker, immensely popular and well-known in the United States. He was a native and powerful Royalist.

Governor Cleghorn, husband of the Princess Likiliki and father of the Princess Kaiuolani, was governor of Oahu and lived lavishly in his bungalow at Waikiki. It meant everything to him to see his daughter on the throne. He was Scotch by birth, and in his youth had been a sailor and wrecked in the islands.

Years after, when I was in Honolulu in the *St. Louis,* he lunched on board with me. As I waited at the gangway to receive him I reflected on the uncertainty of human affairs. I had seen him received on board the *Boston* with the guns and ceremonies due his rank, he himself wearing a gorgeous gold-embroidered uniform glittering with stars and ribands. On that next occasion of our meeting, the old man came slowly down the deck wearing a blue sack suit. The regulations forbade any recognition of his former rank. He was a kind, courteous gentleman and apparently took his changed condition as a part of the day's work. I saw him frequently at that time and I never heard him complain or refer to his past glory.

For months, if not for years, certain Americans had planned for the overthrow of the monarchy with the idea of the United States establishing a protectorate and ultimately taking full possession. Mr. Dole and Mr. Thurston were the leaders of the movement and Mr. Stevens was a zealous coadjutor.

After the *Boston* had been in Hawaii for a few weeks and these gentlemen had got Captain Wiltse's number, so to speak, and found the many weak points in his armor, they began to prepare for eventualities. Captain Wiltse was a Naval Academy graduate of the class of 1856, a classmate of Mahan and Schley. He was a kind-hearted, amiable man, but his was not the far horizon. Like all men of narrow limitations, he was easily influenced.

The rumblings of the revolution grew louder and closer and the air was full of rumors. Mr. Dole and his colleagues were frequent callers on board the *Boston*. In November 1892 Dr. McGrew, a prominent citizen, said to me on the lanai of his bungalow in Pearl Harbor, "In less than three months the United States' flag will be flying over the palace. I know it."

About the same time Mr. Stevens wrote to Mr. Blaine, then secretary of state, "The pear is ripe and only waiting for the plucking."

This was afterwards repeated in congress in the discussion following the new administration's investigations.

I left the *Boston* on January 1, 1893. Part of what happened after that was told to me a few months afterwards by my shipmate, the late Vice Admiral Pringle, then a midshipman in the *Boston*.

Captain Wiltse sent Pringle to the legation to act as aide to the minister. Pringle recounted being with the minister, an old man, lying on the sofa with a handkerchief over his face, much distressed by news just received of the death of his daughter by drowning at Maui. Just then it was announced that Sam Parker, former prime minister of the government, and the British minister, wished to see Mr. Stevens. They were admitted and both men began to plead that he would hold up the landing of the troops. Parker even got down on his knees and said, "For God's sake, Mr. Stevens, do not allow the sailors to land!" Mr. Woodhouse added, "If they land it means the end of the monarchy."

While they were thus entreating, with tears in their eyes, the raucous voice of the marine officer of the *Boston,* Lieutenant Herbert Draper, was heard through the open windows: "Order arms." This was followed by the rattle of rifles on the pavement.

The minister said, "It is too late, gentlemen, the troops have landed."

Captain Wiltse played in hard luck. His cruise ended, he went to Washington expecting governmental recognition, but the administration had changed and Mr. Cleveland promptly disavowed the action of the navy at Hawaii and sent out his *Paramount* commissioner, Mr. Blount, to investigate all the circumstances of the revolution. There were no crosses or medals bestowed in that campaign! Wiltse was absolutely ignored by the administration and returned to New York where he died of apoplexy shortly afterwards—his friends said of a broken heart. The navy "could have better spared a better man."

On January 1, having been detached, I took passage in the *City of Rio Janeiro* for San Francisco. She was commanded by Capt. J. Tremaine Smith, a fine-looking sailorman, well liked by his passengers. Several years afterwards I heard of his tragic death: his body was found one morning in his bunk, his head completely severed. There was some Chinese mystery connected with the murder and I don't know that it was ever solved. The ship itself was wrecked later while attempting to enter the Golden Gate and many lives were lost.

The cruise in the *Boston* had been filled with pleasant experiences and association with a delightful group of officers. Swinburne, Moore, Paymaster Hobbes, Chief Engineer McKean and medical officers Lieutenant Laird and Ensign Rush were all cherished friends and shipmates never to be forgotten.

On January 9, 1893, I was promoted to full lieutenant.

7 Ashore and at Sea in the *Texas* and the *Monadnock*

After a few weeks leave in my hometown Nashville, I was ordered to duty at the gun factory at the Washington navy yard. I was placed in charge by the superintendent, Comdr. Theo F. Jewell, of the manufacture of the heavy caliber guns—ten-inch and 13-inch.

Commander Jewell had been a staunch friend of mine during my last three student years at the naval Academy where he was an instructor in the department of physics and chemistry. I felt that his house was my home at all times. He was an outstanding officer in the navy and rose through all the grades to rear admiral. During his mid-career—in his 40s and 50s—he was justly regarded as a shining light in electricity and one of the foremost officers of his rank.

I found him one of the handsomest men in the navy—tall in stature and of courtly manner. He had great force of character and on board ship was a strict disciplinarian. He was of that brilliant Naval Academy class of 1861 that gave so many excellent officers to the service.

One day Jewell sent for me and asked, "How would you like to go to Chicago to testify in a civil law case regarding the expansion of metal tubes under pressure?"

He explained that Comdr. E. C. Benedict of New York had requested the secretary of the navy, Mr. Herbert, to allow an officer of the gun factory, familiar with measuring the expansion of steel tubes under pressure, to go to Chicago to testify that expansion of one-thousandth of an inch could be easily and accurately measured. The question at issue being the expansion of eight-inch cast-iron gas pipes. Mr. Benedict was, I believe, the president of the Chicago Natural Gas Company.

The trial lasted for several days. The opposing lawyer, General Walker—who had defended Debs in his famous trail and was accounted one of the most skillful cross-examiners in the West—badgered me with all sorts of questions, trying to make me contradict myself and the other witnesses.

Commander Jewell had warned me not to lose my temper on the witness stand. I had said I would not as long as the lawyers did not call me a liar. They didn't go so far as that, although General Walker came near it several times. It was a good show. The crowded courtroom was much interested and from time to time was admonished to keep quiet and order.

When my testimony was concluded Judge Seamans left the bench and congratulated me saying, "I saw the flush coming and I didn't blame you."

Even the chief inquisitor shook hands with me and said, "If you ever need anybody to defend you, call on me."

When I left the witness stand the juror nearest me put his hand to his lips and speaking from the corner of his mouth said, "By God, you are a one-er!"

I remember a few questions and my replies, which give an idea of the manner in which my examination was conducted. General Walker began in a very pleasant manner, but he soon warmed up to the business in hand. "Is it customary for the secretary of the navy to order officers over the country to testify in civil cases?"

"Not that I know of."

"I understand that you and Mr. Heguemburg have been giving little sideshows on the other side. Is that so?"

"You may call it that if you wish. We were having a demonstration to which you were invited."

"I was not invited, and remember, Sir, you are under oath."

"I do not need to be reminded by you that I am under oath. I gave you the invitation myself."

Here Mr. Walker's assistant tried to join in, but was pushed angrily to one side by Mr. Walker as he said, "I can take care of the witness."

Then changing his manner, he continued, "Is this gentleman in court, whom you call 'Commodore', in the navy?"

"No, but he should be. He has all the qualifications of a rear admiral."

Etc., etc.

I write the scene above from memory as I made no notes at the trial. It is substantially correct, although it took place more than 30 years ago and nearly all of the participants in the trial are long since dead. My examination lasted more than an hour. Although the commodore won the first trial of the case, I heard afterwards that it was retried on appeal, and lost. It involved half a million dollars.

The other witnesses for the defense were Professor Haupt and General Smith, an ex-U.S. Army officer who served against Forrest under General Sherman. He told me the following story of a visit he made to General Grant just before the battle of Chattanooga.

General Hooker ("Fighting Joe") sent word to Grant that his force was in a precarious situation and asked for reinforcements. Grant replied, "Tell General Hooker that when two armies are facing each other in battle line, the situation is precarious on both sides. I have no reinforcements to send him."

General Smith was an entertaining man, but naturally did not discuss General Forrest.

After the expiration of my term of shore duty in ordnance at the Washington gun factory I was ordered in 1895 to the new battleship *Texas*, just completed at the Norfolk navy yard.

The *Texas* was supposed to be a prize ship. She was much advertised and there were many applications for duty in her. Her captain was Henry Glass, the executive officer was Lt. Comdr. J. D. J. Kelly; Lieutenant Heilner was the navigator and Absalom Kirby was chief engineer, but in a short time was succeeded by J. A. B. Smith, affectionately known as "Jab".

From the beginning there was no one on board who did not realize that the *Texas* was a goldbrick. In the first place she had been designed in England and her plans had been rejected by the British admirality. It was therefore a nine days' wonder when the navy department bought them—it was said for $10,000.

After commissioning at the Norfolk navy yard she had made the usual trips at sea—a long succession of failures. After weeks of this, the ship was sent to New York to dock. One night while in dock, her bottom caved in! That was the end of the first chapter. She returned to Norfolk to have her bottom repaired and strengthened. Her crew and officers were ordered to other vessels.

It was my lot to be ordered to the *Monadnock*—a Civil War monitor—building for many years at the Mare Island yard where she had been regarded as the navy yard nest egg. I did not want to leave the east coast at that time, so I put the question to the chief of the bureau of navigation.

He said, looking at me in the most disconcerting way, "Why do you object to obeying your orders? Have you any good reason for not wanting to go to the Pacific Sation, or is it simply that you do not want to go the west coast?"

I had anticipated some such question, at least in part, and was prepared to give three reasons, the third being that my last cruise was in the Pacific. The commodore was so stern and unresponsive that I never got beyond the second reason and stopped there, much embarrassed.

"In that case," he said icily, "you will carry out your orders."

On the Norfolk boat that night I found that Lieutenant Heilner was not with us and was told that his orders had been changed at the last moment because his last cruise had been in the Pacific. "My Lord," I said, "that was my third reason for not going!"

I was ordered to assist Lt. J. M. Roper in taking a draft of about 200 men to the *Monadnock* by rail. Roper afterwards lost his life in attempting to put out a fire in the magazine of the U.S.S *Petrel.* He was a fine officer and his death was a loss to the service.

It was a pleasant journey across the continent. Shortly after our arrival the ship was commissioned under the command of Captain Sumner. We made a brief cruise down the coast to San Diego.

In a few months I was again ordered to the *Texas* which, thoroughly overhauled and reconditioned, was at the Norfolk yard. The captain, executive officer, chief engineer and myself were the only officers retained from her first command. When she started out for her second cruise the *Texas* was supposed to be in fine shipshape and "Bristol fashion", so to speak: engines and guns were as fit as their imperfect design permitted, her hull had been stiffened and practically all the improvements recommended by Captain Glass had been made.

But her jinx still followed her. At Newport she ran ashore on Goat Island. It was just about sundown when we passed Castle Hill. The channel was crowded with yachts standing in for their anchorage and I recall how well I thought the captain was handling the ship in the crowded channel way. When we rounded to for our own anchorage, I could see the officers at the War College on the lawn and steps of the college watching us.

All went well until we swung halfway around to the floodtide. The captain and exeuctive were on the bridge and we had a good deal of way on. All the officers were at their stations. I was on the forecastle. I heard the orders: "Full speed astern. Let go the port anchor." The ship continued to forge ahead and a stream of sparks poured from the hawse pipe as the anchor took the chain. By the time the whole cable was laid out the ship was aground almost in the inspector's garden.

It was a curious mishap. At the moment the reverse signal was rung up, a fuse had burned out in the engine room, the lights all went out and the mechanic at the throttle got gallied and put the lever *ahead* full speed. It was hard luck and must have been very mortifying to Captain Glass. An anchor hoy from Providence came down next day to weigh the anchor and pick up the chain. We did not get off until the following day. The New York papers had flaring headlines, *"Texas in trouble again"*.

While we were aground the captain received an unofficial visit from Mr. Henry White and Mr. Bourke Cochrane in company with Lord Russell, the chief justice of England, who was making a visit to America. These gentlemen remained some time on board and seemed to enjoy their stay, although the decks were covered with mud from 120 fathoms of chain cable. That afternoon Mr. White invited the captain and officers to a reception at his house on Halidon Hill where we had the opportunity of meeting Lord Russell in a personal way.

When we received our torpedoes from the torpedo station we returned to the New York yard to have the bow plates straightened and certain rivets replaced. The berth assigned us was alongside the old Cob Dock—no longer existing—where we tied up for repairs. At the same time our chief engineer decided to do some work on the injection valve. We were in 22 feet of water.

Suddenly one morning about five o'clock, just after wash-clothes were triced up and the men were scrubbing decks, the temporary plate on the valve yielded to the outside pressure of 22 feet of water. With a rush, a stream of water 20 inches in diameter poured into the engine room. The ship settled to the bottom in the turbid and foul waters of the Wallabout and remained there until the court of inquiry finished its investigation. No blame was attached to anyone for either the grounding at Newport or the sinking in New York!

However, one important lesson was learned, to wit: all wires leading through watertight bulkheads destroyed their watertight integrity unless fitted with stuffing boxes.

We remained at the yard until the captain reported the ship ready for sea and was ordered by Admiral Bunce to Galveston to receive a silver service, a present from the city to the ship. From thence we went to New Orleans to represent the secretary of the navy at the Mardi Gras festival.

At New York a newly appointed chaplain, Rev. Harry W. Irns, reported for duty. He was known later in the newspapers as the "Fighting Chaplain". He told me an amusing story of how he happened to join the navy. The assistant secretary of the navy, Mr. McAdoo, had taken him to the White House to request an appointment from the president.

Mr. Cleveland received him kindly and said, "There is fine work on board ship for a chaplain. I do not want a mere figurehead in the wardroom. I do not know whether or not I shall appoint you."

The young man, wishing to make an impression at this point and being entirely ignorant of what was expected of him, said: "Mr. President, if God wants me to be a chaplain in the navy, it is certain that the president of the United States will have nothing to do with it."

McAdoo was plainly shocked, the president froze, and the interview ended automatically. "As we left the White House," continued the parson, "I had a distinct feeling that God would not want me to be a chaplain in the navy."

We had a fine run down the coast, but at Galveston, when the anchor was let go, the ship swung to the tide, and then laid her port side gently against Pelican Spit! For our fine captain it was the last straw.

When Mr. Kelley made the routine 8 p.m. report, Captain Glass said to him, "This is the end of my career, Kelley. Read what I shall wire to the secretary: 'In entering Galveston Harbor, got ashore on Pelican Spit. Am hard and fast aground. If ship does not come off in the morning with the tide, shall remove guns, stores, etc.' "

Kelley read it and being of the quickest intelligence said, "If you send *that* despatch, Captain, your career *will* be ended. Let me suggest this." He wrote: "Have touched lightly on Pelican Spit. Will be off next high tide."

And we were. The New York *Herald* wired me to cable a full account of the accident, but I saw too much dynamite in the subject for me to handle under the regulations of the navy.

After a visit memorable for the courtesies and hospitalities of the city, we went to New Orleans and were the guests of the city during the Mardi Gras festivities. Here I met again my fellow-traveler of 1878 in the steamship *City of Rio Janeiro,* Morgan Whitney, then a banker, whom I had not seen in the meantime.

We now received orders from the admiral to join the fleet in New York, stopping for torpedo practice in Port Royal Sound—probably the worst place on the coast for such work on account of the strong tides. In those days the idea of a target practice with guns or torpedoes was to get through with it as quickly as possible. Besides, the expiration of our captain's cruise was at hand and he was anxious to get north.

One day after torpedo practice outside Pensacola, I met one of the navigators from the squadron who had come to the telegraph office, as I had, to get the "tick" for his chronometer.

"Did you hit the target?" I asked.

"Hell," he replied, "Who cares whether you hit the target or not? The question is, Did you get your torpedoes back?"

This was the spirit of the early '90s regarding torpedo practice.

Captain Glass was a Kentuckian who had graduated at the head of his class in 1860 and had taken an active part in all the general engagements in Charleston Harbor in the summer of 1863. His class had a number of distinguished men like Philip Cooper, H. C. Taylor, Pierre Orleans (nephew of Louis Philippe, known at the Academy as "Pete"), Crowninshield, Pegram, Craven and the famous "Joe" Coghlan.

Although his cruise in the *Texas* must have been trying and disappointing in many respects from the beginning, Captain Glass' professional reputation came through every test untarnished. It is a pleasure to recall my indebtedness to him for the many things I learned of my profession under his command.

One day he said to me, "They will never get me east of Benicia again."

He was succeeded by Capt. William Wise, a charming man and a fine character, but with whom I served only a short time before receiving orders to command the torpedo boat *Cushing*.

8 The *Cushing* and the Spanish War

I joined the *Cushing* at Norfolk in May 1897. She was only 100 feet long and 100 tons displacement and drew five feet of water, but she was my first command and I was very proud to report to the department that I had "assumed command". The boat was so small that we were ordered to take only service uniforms to save weight. Then with grotesque inconsistency, the navy yard sent two express wagon loads of blank forms and ship logs—enough for a three-year cruise of a battleship—but no charts!

When I asked the commandant, Admiral Brown, about this he said, "Why do you want a chart to go to New York? I could take that boat up the coast with my eyes shut."

However, I borrowed an old chart from the equipment officer which answered the purpose.

The crew of the *Cushing* was composed of 22 men and two officers, ensigns G. A. Mitchell and F. G. Clark. Our quarters consisted of four bunks in a cubbyhole aft, called a cabin by courtesy. There were transoms on either side and a narrow table amidships filling the floor space. The *Cushing* was our first seagoing torpedo boat.

In New York I received a pleasant note from Mr. Theodore Roosevelt, the assistant secretary of the navy, instructing me to be at Oyster Bay with the *Cushing* June 1st to take him to Newport (where he was to deliver a lecture at the War College) and also inviting the officers of the *Cushing* and myself to breakfast with him before sailing for Newport.

Just before sailing from New York, Lt. Comdr. Cameron Winslow came on board for passage to Newport. He had been the *Cushing's* first captain and was a skilled torpedo boat handler. Thornycroft, the English builder, said he had never seen a better.

At the Norfolk navy yard someone had forgotten to replace the steel diaphragms in the smokestacks, with the result of no forced draft and only about ten knots speed. At Winslow's suggestion, the diaphragms were replaced with asbestos and we had no further trouble—although they were blazing when we reached Newport.

At Oyster Bay Mr. Roosevelt and one or two of his sons came down to the pier to show us the way to Sagamore Hill. Winslow and I had left the *Cushing* earlier and arrived by a different route so were on the veranda when they got back to the house. This was my first meeting with Mr. Roosevelt.

After landing him at the War College in Newport that afternoon, I reported to Comdr. T. C. McLean for duty at the torpedo station and remained there during the summer. The time was passed principally in Narragansett Bay firing practice torpedoes with smokeless powder. There were occasional trips to Perth Amboy, New York, Sag Harbor and Bristol making tidal observations, and transporting powder.

The *Cushing* made the summer record practice, firing more than 400 shots. Captain McLean, in consequence, assigned to the *Cushing* the honor of firing the first Obry gear in the navy. This we did at a speed of 19 knots and at a range of 800 yards—which was considered fine work at that time.

In the Caribbean Sea war clouds were gathering. We heard rumors of war with Spain, but were skeptical. I had not forgotten Captain Wiltse's dictum about the "first crack of a gun". Four torpedo boats—the *Porter, DuPont, Ericsson* and *Cushing*—assembled at the torpedo station and began fitting out for distant service. We heard that the flotilla would soon sail for Key West under Lt. Comdr. W. W. Kimball.

In the middle of July, Commodore Dewey had come to Bristol to conduct the speed trials of the*Du Pont*. This was my first meeting with him, and he had not then sprung into fame. I was much impressed with his smart, alert appearance and his affability.

The *Cushing*'s two officers were now detached and Ens. Cabell Breckenridge replaced them. Alas, poor Breckenridge! If only sometimes we could gaze into the crystal!

The last of September 1897 the four boats—the original Torpedo Flotilla—assembled in the basin at the lighthouse depot at Staten Island. We sailed for Hampton Roads on October 2, the *Cushing* leading out, with Kimball on board. As it came on to blow heavily the commodore (Kimball's courtesy title) decided to run in under the lee of Lewes breakwater at the entrance of Delaware Bay.

The boats attracted much interest from the lighthouse men and coast guards, some of whom came on board. I heard one of them say on the deck of the *Cushing,* "I'd just as leave go to sea on a whale!"

The *Cushing* did not look unlike one. We were much smaller and lower in the water than the other boats.

At this time the North Atlantic Fleet, under Admiral Sicard, was anchored off the southern drill ground, 36 miles east of Cape Henry. One afternoon Kimball came on board the *Cushing,* then anchored inside the bar at Hygiea, with urgent despatches for the admiral and orders to deliver them without delay and return to Hampton Roads.

We were out all night, and I remember that faithful Peter Ailnas, one of the seamen, remained at the wheel until we returned at 6 a.m. He is now a grandfather living on his own farm in New England and I hope he will read this acknowledgment of his services on that occasion. I had a letter from him the other day.

We soon heard that the despatches to the commander in chief instructed him to send the *Maine* under Captain Sigsbee at once to Key West. It began to look as if trouble were in the offing.

In a few days the division of torpedo boats went to City Point to escape a cyclone on its way up the coast, which proved to be severe and destructive. From City Point we continued to Richmond and remained there until the weather abated.

Our run down the coast to Key West was a real torchlight procession. Wherever possible we went through the inside passages, stopping at all the principal towns and cities, receiving unbounded hospitality everywhere. Jack Fremont was in command of the *Porter,* Usher of the *Ericsson* and Spencer Wood of the *Du Pont.*

Everyone onshore wanted to know our ultimate destination, and no one accepted our protestations of peaceful intent and ignorance of ulterior motives. It was not until much later that we knew that sending the flotilla to Key West was Mr. Roosevelt's idea, in order to have them near Cuba in the event of war with Spain.

The flotilla arrived at Key West late in the afternoon of December 31. A motley crowd of "Conchs" and "Kingfishers" were at the navy yard dock wrapped in dingy shawls and coats, shivering in the evening chill.

Commander Forsythe, the commandant, repeated the rumors of war with Spain which we had heard at Jacksonville and Fernandina and said he was confident that the flotilla would not get west of Key West. In a few days the North Atlantic Fleet arrived off Sand Key and then went to Dry Tortugas to wait for something to turn up.

Sometime in January the *Ericsson* and *Cushing* were sent to Tampa by the commander in chief, but the day we arrived there the *Cushing* was directed by wire from Captain Sigsbee to return to Key West immediately. On approaching Key West by the northwest passage, we sighted the *Maine* standing out of the harbor. She signaled to the *Cushing* to come within hail. Captain Sigsbee slowed down and told me through the megaphone that there was important mail at Key West for me and to familiarize myself with it immediately. The *Maine* then steamed ahead—on her last voyage.

I found on opening the mail that the *Cushing*'s captain (myself) was designated by name by the navy department to maintain daily communication by cable with either the *Maine* or Consul Gen. Fitzhugh Lee, and in the event of important messages, I was to report them to the senior officer afloat at Key West. If I deemed the matter urgent I was to cable the department and to report by torpedo boat to the commander in chief, who with the North Atlantic Fleet was now at Dry Tortugas awaiting developments. Daily I was to send some message by cable to General Fitzhugh Lee, to which he would reply. Any interruption of the cable service was to be reported at once to the department.

Things settled into a dull routine. The admiral came in from Dry Tortugas and took up his quarters in the *Fern,* whose captain was W. S. Cowles, Mr. Roosevelt's brother-in-law. The *Fern* was tied up at the dock near the *Cushing*.

In the *Texas* had been two young officers of whom I was fond—Ensigns Breckinridge and Worth Bagley. Both were of exceptionally fine metal; neither lived through the summer.

Breckinridge had been in my gun division in the *Texas* and we were close friends. I had gladly approved his being ordered to the *Cushing*. He had joined at Newport. Our relation was that of brothers, rather than senior and junior officer. It seemed to me he embodied in his character all the finest and truest traits of young manhood. He was without guile or fear and his word was hidebound. He was a worthy scion of distinguished stock and had he lived, would have won a high place in the service to which he was devoted. One of the most lovable men, he was the salt of the earth and sea.

One night, February 10, Admiral Sicard sent for me and said I was to leave for Havana at daylight the next morning with an important communication for Captain Sigsbee. On returning to the *Cushing* I told Breckinridge, who was the executive officer, to have everything ready to go to sea by daylight next morning and that we were going to Havana. We were both glad to get away from the dullness of Key West.

It was broad daylight when the *Cushing* headed out past Fort

Taylor. The wind had increased during the night and outside of Sand Key Lighthouse, was blowing half a gale against the Gulf Stream current, making a heavy sea. All went well until about noon, or afterwards. The highland back of Matanzas had just been sighted. Breckinridge was forward at the conning tower and I was sitting in a chair aft reading, with one arm around the signal mast. A messenger came aft from him and reported: "Mr. Breckinridge says he has sighted smoke ahead.

I replied, "Tell him I think that is land and not smoke."

I saw him deliver this message to Breckinridge and saw the latter turn to come aft. He had on his raincoat and high rubber boots, for it was very wet and slippery forward on the steel deck. He had taken only a few steps toward me when the *Cushing* took a deep and violent roll to starboard. Breckinridge was thrown heavily against the copper lifelines, which snapped, and my friend and comrade went overboard.

Every effort was made to save him. He was much beloved by the crew and at one time there were three men in the water struggling to rescue him. Although we succeeded in getting him on board in about 20 minutes, life was gone. He was the first sacrifice in our war with Spain.

"And all the trumpets sounded for him on the other side."

The *Cushing* arrived at Havana in the early afternoon and anchored near the *Maine*. Captain Sigsbee and all the officers were, of course, sympathetic and kind. They relieved me of all arrangements concerning Breckinridge, whose body was taken ashore to be sent home after a brief ceremony by Father Chidwick. Breckinridge's death occured on Friday, February 11. I returned to Key West two days later.

It is worth noting that the night before leaving Havana I was in the wardroom of the *Maine* to say good-bye to the officers. We discussed the possibility of an attack on the *Maine* if war was declared between the United States and Spain. I remember Lieutenant Commander Wainright, the executive officer, saying, "Our guns command every fort in the harbor, and they could not bring a single one to bear on us."

There was not a thought expressed about the destruction of the *Maine* by a mine! That night I dined with Captain Sigsbee and Gen. Fitzhugh Lee onshore and sailed the next morning for Key West.

In obedience to my instructions, the consul general and I had been exchanging daily messages by cable. They resembled a code and made no sense, but they served their purpose. For instance I cabled: "Fisheries conventions today."

General Lee to *Cushing:* "Hope good results."

Cushing to General Lee: "Price of fans has advanced."

General Lee to *Cushing:* "Felicitations, etc., etc., etc.,"

At nine on the evening of February 15, some 63 hours after the *Cushing* had sailed, there came the great explosion that shook the world and these inane but necessary messages ceased.

About ten that evening, after I had turned in, Captain Skelling, our confidential agent at Key West, came to the dock to see me. He said, "I have a most important message from our agent in Havana, a man who has never failed us. He cables that the *Maine* is blown up and adds, 'It is a curious sight to see the crowds on the marina watching an American man-of-war sink.' "

By the light of an oil lantern on the dock he read the cable to me. As my orders were to report to the senior officer *afloat* any important news from Havana, I at once informed Captain Cowles in the *Fern,* which was on the opposite side of the dock, and suggested that before communicating with Admiral Sicard—who had returned to Dry Tortugas—we three go to the cable office and wait for the confirmation of the appalling news.

While waiting in the dimly lighted cable office, we sat grouped in front of the operator. Presently the instrument began to click. I was watching the face of the operator and as the message continued I noticed he looked at Captain Skelling, himself an operator who was intently reading the instrument, and raised his brows. When the message was taken down, he handed it to Skelling, who handed it to Cowles, who passed it on to me.

It ran as follows:

Secnav
Washington, D.C.
Maine blown up in Havana Harbor at nine forty tonight and destroyed. Many wounded and doubtless more killed or drowned. Wounded and others on board Spanish man of war and Ward Line steamer. Send lighthouse tenders from Key West for crew and the few pieces of equipment above water. No one has clothing other than that upon him. Pûblic opinion should be suspended until further report. All officers believed to be saved. Jenkins and Merritt not yet accounted for. Many Spanish officers including representatives of General Blanco now with me to express sympathy.

Sigsbee

February 15th, 1898.

It not infrequently happens that when a man achieves distinction there are those who belittle what he has done. In the case of Captain Sigsbee it was said by some of his contemporaries that he never wrote the famous "Suspend Judgment" message and that it was composed in Washington to save Sigsbee's face! That is not true.

At that moment only four persons in the United States knew that an American battleship had been blown up in a friendly harbor. I suggested that Captain Cowles send immediately for Usher to take the *Ericsson* at once with the news to the commander in chief at Dry Tortugas. Usher being senior to me, I could not give the order myself.

The next morning the whole fleet was assembled off Sand Key Light. Then came Admiral Sicard's hour of great trial. He was an ill man when he came south and, loath as the department was to relieve him, it was necessary in the interests of the service. I carried him the telegraphic orders a few nights afterwards to report to a medical board of survey on board the flagship.

The admiral was living at the Key West Hotel. It was nearly midnight. He came out into the hall and read the message by a flickering gas jet, then turned to me and said in his peculiar voice, "Thank you, Gleaves, good night."

It was dramatic. I have never forgotten it—the end of a man's hopes and aspirations after 40 years of service, at the moment when the prize for which he had striven was almost in his grasp—the command of a fleet in action!

Admiral Sicard was subsequently relieved by Capt. W. T. Sampson, at that time commanding the *Iowa,* who was immediately appointed acting rear admiral.

That evening the *Olivette* arrived at Key West from Havana with the survivors of the *Maine.* Lieutenant John Hood gave me a message to put in code and transmit to the secretary of the navy, which ran as follows:

Cipher code sunk with *Maine* but easily recovered by diver. For that reason American wrecker desirable. *Maine* was probably destroyed by a mine. It may have been done by accident. I surmise that the berth was one planted previous to her arrival, perhaps long ago. I can only surmise this.

Sigsbee per Hood.

The death of Breckinridge had prevented the *Cushing* from being alongside of the *Maine* when she was destroyed, for it was Admiral Sicard's intention to have me remain in Havana several days. Captain Sigsbee told me on arrival that but for Breckinridge's death he would have had me tie up alongside the *Maine*.

After the destruction of the *Maine* a notable change took place in all the government activities at Key West. Everyone felt that it was only a question of a short time before hostilities would break out. The fleet shifted its base from Dry Tortugas to the waters outside Sand Key. Vessels bringing supplies arrived daily, men-of-war of all classes were hastily put in commission and sent to the commander in chief.

A naval base was established in command of Commodore Remey. The cable office was reinforced by many operators and stenographers, and ship-chandlers onshore busied themselves with replenishing their stores. Every evening in the Key West Hotel a little group of Cubans assembled for a conference behind closed doors. Journalists began to arrive along with a regiment of lesser press lights. Harbor and town awoke from a 24-year sleep—not since the *Virginius* affair had Key West been so lively and agitated.

One day I received a letter from the captain of a Spanish gunboat in Cuban waters expressing his regret at the *Maine* explosion.

Captain torpedo boat *Cushing*, Havana

Sir:

In the name of my officers and men, deeply affected for the catastrophe of your armoured cruiser *Maine,* I have the honour to send you and brother officers and men the expression of our true condolence.

Yours sincerely,

Juan de Carransa
Lieutenant 1st class,
in command of H. M. C. Gunboat
Diego Velasques

Cienfuegos, 16 February, 1898

This I thought significant and sent a copy to the secretary of the navy. It seemed to me a strong indication that the Spanish naval officers at least had nothing to do with the destruction of the *Maine*.

Admiral Sicard had, of course, ordered a court of inquiry on the *Maine* at once and the members were carefully selected. Captain Sampson was president, Capt. French Chadwick and Comdr. W. P. Potter, members, and Comdr. Adolph Marix, judge advocate.

The court in its report, dated March 21, 1898, found that the *Maine* was blown up from the outside, but did not fix the responsibility. It stated "that in its opinion the ship was destroyed by the explosion of a submarine mine, which caused the partial explosion of two or more of the forward magazines" and that it had "been unable to obtain evidence fixing the responsibility for the destruction of the *Maine* upon any person or persons."

In the month preceding the declaration of war, the fleet was anchored off Sand Key Light and torpedo boat patrols were established nightly. This was arduous service for the boats, especially the small *Ericsson* and *Cushing,* and the sea was rough. Midshipman Henry Mustin was sent to the *Cushing* as temporary relief of Breckinridge, and Mustin was succeeded by Midshipman David F. Boyd. Both of these young officers were admirably suited for the duty.

The joint resolution of congress for intervention, authorizing the use of our land and naval forces, was passed on April 19 and signed by the president the next day. On April 21 the respective ministers were each withdrawn. On Sunday, April 24, Spain officially recognized the existence of a state of war and on Monday congress, in response to President McKinley's request, declared by a joint resolution that war existed and had existed "since the 21st day of April, A.D. 1898 including said day."

A few days before, the ships had been painted grey and cleared for action. All spare spars and boats, riggings and furniture were sent ashore to the naval station. On April 22 the fleet, under command of Sampson, left Sand Key for the blockade of Havana and other Cuban ports.

Admiral Sampson's request to bombard the Havana forts had been turned down and instead he was ordered to blockade the north coast. In the original order of sailing from Key West the *Cushing* was stationed at the head of the fleet. This position of honor was so assigned as she was the only boat that had direct torpedo head fire, but Lt. John C. Fremont claimed it by virtue of his seniority and the formation of the flotilla was accordingly changed. The night before sailing, Ensign Baldwin, who had succeeded Breckinridge, fell through the main hatch and broke his ribs. The *Cushing* was held back by the admiral until Baldwin was replaced.

This was my first great disappointment of the war. A few days afterwards the *Cushing* was sent with the mail to the flagship off Havana and on the return trip to Key West, while chasing a suspicious-looking steamer, was totally disabled by the blowing out of a high-pressure cylinder head. The damage was temporarily repaired by cutting out the defective cylinder, but speed was reduced to twelve knots until a new cylinder head was received from the Herreschoffs. It did not arrive in time for us to join the fleet before the Battle of Santiago.

On the day the fleet sailed for Porto Rico I took messages to the admiral off Sand Key about ten that night. He asked me how much speed I could make and flatly refused to accept the *Cushing* as an escort with only twelve knots. A representative of a newspaper syndicate was in his cabin, begging for a passage to San Juan.

During the short period of the war, the *Cushing* was employed variously in patrolling, scouting and blockading and made several trips to the north coast of Cuba. The service, while important, was not interesting. At Sagua la Grande we captured and destroyed a number of small vessels which had been engaged in landing cargoes of steamers anchored outside the reefs. We were on this duty when news was received that the protocol was signed, the "War" was over, and all vessels ordered to return to Key West.

The *Cushing* was towed as far as Hatteras where we cast off and proceeded to New York, arriving August 24th. Our cruise had lasted 16 months and we had made 8,185 miles. On 10 September 1898 I was detached from the *Cushing* and granted leave of absence.

I received the following letter:

The Phaeton
539 West 112th St.
New York City
February 12, 1914

Dear Gleaves:

I take pleasure in sending you, by this mail, my photograph and a facsimile of my first despatch reporting the loss of the *Mainė*—all according to promise. If the photograph does not suit, I will get you another one. The one sent was taken in 1905, just before I left New York in command of the John Paul Jones Expedition to France.

It has always been a distinct gratification to me that you, personally, were so closely connected at Key West with the transmission and cognizance of my despatches concerning the loss of the *Maine*. Those were indeed "troubled times", my dear Gleaves. With kindest regards to Mrs. Gleaves and yourself, I remain, in heartiest friendship,

Sincerely yours,

Charles D. Sigsbee
Rear Admiral Retired U.S.N.

To Captain Albert Gleaves, U.S.N.
Commandant, U.S. Navy Yard
New York

9 The *Alabama* at Philadelphia

After being detached from the *Cushing,* I served in the Washington navy yard until April 28, 1900. My shore duty having then run its course, I was ordered to the *Alabama* as navigator. She was then fitting out at Cramp's shipyard, Philadelphia. I reported for duty May 1, 1900, but had not been in Philadelphia long before receiving another order to the battleship *Indiana* at League Island for temporary duty as navigator, to fill an unexpected vacancy.

On May 25 I was promoted to lieutenant commander.

Captain F. W. Dickens commanded the *Indiana* and Lieutenant Commander Dillingham was executive. We left Philadelphia June 1 and after coaling at Hampton Roads, joined Admiral Farquhar at Newport. At Hampton Roads the captain did a pretty piece of seamanship in putting the *Indiana* at full speed alongside a collier just at the slack of the tide—a difficult thing to do, as any sailor knows.

Captain Dickens' mannerisms had given most people an incorrect idea of him. During my six weeks with him in the *Indiana* I learned his worth, for he had an iron nerve and accurate judgment. He had occasion for both several times and I never saw him hesitate to take chances or do the wrong thing.

At Rockland, for instance, he took the ship into the inner harbor in a thick fog while other vessels anchored outside. When I asked him, on approaching the breakwater, if we would anchor outside, he replied, "No, we were ordered to Rockland *Harbor*. If we stop before we get there, we don't get there".

On another occasion at Newport when the flagship *New York* made an error in signaling our anchorage, it became necessary to turn the ship suddenly with scarcely room between the shoal off Rose Island and the *New York*. Without a moment's hesitation the captain ordered the helm put over and simultaneously reversing one engine, with full speed ahead on the other, he swung her around. Admiral Farquhar stood with his staff on the poop of the *New York* watching the maneuver as the *Indiana* almost grazed her side in turning completely around.

Captain Dickens wore long side-whiskers, of which he was proud. Like so many of the older officers of that date he clung to them as tenaciously as they all did to sails. He was a fine type. My cruise was all too short with him. In the middle of August I returned to duty in the *Alabama* under Captain Brownson.

The *Alabama* was number 290 on the books—the same number as the famous Confederate cruiser of that name—and she was not commissioned until the 16th of October 1900. At that time she was considered the finest ship in the navy, and every man and officer felt a pride in being on board. She was 12,000 tons displacement and carried a battery of four twelve-inch guns and 14 six-inch. Her speed was 17 knots.

While fitting out at Cramp's we saw much of the Russian naval officers who were there in connection with the building of the *Variag* and the *Retrizan*. War with Japan was frequently discussed and we sometimes joked with Captain Behr, who was to command the *Variag,* on the possibility of the sun flag someday flying at the peak of the *Variag.*

The Russians were jolly fellows and we were on friendly terms with them. Captain Behr went down in command of the *Osliaba* at the battle of Tsushima. When last seen alive he was smoking a cigarette on the bridge as his ship sank beneath him.

The Russian naval attache, Count Fersen, went with us on the trial trip. He was especially interesting to me on account of his name. He was a big man, red-whiskered and fond of the "high life". In the battle with Togo he was captain of the *Jemjugd,* and after the fight attempted to escape to Vladivostok, but lost his ship on the rocks off Manchuria near the entrance to Vladivostok harbor.

It was not until the 13th of December that we got away from Cramp's. Dr. Weir Mitchell came on board that afternoon as the captain's guest for passage to New York, and I have never forgotten his entertaining stories and the delightful dinner in the cabin the next night when we passed out of the capes.

The doctor told me an interesting story of my wife's father, David Porter Heap*, who was his classmate and close friend at Jefferson College. Heap had asked him to act as his second in a duel with a fellow student who he had challenged, but Mitchell arranged matters without arms.

*Afterwards consul general at Tunis and Constantinople; during the Civil War a major and paymaster in the army and aide to Admiral Porter.

Our cruise along the coast in the *Alabama* was uneventful, save for the target practice off No-Man's-Land in the summer of 1901. Admiral Higginson who had succeeded Admiral Farquhar as commander in chief kept the fleet persistently at drills—night and day—landing five-inch guns, exercising at fleet tactics, practicing with guns and torpedoes.

He conceived the idea of using as a target a condemned lightship obtained from the lighthouse department. This was easily converted into a target by a spread of canvas 15 feet wide and 60 feet long. When in position she looked as big as a battleship and at a distance of 2,000 yards seemed so close, we thought it would be child's play to hit it. The game was to pass in front of the target in column of vessels, each ship in turn firing her twelve-inch guns.

The flagship *Kearsarge* led, of course, and the ships astern expected never a chance. The opening range was 2,000 yards with the target on the bow, decreasing to 1,800 abeam, then increasing again to 2,000. It seems incredible, but the *Ram's Island,* the lightship, was not touched. The admiral was so disgusted and disappointed that he made a general signal "Melancholy", then ran the *New York* close to the lightship and sank her with six pounders. This was the most important event of our cruise, for it opened the eyes of the navy to our inefficiency with guns.

After the Battle of Santiago Lieutenant Niblack had found that, notwithstanding the destruction by gunfire of the Spanish ships, Sampson's fleet had scored only four percent of hits. To appreciate the improvement in naval gun practice since the firing at the *Ram's Island* which the fleet could not hit at a distance of 2,000 yards, it may be stated here that our 14-inch 45 caliber guns now have an effective range of 35,000 yards. The heavy cruisers, armed with eight-inch guns have a range of 36,000 yards.

About this time the ships on the China Station were carefully studying the problem of target practice under the direction of lieutenants Sims and Chapin. The former had been in close contact with Commander Percy Scott of the Royal Navy who had developed a system of instruction destined to revolutionize the naval gunnery of the world.

Lt. Bradley Fiske, of our navy, had previously invented two important accessories—the telescopic sight and the range finder—without which modern naval gunnery were impossible. Of what avail were guns with a range of 15 miles if they could not hit a target at a distance of one mile? Thus it was that our gun practice was brought to its present excellence and it is to Sims and Fiske that the credit is due, for they did more than any others to bring about this consummation.

Personally, an interesting event of that summer was meeting Captain Joshua Slocum who had just returned from his famous voyage around the world in his little sloop, the *Spray*. There is an old saying among sailor folk that you are sure to get into trouble if you go to sea long enough, and several years later poor old Slocum was lost in the West Indies where he had gone from his farm at Gay Head in one more cruise with the *Spray*. We corresponded almost to the time of his death, and some of his letters are classics—just as is his narrative of the voyage of the *Spray*.

He was an admirer of President Theodore Roosevelt, and when the latter was elected in 1904 he wrote me the day after the election: "My, my, what news we have this morning. I am full of gratitude to God. Every breeze is a fair wind in an honest man's sails. Until at last the hurricane of slander and vituperation let loose from the windbags to dismast his ship only sent her bounding more joyously into port." No one but a sailor with salt in his heart could write such lines.

A short time before his last voyage Captain Slocum wrote to me from Tisbury, November 2, 1905:

> The *Spray* is fitted for the West Indies, with provisions on board for a crew of one—no exploit—I go simply to get a dollar and to taper off like, while I may. I expect to come on the coast in the spring in time to arrange my boats for summer, and by the way, to teach youngsters something of navigation, enough at least to get them interested in the art as we sail along. My wife joins in kindest regards to you and yours.
>
> Joshua Slocum
>
> P.S. I don't blush the deep crimson that one might think I should handling such papers as Edwin Arnold's for this reason: it seems entirely the exploit of someone else. I forget I was there, still it all flashes before me as reality of the days when I was keyed up and not slack in stays. To come again into that state I would sail again, but that state might not come again.

It did not, unfortunately, and like Edwin Lear's sailor, "he never came back, he never came back."

At Old Point on our return from sea on the 14th of September, we heard of the death of President McKinley and sent sailors and marines to Washington to join the funeral escort. Our captain commanded the bluejacket battalion.

On October 25, 1901, at New York I was greatly surprised to receive a telegram from my brother-in-law, Comdr. R. F. Nicholson, who was the detail officer of the navy department, saying that the secretary of the navy, Mr. Long, had appointed me to command the *Dolphin,* which was known in the service as the president's yacht. Thus ended my duties as subordinate on board ship—thereafter the cabin for me.

The wardroom officers gave me a champagne farewell when I left the ship, and Captain Brownson went with me to the Fall River steamer in which I took passage to Boston where the *Dolphin* was refitting in the dry dock. On the way to the steamer the captain said, "I have serious doubts of your success as a captain because you are not simpatico with the men. You are too severe."

A year later, when in command of the *Mayflower,* I recalled this remark to him. I said, "I think you will acknowledge you were mistaken, or I would not now command the *Mayflower.*"

We were in my gig, returning from the conference on board the flagship. He gazed over the rail at the lighthouse on Montauk Point and replied, "Well, I don't know."

He always died hard!

I learned more of my profession from Captain Brownson than from any other officer with whom I ever served, and my experience has included service with many types of high degree. Captain Brownson had the happy gift of drawing men to him and knowing how to lead them.

After he had retired, President Roosevelt who had a great admiration for him, reappointed him to be chief of the bureau of navigation. Shortly afterward they failed to agree on a question which Brownson thought vital to the discipline of the navy, and Brownson resigned his position in the department. Afterwards Colonel Roosevelt is reported to have said of Brownson, "He and I had a serious difference of opinion on a point of administration, but if I were president and the country engaged in war, I would immediately appoint him commander in chief of the fleet."

The question at issue was whether or not staff officers should have positive rank and whether the surgeons should command our hospital ships. Dr. Rixey, who was the surgeon general of the navy, made a strong and bitter fight for his corps and won out, upon which Brownson resigned.

10 In Command of the *Dolphin*

On 2 November 1901, I relieved Commander Southerland at Boston of the command of the *Dolphin*. The ship was in the old stone dock at the time under orders to go to Washington where I thought we should spend the winter. However, on reporting to the secretary of the navy, Mr. Long, I found we were to be at the Washington yard only until after New Year's Day and then go to the West Indies to do surveying for the general board. On the way we were to run a line of soundings from Cape Hatteras to Porto Rico.

It was the middle of January 1902 and the Potomac River was full of ice when we sailed for Porto Rico. We had rough weather even after crossing the Gulf Stream, and the ship—of only 1,700 tons—was lively and uncomfortable, although her motion was easy. We had a Sigsbee deep-sounding machine and sounded every four hours. On the 18th, 90 miles off the northwest cape of Porto Rico we got 4,662 fathoms, the greatest depth discovered in the North Atlantic Ocean. I have recently seen in the New York *Times* that this has been confirmed by the Smithsonian Institute.

At this time the civil governor of Porto Rico lived in the "Pink" Palace. The military governor, a lieutenant colonel, lived in the Casa Blanca, while the senior naval officer had to take what was left—although he was a post captain and much senior to the army man. The residence assigned to him had formerly been the captain of the port's office and was built over a city sewer.

When in Porto Rico the following year in the *Mayflower*, I pointed out this injustice both to Admiral Taylor and Admiral Dewey, but my comments did not register. I remember Admiral Taylor said it was one of the strongest characteristics of the navy that we did not seek preferment. So Capt. Yates Stirling continued to live over the city sewer, and one of his daughters had typhoid fever in consequence.

Our surveying ground was the southwest coast of San Domingo including Saona Island. We were to investigate the narrow passage between the two, examine a reported shoal 100 miles southeast of Saona Island and develop the 100 fathom curve in Mona Passage. There had been no surveys of this part of the coast for 70 years and the old Spanish charts were unreliable.

I look back upon that winter's work as one of my happiest experiences. The weather was ideal. The sea always calm, clear and blue. The work was interesting and officers and men enthusiastic. The whole job was finished in record time, including the smooth chart which had been carried on from day-to-day by the skillful draftsman from the hydrographic office—unfortunately I do not recall his name. We were very proud of our accomplishment and got lots of kudos from the bureau of equipment, and mention in the secretary of the navy's annual report.

The cruise was supplemented by a trip around Cuba with Admiral Bradford who joined us at Key West for the purpose of inspecting the sites of several proposed coaling stations for the United States to be selected by him. We went to Havana, Cienfuegos, Guantanamo and Nipe Bay. It was a delightful cruise at the most perfect time of the year in the West Indies.

I had had misgivings on hearing that Admiral Bradford was coming to the ship, for I had not forgotten Trenton days with him. I made up my mind to do my best for his entertainment and comfort and must have succeeded as he offered to give my requisitions for several things—hitherto disapproved—a fair wind. He asked what I wanted especially for the ship. I said, "Four things: a piano, a new library, new upholstery for the cabin and the fourth I can't remember now, but when we get back to Washington I'll come to your office and remind you of it."

He took it good-naturedly and allowed us all I asked, but told his assistant in the bureau it had been an expensive trip for the government. Incidentally, he presented me with a silver match case.

I find it difficult to avoid being chronological, and yet do not want my recollections to appear like a log book. After our winter in the West Indies the ship was kept busy with official functions. Back in Washington the secretary decided to entertain the president and cabinet at a dinner on board at the navy yard. I never saw Mr. Roosevelt in finer form than he was that night. He kept the table in a roar with funny stories and interesting reminiscences. He called the secretary of agriculture, "Old Cornstalks" (James Wilson), and requested that the band play "Garry Owen"—one of his army favorites.

Mr. Hay, the secretary of state, however, was as silent as an oyster. Even Mr. Leslie Shaw's jokes and Mr. Long's puns failed to arouse him. Perhaps it was because there was no wine, for Mr. Long—being president of the Temperance Union—thought it inconsistent for him to serve wine and as Admiral Terry, commandant of the yard, remarked afterward, "White Rock flowed like champagne."

After dinner the crew staged a boxing bout on the poop, and one of the lady guests remarked that there was more blood shed that night in the United States Navy than in the Spanish War. We danced the lancers and the president was lively and full of fun.

A few days afterwards we took Admiral Dewey and his staff down to the southern drill to inspect the North Atlantic Fleet under Rear Admiral Higginson.

A French mission had come over to unveil the Rochambeau statue in Washington accompanied by some of the families of Rochambeau and Lafayette. When it was arranged for the French flagship *Gaulois* flying the flag of Rear Admiral Fournier to visit Annapolis, the president decided to return the admiral's official visit to him there and made a serious ceremony of the event. He came to Annapolis by train and the *Dolphin* took him and his party from the Naval Academy to the *Gaulois,* which along with the *Kearsarge,* at that time Admiral Higginson's flagship, and the *Alabama* and *Olympia,* were anchored about four miles out in Chesapeake Bay.

The president was accompanied by the secretary of the navy, secretary of war and the French ambassador, M. Jules Cambon. The rest of the party preceded him and were on the quarterdeck to receive him when he arrived. All the presidential honors were rendered by the ships, both on his arrival and his departure.

After an elaborate and characteristic French luncheon of many courses in the admiral's cabin, Mr. Roosevelt got into the *Dolphin*'s handsome 14-oared, silver-trimmed barge at the gangway with M. Cambon and some of the cabinet officers. The ships manned yards and rail and each fired simultaneously the national salute of 21 guns and cheered ship.

It was a fine clear day in May and a light southerly wind drifted the white smoke of more than a hundred guns around the barge. When we shoved off from the *Gaulois,* the president was in high spirits. He placed his hand on the ambassador's knee and with gleaming teeth said, "They say this is a relic of barbarism, but I love it!"

Later in the month the *Dolphin* went to West Point to bring the French commission to New York where they were to land at the Battery and be received officially by the city. The commission had luncheon on board as we passed down the Hudson.

An amusing incident occurred as we approached the ships of the Atlantic Fleet anchored off 23rd Street. The ambassador came on the bridge and, being very tall, was an imposing figure in his full diplomatic uniform. He was followed by an attache of the French embassy with Madame Cambon—the latter insisting on coming on the bridge also. In a few minutes Admiral Fournier in his full dress appeared and asked me if I had given madame permission.

"No," I said. "The attache brought her on the bridge."

"Well," he replied, "we are going to pass through the fleet, salutes will be fired and the bridge is not the place for a woman."

Saying which he crossed over, and a lively interchange took place between the lady and the admiral. This resulted in the attache escorting her aft to the poop to the evident amusement of the ambassador who had not said a word, evidently considering the case one to be settled by the navy without diplomatic interference.

For the navy's part in the entertainment of the visitors, the admiral and the captains of the big ships were decorated by the French government with the medal of the Legion of Honor. I was made a chevalier, "the lowest order of French nobility" as my impertinent young daughter Anne commented.

At New London the president came on board to see the annual boat races between Yale and Harvard. It was a fine day and many guests were on board. About seven bells, the traditional time when the sun is over the foreyard, I asked the president if he would join a party in my deck cabin.

He said, "You know I do not drink, but I don't object to watching others."

When he entered the room General Wood offered him the bottle of King William, which he declined, and said as his teeth snapped, "But I love to see you drink."

One night several years afterwards when dining at Sherry's with Mr. John Spotswood Bowers, who had been Mr. Roosevelt's lawyer in the famous libel suit, I related this incident. Mr. Bowers said, "What a fine witness you would have made for the defense!"

On June 29, 1902, I was relieved of the command of the *Dolphin* by Lieutenant Commander Stoney and transferred at once to the *Mayflower* which was lying at an adjoining dock at the New York navy yard. My orders authorized me to take anything out of the *Dolphin* I desired for the *Mayflower* and when Stoney was next at the department he told the secretary I had taken everything except the rudder and smokestack!

Stoney was one of the characters of the service and a humorist to the last. Just before his death on board the *Santee,* then under his command, his family was at his bedside waiting for the end. The surgeon in attendance said, "It is all over."

At these words, Stoney opened his eyes and said, "I missed fire that time, Doc."

Then he died.

11 The *Mayflower* and Presidential Service

The command of the *Mayflower,* the vessel selected by President Roosevelt for his special use, was considered a great prize in the navy. I was lucky enough to be the first to get it. She was English built, of 3,000 tons, a nominal speed of 21 knots. During the Spanish War the government had bought her from Mr. Ogden Goelet. She was luxuriously fitted out. Most of the furnishings had been stored at the New York yard but were replaced when the ship was commissioned for special duty in 1901. She was a beautiful craft and although at first we had trouble in bringing her up to her contract speed, when this was corrected she proved satisfactory in every way.

Shortly after taking over the *Mayflower,* I had a night of great adventure. I was sleeping in the president's cabin in the stern. About one a.m. I was awakened by smoke and the smell of burning rubber. I got up and found the quarters full of smoke, the bed in the adjacent room and the brocaded paneling of the bulkheads blazing. All the woodwork was saturated with kerosene and the decks were covered with it. I realized immediately the desirability of not sounding a general alarm, so with the help of the executive officer, Lt. Comdr. Woodward Phelps, and the master-at-arms the fire was put out and the quarters locked up.

The next morning I reported the matter privately to the commandant and then to the navy department. Mr. Cortelyou, who was at Oyster Bay, cautioned the utmost secrecy and I doubt that the president ever knew of the near destruction of the ship. The point was to keep it out of the newspapers, which were severely critical of Mr. Roosevelt for using the ship at all. This we succeeded in doing.

Much of the criticism was unjust. For instance, he was accused of entertaining his friends on board at government expense, while as a matter of fact he insisted on paying for everything—including the laundry.

It was never known who was responsible for the fire, but there is no doubt of its incendiary origin. Strangely enough the *Mayflower* ended her career by fire 30 years later when she was burnt to the waters edge at the Philadelphia navy yard.

We spent the summer in Long Island Sound and adjacent waters. There were frequent parties on board and luncheons and dinners ashore. We had the opportunity of meeting many noted men and women who as guests of the Roosevelts enjoyed the short trips we made out of Oyster Bay.

I think the president became restless under the almost uninterrupted fire of the press. One day he told me he wanted the ship to have regular target practice and also a heavier battery. Representatives of the press were notified of the gun practice. The navy department sent a regulation ship's target and we conducted a fair practice near Orient Point. The president was so delighted that he gave $35 to the winning crew of the six pounder—at that time her heaviest gun. To avoid conflicting reports in the press, he said to me, "Caution the officers to agree on what they say to the reporters, and remember Lord Melbourne's advice to his cabinet."

When the annual maneuvers of the fleet came off in Buzzard's Bay, the *Mayflower* was sent to join the admiral, and after that to the navy yard at New York. Admiral Barker was the commandant—a stickler for the regulations. On taking command of the fleet, he prefaced his first general order thus: "No law of congress is a dead letter."

Everyone knew he referred to the law relating to the use of spirits on board ship, but both the president and Mr. Long made an exception in the case of the *Mayflower*.

The admiral asked me, "Do you have whiskey in your mess?"

"Yes, sir."

"Isn't the ship a naval vessel?"

"Yes, sir."

"Then I do not understand why you do not obey the law."

I replied, "Recently at New London the president had a distinguished guest on board the *Dolphin* and sent to me for a bottle of Scotch, although he does not drink himself. I would have been embarrassed if I hadn't had it."

He replied after some reflection gazing over the rail at the crowded traffic in East River, "I think I would have sent for the surgeon and had him prescribe it."

"Well, if I had, Admiral, I would have lost my job."

In December 1902 the *Mayflower* took Admiral Dewey and the general board to Culebra to review the ships of the north and south Atlantic and the European squadrons. It was Admiral Taylor's idea to assemble all the available ships and to exercise them as a fleet. One day's exercise—in a run over to St. Thomas—demonstrated the futility of this, for at that time the fleet, made up of various and diverse classes of ships, was without form and void—so to speak.

It had been the intention to spend several weeks in the Caribbean, but Admiral Dewey got restless and decided to return to the United States. One day at luncheon he astonished everyone by asking the chief of staff, Captain Swift, how long it would take to "close up and sail for home."

Captain Swift said, "By pushing everything and everybody, we should be ready in ten days."

The admiral exploded, "Ten days! Hell! Get everything ready at once. I shall sail tonight at eight."

And we did.

When the North Atlantic Fleet, under command of Rear Admiral Barker, sailed for a cruise to the Azores in the summer of 1903, the president granted my request to go with them. I think he was glad to get the ship out of sight.

Trouble had been brewing for some time on the Isthmus of Panama over the approaching crisis of our negotiations with the French and Colombian government for taking over the canal. Here was another opportunity for the *Mayflower* to disappear from the coast.

After returning from the Western Islands we sailed from Washington to Colon with Rear Adm. J. G. Walker, Rtd. and Rear Admiral Coghlan—who hoisted his flag temporarily in the *Mayflower* as flagship of the Caribbean Squadron. Mr. Gudger, our consul general at Panama, was a passenger. After a rough passage as far as the Bahamas, making at least two of the guests seasick, the weather moderated.

According to our latest news when leaving Washington a rebellion was brewing in Panama. When we should have sighted Manzanillo light at midnight (14 November 1903) and did not, I decided to lay off until daylight, in case the light had been purposely extinguished, and so informed Admiral Walker. He was sound alseep on the sofa in the after cabin but woke up instantly when I entered.

His reply was characteristic: "I must say, Gleaves, I take considerable satisfaction in the fact that this is your funeral and not mine. I do not care what you do as long as you get me to Colon in time to get the ten o'clock train for Panama."

Colonel Shaler was the superintendent of the Panama railroad and lived in a beautiful bungalow in Colon close to the beach, surrounded by palm trees and facing the Atlantic Ocean. He was a Confederate veteran and a man of engaging personality. It was his custom to have the officers of the army and navy who were on duty at the isthmus to Sunday luncheon with him. When we went out to the table the first time Colonel Shaler, as was his custom, said grace. He then said, "Admiral Walker, I shall ask you to play lady."

As we sat down Admiral Coghlan said to Walker as he spread out his napkin, "Admiral, I have often heard of your playing with the ladies, but not playing lady."

Walker, not at all disconcerted, replied, "Well, Joe, I never played with them as much as I would like to."

In December Admiral Coghlan sent the *Mayflower* to the Gulf of Darien to investigate reported landings of the Colombians on Panama soil. We went as far into the gulf as the mouth of the Atrato River. The weather had cleared and the scenery in the gulf was beautiful.

When Lieutenant Poor returned from his investigations at Turbo he brought with him an Englishman who said that two Colombian gunboats had been there a few days before and landed troops. We then returned to Colon, but a week later the prefect of Colon informed the admiral that the Colombians were landing at Tiburon at the Isle of Pines.

The admiral had shifted his flag to the *Prairie* and when he gave me my orders said, "If I were going I would clear ship for action."

I asked, "Would you open fire on a landing party on a Panama beach?"

"That," he replied, "would depend."

There was nothing in my written orders to warrant hostile action.

At daylight the next day we were at the Isle of Pines. We got inside the breakers and narrowly escaped getting ashore. Obtaining no satisfactory information from the natives, we returned to the Gulf of Darien to look in at a Colombian camp reported as established by the yacht *Atalanta.*

Sighting a column of smoke in the northeast, we turned and headed for it and found it was the Colombian gunboat *Pinzon* formerly the *Atalanta.* Her ports were open and her decks crowded with soldiers. The *Mayflower* was cleared for action, ammunition got up and the men stationed at the guns. No salutes were fired and nothing happened. When I saw her anchored on the Darien shore and showing no hostile intent, I returned to Colon.

The American attitude had greatly incensed the Colombians, who resented our increased naval forces on both sides of the isthmus, the additional marines arriving in the transports and the visit of the *Mayflower.* Each event was considered an insult from the "Colossus of the North". The *Mayflower* remained in isthmian waters several weeks during which time, to quote Captain Wiltse at Honolulu, "we made history".

Admiral Walker had the most extraordinary power direct from the president, whose personal representative he was, and all officers of the government—diplomatic, navy and army—were subject to his orders. It is not for me to discuss the Panama Canal question. The president expressed the entire subject in a nutshell when he said (if correctly reported), "I wanted the Isthmus and took it."

That was a matter for statesmen and diplomats. Commissioners from Panama and Colombia came on board to interview the admiral. A German steamer came from Cartagena, and lest she have troops on board the *Mayflower* lay across her dock which forced her to anchor in the bay. General Reyes, the famous ex-president of Colombia, arrived in the French steamer *Canada* and the admiral took me with him to call—unofficially, of course. The general was on his way to Washington on a diplomatic mission and had no wish to go ashore at Colon. As a matter of fact, the admiral would not have permitted it anyway.

We cruised to Chiriqui Lagoon and planted buoys on shoals. The weather continued bad with stiff northerly winds, rain, thick fogs and heavy seas. It was terribly hot and the mosquitoes were bad. Henderson used to say that God made flies to make us thankful they were not mosquitoes.

On 21 January 1904 the *Mayflower* was ordered to return to the United States and to dock at Norfolk. The night of February 7 Mr. Roosevelt sent for me to come to the White House. He told me that he had decided not to use the *Mayflower* any longer and that he would give me any shore duty I wanted "that was legitimate."

I wanted the Gun Factory, but Admiral Taylor objected because I did not have enough rank. He suggested that as I was a lieutenant commander, I should go as inspector of ordnance at the Torpedo Station, Newport, Rhode Island—of which I had never thought. However, no changes were to be made for several months, and we soon received orders to Charleston, SC, to pick up Admiral Dewey and the general board for their annual visit to the fleet in the West Indies.

We left Charleston February 23 and while going down the river Admiral Dewey, standing by me on the bridge, called my attention to the deserted wharves, the dilapidated piers and the general air of decrepitude and idleness along the waterfront of the city.

The admiral, commenting on the sad appearance of this view, said, "Gleaves, it is a judgment of God. I had a classmate from Charleston named Porcher. After the attack on Fort Sumter I asked him if the South seceded, would he remain in the Union navy. His reply was, 'I would rather break rocks in the streets of Charleston than fight against my own people.' "

I thought of Mr. Robert Cave's remark at the unveiling of the Lee statue in Richmond ten years before (1894): "I am not one of those," he said, "who speak of Appomattox as a judgment of God. I do not forget that a Suvorov triumphed, a Kosciusko fell; that a Nero flourished and a Christ was crucified."

On the run south, the *Mayflower* made her best speed: in the Crooked Island Passage she made 16½ knots. When I reported this to Admiral Dewey and said I was now ready to sing my Nunc Dimittis, he smiled and asked, "How much of that is due to current?"

At Guantanamo we found Admiral Barker's fleet composed of his own ships and Sigsbee's squadron of cruisers, besides a collection of yachts, colliers and supply vessels—a total of 19. Later several ships from the South Atlantic and Mediterranean joined up. I supposed Admiral Taylor, the chief of staff, was ready to sing a Te Deum, for he had longed to get the ships together and keep them together for maneuvers. But the time was not ripe for that. The collection of ships was too ill-sorted for fleet tactics, as was soon demonstrated by a collision between two battleships in the simplest of maneuvers.

Our cruise in the Caribbean did not last long. Admiral Dewey decided to visit San Domingo, Jamaica and Cuba, and then return home. In the afternoon of March 4 we anchored off San Domingo City and were informed by the health officer that a skirmish had just occurred between the government forces and the rebels. We sent a boat ashore for the consul and at the same time manned the guns lest we should be fired on. Nothing happened.

At Port Antonio we fell in with an American yacht whose owner was anxious to salute the admiral's four star flag. I lent him one and he gave a fine demonstration and was very proud. I went with the admiral to return his call and learned that he was a Civil War veteran—one of the few who went in as a private and came out as a private.

When he said he was at the Battle of Nashville, I said I also was there "in arms". My joke did not register for he replied, "I suppose you were with Wilson on the right." If General Wilson had commanded the infantry, I would have thought my host too was joking!

At Havana I played jai alai and won several dollars. We remained three days and then sailed for the United States.

On 1 June 1904 the *Mayflower* sailed from Old Point for a summer cruise to Europe with the North Atlantic Fleet, stopping at Martha's Vineyard for target practice with the *Illinois.* Here we lost our popular and able first lieutenant, Hilary P. Jones, ordered to command the *Scorpion* in the West Indies.

On June 20 we sailed from Newport for the Azores. Mr. James Gordon Bennett's yacht, the *Lysistrata*—the sister ship of the *Mayflower*—came in and anchored near us the night before we went to sea and was there when we cleared the harbor. The voyage across the Atlantic to Horta was rather rapid, averaging 14 knots.

Our consul at Horta, Mr. Benares, told me that the *Lysistrata* had arrived a few days before and sailed immediately for the channel, and that Mr. Bennett seemed much pleased that he had beaten us across, having sailed from Newport six hours after we did. He said Mr. Bennett wrote no letters at Horta, but sent "about 100 cables."

From Horta we continued to Gibraltar where we found the European Squadron under Rear Admiral Jewell and a division of the British Channel Squadron under Rear Admiral Walker, popularly known in the English navy as "Hookey" Walker. We did not remain long at Gibraltar.

I accompanied my admiral to a garden party at Government House given by the governor, Sir George White, the defender of Ladysmith. At a luncheon to the field marshal on board the *Olympia,* I was seated next to him. Afterwards I mentioned to the admiral that I was rather out of my latitude considering my rank. He replied, "I put you by the general because you talk."

At this time Rear Admiral Chichester was in command of the Royal Naval Station at Gibraltar. He was genial and cordial and as popular with all Americans as with his own people. One day at the officers' club he told me of his famous interview with Admiral von Diedrich just before the taking of the city of Manila. His account was almost word-for-word as Admiral Dewey's flag lieutenant, Brumby, had told me on his return to the United States in 1898. Admiral Chichester said that for this action the queen had decorated him and also made him one of her honorary aides-de-camp. The citation stated: "for services rendered the British Empire."

In a few days Jewell sailed to join Admiral Barker, the commander in chief of the North Atlantic Fleet then at Trieste, and attached the *Mayflower* temporarily to his force. We passed "up the straits" over the old trails I had traversed so many times in other years and worked out a search problem in the Adriatic. The admiral assigned the *Mayflower* to the Eastern section for, as he told me later, he thought I would be interested in the battle waters of Lissa. This was considerate.

The American fleet was anchored outside the breakwater at Trieste. It was composed of the *Kearsarge, Alabama, Connecticut, Illinois, Missouri* and *Iowa.* The visit of our ships to Austrian waters was accepted by the government as a friendly gesture, and there was much entertaining afloat and ashore.

The military governor came down from the army maneuvers in the mountains and gave us a banquet at the palace. Admiral von Jedina, the commander of the naval station, entertained the fleet at his headquarters in the Villa Neckar, once the residence of Pauline Bonaparte.

He made a fine speech in which he emphasized the exploits of the American navy. As a boy at their naval academy he had been thrilled by the story of the battle between the *Alabama* and the *Kearsarge.* Now he was glad to see two ships bearing those names lying side by side in the harbor of Trieste, flying the same flag.

Admiral Barker replied that United States naval officers could never forget the immortal words of Admiral Tegethoff at the Battle of Lissa: "Ram everything grey."

The stay of the ships at Trieste was a real holiday. The officers and men of the two navies fraternized and found much in common to discuss, although at a dinner on board the *Mayflower* the ghost of Martin Kosta appeared for a few anxious moments but was quickly banished.

On July 24 the ships went to Fiume. Hungary was as cordial as Austria. The ice machine of the *Kearsarge* had broken down and the ice obtained from shore proved to be infected. Typhoid fever appeared in due course and a number of officers and men became ill and were transferred to the hospital onshore.

Baron Rozner, the governor of Fiume, gave a reception to the officers at the palace. The gardens were illuminated with colored lights and a concert was given by singers from the Royal Opera in Budapest. It was a gala affair.

Admiral Barker gave his return dinner on board the *Mayflower*. It was discovered, just as the guests entered the dining room, that the ship's printer had put on the menu cards "Fiume, Austria"—which was a serious breach of etiquette. Luckily the type had not been pied and the error was soon corrected. An Austrian officer, when told of the mistake, said to me with much fervor I thought, "I wish to God you had not changed them."

As the typhoid fever continued, the *Mayflower* was sent back to Trieste with three new cases and orders to remain there until the fever was over. Barring the typhoid, our second visit to Trieste was as interesting as the first.

One day the *Lysistrata* came in and anchored near us. As the New York *Herald* had always been a strong and powerful friend to the navy, and Bennett himself had served in the navy during the Civil War, I had no hesitation in sending an officer on board with the usual tender of services accorded a man-of-war.

In the afternoon Mr. Bennett, accompanied by his two guests—one of whom was the Count of Grammont—returned the call and invited Lieutenant McDowell, our first lieutenant, and myself to dine that night on board the *Lysistrata*. Towards sundown a strong bora came on to blow with great force and continued all night with such violence as to prevent leaving the ship. Both ships had two anchors down and rolled deeply in the short heavy sea.

The following day when "the harmless storm was ended" Bennett sent word that he would like me to come on board as he was going to put his ship alongside the pier, which he did at speed and in fine sailor-like manner, handling the ship with skill and judgment.

He was a fine, handsome figure standing on the bridge and his ship was completely and luxuriously equipped—even to a dairy. He kept two cows on board and would send them back to his farm at Beaulieu from time to time and receive fresh ones. These cows were milked by electricity.

The corridors, stairways and salons were lighted by the owl figures, which always adorned the editorial page of the *Herald*. Bennett told me that the idea was suggested by an incident of the Civil War. The ship he was serving in was saved from a surprise attack from shore by the hooting of owls in the swamps, disturbed by the advance of the Confederates. They are still on the gateposts of Bennett's former home in Newport.

During these days I saw much of Admiral von Jedina. We frequently walked or drove over the mountains. He was an accomplished and cultured man and fond of Americans. When naval attache in London, he was Lieutenant Cowles' best man when the latter married Miss Anna Roosevelt, sister of Theodore Roosevelt.

As a midshipman he had served on the staff of Maximilian, then the commander in chief of the Austrian navy. In December of 1866 he was a midshipman in the frigate *Elizabeth* sent to Vera Cruz to bring the emperor back to Austria. While Jedina was ashore with a boat in waiting, a courier arrived with a communication for the captain of the *Elizabeth* and requested Jedina to send it off immediately. Jedina replied that his orders were positive to wait for the emperor and no other boat was available. The courier informed him that the emperor was not coming and was so emphatic that Jedina consulted with the prefect, whose office was nearby. The latter replied that it was true he was not coming.

"As a matter of fact," von Jedina said, "Maximilian, whom the Mexicans wanted to escape from the country, had got to Orizaba, halfway to the sea, when he decided that rather than face the ridicule of the world over the fiasco of the attempt to establish a French empire in the Western Hemisphere, he would remain and take the consequences."

From Orizaba Maximilian went to Puebla, assumed command of the so-called Mexican army of some 3,000 men and marched to meet the enemy. He was surrounded, captured and shot by a firing squad at Queretaro. Jedina had witnessed the embarkation at Miramar of Maximilian and Carlota in an Austrian frigate that sailed in company with a French frigate as a *convoi d'honneur*.

Our enforced stay at Trieste gave me an opportunity to do a lot of sightseeing. I went to the caves of Adelsberg, to Goritza and to Vienna with Stephen Bonsal. At Vienna our consul general, Rublee, took me to Schonbrunn and thence to the banks of the Danube. On the way back to town we passed the Emperor Franz Joseph who was driving out to Schonbrunn, between lines of soldiers on both sides of the streets. He was a fine looking old gentleman, but truly a man of sorrows, with many more to come.

When I went back to Trieste from Vienna, Archduke Ferdinand and the archduchess were on the same train. I did not know it at the time, and only learned when I asked someone at the station the cause of the excitement, bustle, red carpets, the troops and the sailors.

At Goritza, where I dined with our consul, I saw in the crypt of the chapel on the side of the mountain a tomb inscribed, "Louis XIX". Who was Louis XIX? It was many years before I discovered the answer. He was the son of Charles X who was expelled from the French throne in 1829 and recognized only by a few Royalist—and that only for a short time.

Near Goritza is the castle of Wallenstein, now the beautiful property of a rich resident of Trieste. It has ever since been a matter of great regret to me that sailing orders prevented my accepting an invitation to lunch at the famous chateau, then owned by the Baroness Bianchi.

In the latter part of August the Austrian fleet under Admiral von Ripper arrived and I never saw ships handled with more skill and boldness as they came into port—the destroyers dashing to their berths inside the mole, the battleships anchoring simultaneously outside.

Admiral von Ripper was the officer who suddenly appeared at sundown off Santiago just after the battle. The Americans thought a fresh Spaniard had joined up, as the Austrian and Spanish flags were very much alike. Admiral von Ripper told me he ordered his band to play "Hail Columbia" as loudly as possible and not to stop playing under any circumstances while he hoisted the American flag at the main truck and turned the search lights on it. As it was, his ship came near getting a broadside from the *Brooklyn.*

August 18 was the emperor's birthday and Admiral von Jedina invited me to attend mass with him and hear the Te Deum at the church of San Antoine. When I left the *Mayflower,* I gave orders that a salute should be fired after the Austrian guns, following the motions of the Austrian flagship in every particular.

I really didn't know what I was in for, because during the mass, every time the host was elevated, the Austrians fired 21 guns, as did also the *Mayflower.* The admiral leaned over to me in the chancel and said, "The salute at noon would have been sufficient."

I replied that it was too late to stop the firing. Besides, as my old Captain Wiltse would have said, "It was not only my duty, but my pleasure."

After the ceremonies at the church I took the review of the Landwehr with the admiral, and for the first time saw the absurd goose step.

The typhoid patients were returned to the ship as soon as possible, but Lieutenant Clement did not recover. When his body was shipped home, someone in the navy department wired his father that the body was on board a "cattle steamer" which was the finishing stroke for his heartbroken mother and involved me in a correspondence which need never have been necessary if only there had been in the department a "Bureau of Imagination". I have forgotten how many officers and men died, but it was not until September 8 that the survivors were all on board and we sailed for Palermo.

The Persians have a proverb: "This too will pass away". Although we had been well treated at Trieste and had made hosts of friends, we were glad after two months to begin our return voyage to the United States. We stopped at Algiers, on my request. A more attractive place does not exist in the Mediterranean.

I received a cable to go to Genoa to get a sick paymaster. We had rough sea during the passage, which was not a long one. Arriving in Genoa, we found the city under martial law owing to riots and disorders. There were four Italian warships in port, and they landed sailors to preserve order. As I refused to pay the coal contractor "for stowing coal" which his men would not stow, I sailed from Genoa leaving an unpaid bill and told the contractor to take it up with secretary of the navy. I never heard anything more of it.

After short trips to Gibraltar and Horta we arrived at Norfolk on 15 October 1904, and were ordered to New York the same day. Shortly afterwards the navy department ordered the ship to be put out of commission and it was rumored that she was to be used as a coal hulk. Presumably this was a reply to the critics. However, she was spared this ignominious fate by being recommissioned for the use of the Russian Commission at Portsmouth, under the command of Capt. Cameron Winslow.

As I had completed four years at sea I was detached and ordered home on leave.

While in command of the *Dolphin* and *Mayflower*, as the president's yachts, before going on active service to the isthmus, I had opportunity to finish my first book—the biography of James Lawrence. President Roosevelt helped me with advice in seeking a publisher. He told me that his "best book" (so he called it), *The Naval*

War of 1812, had been published in 1889 at his own expense. He could not find a publisher to risk it.

In working over my book I ran across one called *Smith Brunt,* a naval story partly about Lawrence and his fight with the *Shannon.* I wrote to the author, Waldron Kintzing Post, for verification of certain words he had ascribed to Lawrence. His reply was a peccavi—pleading the temptations of historical fiction—and an invitation to dine and talk it all over.

The result was a friendship for the rest of our lives. He aided me in getting the book published by Putnam—without any expense on my part. They had published the *Naval War of 1812* and apparently had more confidence in me than in T. R. at the age of 30. Also, after I was ordered to Panama during the process of publication, Post read and corrected the proofs sent to him during my absence.

On one of those yachting days on the *Mayflower* we took to an American's Cup race a party including, among many other distinguished persons, Admiral Dewey and Sir Thomas Lipton. I heard the admiral inadvertently canonize the owner of the *Shamrock* by addressing him as "Saint Thomas".

12 Newport's Torpedo Station the *St. Louis*

My intention to write only of my sea experiences will have to be broken here in order to speak of my connection with the development of the torpedo in the navy.

When Admiral Taylor decided that I was to go as inspector of ordnance in charge of the torpedo station, I was greatly surprised as I was not a torpedo expert, although I had several years duty with the manufacture of modern naval ordnance. I had declined the post of naval attache at Berlin on the ground of expense, so felt I could not decline this desirable alternative. The president told me when I accepted that he was "as pleased as Punch."

The condition of our torpedo equipment at this time was lamentable. Admiral Higginson would have said "melancholy". We were further handicapped by our dependence upon a manufacturing firm which had the sale rights of the Whitehead in this country. The Honell torpedo, although wonderfully promising, could not be relied upon. It was eventually bought by the Bliss Co.

After a long study of the question, the chief of the bureau of ordnance, Admiral Mason, consented to let me see the president on the subject and tell him that he was willing that I go to Europe to study the foreign methods of making torpedoes. The president heartily agreed and gave me personal letters to each of our ambassadors at London, Berlin, Paris and Vienna. At my request Lt. Gregory Davison from the torpedo station was ordered to accompany me. He was not only a torpedo expert in the full meaning, but had practical knowledge and skill in mechanical engineering and was also a fine draftsman and mathematician.

We were abroad six or eight weeks visiting the torpedo factories of the various countries to which we were accredited with the exception of Woolwich to which, for some reason, we were not admitted. I had always suspected that certain formalities had not been observed—perhaps the omission of the formal call at the Admiralty or even perhaps our lack of a morning coat and pin striped trousers (for the English are meticulous in certain habits of appearance). I regretted not meeting Lord Fisher more than not seeing the Woolwich torpedo.

In London I stayed with our naval attache, John Gibbons, who was one of my oldest and dearest friends, and am certain that the exclusion from Woolwich was not due to any lack of effort on his part.

At Toulon, Kiel, Spezzia and Fiume every courtesy was extended us. Our trip abroad was satisfactory and beneficial and met with the approval of the bureau of ordnance in Washington. In London I closed an order for Whitehead torpedoes with the Vickars' people and in Paris brought a few mines. It was interesting work. We were especially interested in the construction and layout of the torpedo factories and facilities and were allowed to study these freely with the exception mentioned.

While we were in Europe, work was progressing on the new factory on Goat Island which, due to the efforts of Senator Wetmore, had been authorized by congress. Our experience abroad taught us much that was immediately put to use for completing the work in Newport.

The social side of our trip was no less instructive or entertaining. Thanks to the president's letters, I recall a dinner and reception at the ambassador's given for the delegates to the Red Cross convention. Royalty was present and it was interesting to note that the ambassador and Mr. Reid received them on the grand stairway. Of the distinguished people there I remember only the Pauncefotes, Admiral of the Fleet Wilson and Dr. Nansen, the Arctic explorer. The strong, rugged faces of the last two impressed me deeply.

At a luncheon given to Davison and myself at the Central Service Club by Lt. Trevor Dawson of the Vickars Co. we met Admiral Jellicoe, Capt. Percy Scott and Capt. Bernard Curry—and others whose names became well-known in the World War.

It was curious to note the reaction of the various ambassadors to the president's personal letters recommending Davison and me to their good offices. Only one did not respond, but as Captain Cloman, our military attache in London said, "The ambassador is getting these letters of introduction constantly, and ordinarily the visitors are satisfied with a visit to the Royal Mews," (which would explain any apparent lack of interest).

It is a pleasure to speak of the courtesy of Mr. Charlemagne Tower who took a real interest in our mission and did much to aid us. In Italy the ambassador was absent, but Mr. Hitt took us to dine one memorable evening at the famous cafe in the Albian Hills. The drive across the Campagna is one of the most pleasant recollections of that tour.

On our return home I went at once to Washington and gave Mr. Roosevelt a rather detailed account of our experience. He appeared especially pleased to hear of the attention we received in Germany.

I found the torpedo factory nearly completed. It was intended only for the construction of 50 torpedoes at first, but designed for expansion since it was necessary to be modest in requests for appropriations to begin with. Senator Wetmore thought if we asked for the modest sum of $50,000 he could get it at the next congress, which he did. At the beginning of the World War this factory had a capacity of more than 300 torpedoes annually, and the government could fix its own price for what it bought.

In the spring of 1903 I had been onshore longer than at any other time before or since and was anxious to get to sea. Admiral Brownson, about to sail for the China station, invited me to go with him as his chief of staff. I declined as I felt my work at the torpedo station was not finished.

A year later when the factory was practically finished, I was ordered to the *St. Louis*—a 10,000 ton, 21 knot ship armed with six-inch guns. She was at Bremerton, and I crossed the continent on the Canadian Pacific. I knew I could not expect to remain very long, as I was well upon the list of commanders and the *St. Louis* was rated a commander's command.

The Bremerton navy yard had only a few years before been cut from the forest primeval and was not the fully equipped yard it is now. I was fated to remain there, off and on, more than half the cruise. Although the ship was new, her boilers were in deplorable condition when I assumed command. I asked for a statutory survey which was granted, and the repairs authorized were not completed for eight months.

Before the main work was commenced, temporary repairs were ordered and the ship was sent to Honolulu to bring Mr. Garfield, then secretary of the interior, to the United States. Upon our return we put in at San Francisco and found there the U.S. fleet under Rear Adm. C. S. Sherry, just returned from its famous voyage around the world. Gun salutes were exchanged between the secretary and the admiral.

The secretary of the interior has no distinguishing flag, or at least he had none at that time. As the secretary had considerately excused the admiral from making the first call, and furthermore wished to make a personal visit on several officers, I decided to fly the jack in the bow. When we got on board the *Connecticut* the admiral asked me, out of the hearing of the secretary, "By what authority are you flying the jack?"

I replied, "My own, Sir". I expected to hear from the navy department about this, but I never did.

The fleet sailed at noon and the following morning the *St. Louis,* flying the flag of Rear Admiral Swinburne, sailed for Puget Sound where for several months she remained under repairs.

While the *St. Louis* was at San Francisco, President Taft made a visit to the city. At the banquet in his honor, the Dutch minister in his speech stated that the popularly held idea that France was the first nation to salute the new American Stars and Stripes flown by Paul Jones was a historical error. He claimed the flag was first saluted by the Dutch government when Paul Jones was in the *Texel.*

I had requested the I might cruise in the South Pacific to Tahiti, the Marquesas, Hawaii, Samoa and the Fiji Islands but on account of the coal question, the first two groups were cut out of the itinerary by the navy department. We sailed on the South seas cruise on 7 June 1909. Our complement was 21 officers, 506 bluejackets and 44 marines.

The cabin mess attendant was a young negro from New Orleans known on the ship as Lijah. We had gotten under way from Port Madison at early daylight—about 3:30. It was glorious weather, perfectly free from fog. In such weather, rare enough in the vicinity of Mt. Rainier, the navigation of the sound presents no difficulties.

After breakfast I was reading in the cabin when Lijah, looking out of the air port, called to me, asking why we were so close in to land. I saw we were running almost along the beach, when we should have been in the middle of the sound. It was a close call and I always had a feeling of gratitude in my heart for our mess attendant.

We stopped to dock at Mare Island and then continued to Honolulu, and had two more close calls. One has been related in the Naval Institute, the other may not enter here—but there were other annoyances.

On one occasion the officer of the deck requested permission to set the clocks back 25 minutes. I replied to do so at 11 a.m. After breakfast I noticed that they had already been changed.—the reason given was that the order was understood to apply to future clocks! Another time a man was to be released from confinement at 7 a.m. At 7:30, no report having been made, I asked why. The reply came, "He has been released now." War is not the only thing that's hell. Trying to get a ship's company into shape and proper performance of duty is hell also. An old boatswain once remarked, "It's a good man in the navy who does what he's told."

On June 25 we picked up the first northeast trades and topping seas and carried fine weather into Honolulu. Admiral Ishii's training division, which we had met in Seattle, was in port and certain newspapers sent out cablegrams that the *St. Louis* was trailing the Japanese ships.

At Honolulu there were the usual gaieties onshore, but I was anxious to get on with the cruise in the South seas. For eleven days we rolled deep in heavy quartering seas as trade winds blew strong. Gradually it faded out as the ship approached the doldrums, then after we had crossed the belt of calms, it blew again—cooling off the ship which was 123° in the passages while on deck the tar boiled out of the seams. I was much impressed with the accuracy of Commodore Wilkes' charts on which we navigated through the islands on either side of the line. These charts were made 40 years before with instruments of that time which lacked the modern refinements.

Suva, our port of destination, lies on the Koro Sea which is entered by channels through dangerous reefs. On the 14th we crossed the 180th meridian and gained a day. The scenery around the harbor is very beautiful and the town of Suva attractive, possessing among other things a Carnegie library.

It had been a long time since Suva had been visited by an American man-of-war and the *St. Louis* was received with enthusiasm and boundless hospitality. Dinners and receptions were exchanged with the governor and other officials, but the red letter day was when we made a visit by a native motorboat inside the reefs to Mbau, many miles distant, once the home of Thackenbau, king of the Cannibal Islands. His house is now occupied by his son, who was absent but who had turned it over to the vice-consul for our entertainment. The walls were decorated with war clubs, braided mats and sennito, not to mention a certificate of the king's conversion to Christianity—presented by missionaries—and another to indicate that he was a loyal subject of Her Gracious Majesty. Nearby were the timbers of a French man-of-war, wrecked on the island many years before, the crew "disposed of" by the natives.

At Fiji during a luncheon given to the officers onshore, I had to respond to the mayor's toast and unfortunately in my remarks gave the precedence to "His Worship" instead of to "His Grace the Bishop of Polynesia" which disconcerted the latter to a visible extent.

From Suva to Samoa was a short run. On the way we picked up our lost day! The governor of Samoa at that time was Captain Parker of the navy who invited me to go to Apia with him in the *Annapolis.* I had to decline and instead sailed for Honolulu where we arrived on August 15. There I learned that although Samoa and Honolulu were American, native articles from one port to another were dutiable. A great row was raised by the energetic collector of customs at Honolulu because some of the crew had sold tapa cloths to Chinese traders in Honolulu. This was reported to the collector who, of course, had the law on his side. The chief culprit was the master-at-arms. After the affair was settled, he and the district attorney became such good friends that he presented the small daughter of the D.A. with a gold watch.

I was now nearly at the head of the list of commanders, and shortly after our return to Puget Sound was detached from the *St. Louis* and ordered to Washington. The wardroom officers rowed me ashore in the gig. Lieutenant Commander Pratt pulled stroke and as the bow touched the dock the paymaster who was at the bow oar, unshipped the pennant staff, disconnected the pennant and presented it to me as I stepped ashore. The officers stood up and gave three cheers, which supplemented those of the crew when I went over the side of the ship.

In due course I arrived in Washington and when I called upon Mr. Winthrop, he asked me if I would like to come to the navy department as his aide—a complimentary detail which I gladly accepted. Later he told me he had selected me on account of the beautiful condition in which he found the *St. Louis* when he inspected her at San Francisco.

However, there was very little to do, and I was eager to get to sea again although I had been made a member of the general board—the great naval Sanhedrin. After passing my examination for captain, I was at once ordered to command the *North Dakota*—our newest and biggest battleship fitting out at the Boston navy yard.

13 The *North Dakota* Command

The *North Dakota* and the *Delaware,* sister ships, were our first super dreadnoughts. They were 22,000 tons, armed with twelve-and five-inch guns, speed 21 knots and heavily armored on the turrets and sides. Although the *North Dakota* had been completed and turned over to the navy department, many interior changes were decided upon by a board convened at the war college.

When I joined her at Boston she was being ripped to pieces by the yard mechanics. The noise of the pneumatic riveting made the cabin uninhabitable, so I lived on board the old receiving ship, *Wabash,* with Captain Helm. The changes in the *North Dakota* improved her battle efficiency, but it always seemed to me that a great waste of money might have been saved if the mistakes in the design had been corrected before the ship was finished.

Finally, with new casemates and new positions for the five-inch guns, we escaped from the muggy weather of the navy yard and reported for duty in the North Atlantic fleet, then under Rear Adm. Seaton Schroeder.

In the shakedown cruise that followed, the ship scored at target practice and with the *Delaware* stood at the head in the annual competitive gun practice off the Capes of Virginia. The *Delaware* had orders to rig the target for the *North Dakota* and have it ready at 7 a.m. on the day of the practice. When the time expired and apparently no preparations had been made to carry out this order, the flagship signaled to the *Delaware,* "Why have you not carried out your orders to rig target?"

Delaware replied, "Will explain by letter later."

Flagship replied, "Explain by signal at once."

It so happened when the *Delaware* went on the range, after the *North Dakota,* she made a splendid score and demolished the target, whereupon her captain, Gove, signaled—unofficially of course—to the chief of staff, "We may be slow in putting up targets, but we are hell in knocking them down."

Satisfaction over the result of our firing was marred when at the end of practice an acetylene tank in one of the boiler rooms exploded. The inexcusable mistake of locating the tank over a boiler cost the lives of three men, but brought the Medal of Honor to two other enlisted men who tried to save their lives. The material damage, however, was soon repaired and the ship was not delayed when the fleet sailed for Europe.

The *North Dakota* had turbine engines and also in-turning screws—the third ship I commanded with this mechanical atrocity, now happily abandoned. However, I could always count on her doing the opposite of what was expected of any other ship when the helm was used with the engines. Her backing power was so much less than that of her sister ship, the *Delaware,* that the admiral increased the cruising distance between ships of the first division from 400 to 500 yards.

About this time, on the suggestion of Admiral Schroeder, the navy department ordered the terms "left" and "right"—to designate the direction of turnings—substituted for "starboard" and "port"—which had always meant the helm and therefore opposite to the turn. It was hard to get accustomed to the change, and I began to think naval constructor Woodward not far wrong when he spoke of steel ships and wooden men.

When Secretary Meyer visited the *North Dakota* at Newport in the summer, he promised to remember me in selecting the ship to represent the navy at the coronation of George V. He kept his word, and one day at Guantanamo the flagship signaled for all ships having English gold to transfer it to the *North Dakota.* The North Dakotans were proud and jubilant, and congratulations began to pour in.

A day or two later the order was cancelled and the *Delaware* was substituted. It developed later that someone in Washington persuaded the secretary that as the *North Dakota* was the first man-of-war with turbines, they should be disassembled and overhauled before sending her on distant service. This ended our part in the coronation and when the turbines were examined they were found to be in excellent condition.

In November 1910 the fleet, composed of 16 battleships, sailed for the English channel. Upon arrival off Ushant, the division proceeded independently to the ports they were to visit—Howard's division went to Brest; Vreeland's to Cherbourg; Murdock's to Gravesend and the commander in chief's to Weymouth. Each division was to remain three weeks in port and then shift with the ships across channel.

This was a generous allowance for port for the visitors, but rather strenuous for our hosts, who no sooner finished entertaining one division when they had to begin with another, making their share of the fleet's entertainment six weeks on end. It has always seemed to me that the visit of the fleet was badly arranged. It would have been better and easier for all hands if eight ports had been visited instead of four, and the kaiser's feelings would not have been hurt by the omission of a visit to Kiel.

It is not often the navy confuses a program of any sort, but so far as the first two divisions were concerned, the affair was not pulled off satisfactorily. The first division arrived in the channel a day ahead of schedule, whereupon at the request of the Admiralty, the naval attache in London, Captain Simpson, wirelessed Admiral Schroeder it would not be convenient to have the ships at Weymouth until the day agreed upon and requested him to anchor at Torbay, a few miles from Weymouth, until the following day.

This was done, of course, and the next forenoon the first division passed the channel ships coming out of Portland in formation. We took their buoys in Weymouth harbor almost before their moorings had cooled off and were comfortably and skillfully berthed by British naval officers sent on board our ships for that purpose, but we all felt that a mistake had been made. Murdock's division passed on up the channel to Gravesend.

Official and personal invitations poured in. The Admiralty showed keen interest in the design of the two superdreadnoughts and sent officers down from London to study them. Our ambassador, Mr. Whitelaw Reid, the Duchess of Marlborough, Lord Northcliffe, the lord mayor of London and the United Service Club were among our official hosts in London.

Admiral Schroeder's division—composed of the *Connecticut* (Flag), *Delaware, North Dakota* and *Michigan*—attracted hundreds of visitors to Portland harbor. The officers went to London or made excursions into the country and generous shore leave was given the men. There were luncheons, dinners and teas. We felt that the visit of the fleet had a salutary effect in bringing together the officers of the two services, and to quote the navy regulations: "in cultivating friendly relations with the habitants on shore."

A British ship was told off to be the "running mate" of each American ship. The *North Dakota*'s vis-a-vis was the *Collingwood* commanded by Capt. W. C. Pakenham—one of whose forebears was the hero of Salamanca, Sir Edward Pakenham, who afterwards fell at the head of his troops in the battle of New Orleans.

Captain Pakenham was a charming and attentive host. He and I walked together through the beautiful countryside of Dorset and one day made an excursion to Corfe Castle, accompanied by Captain Heath. Both officers distinguished themselves in the battle of Jutland. Even in 1910, the year before Agadir, more then one captain said to me, "War is inevitable." But I never heard the question discussed with acrimony.

Most of us thought that three weeks was rather long for a courtesy visit. It was more like a visitation, but the visitors enjoyed it even if it was a bore to our hosts who had to go through the same thing with another division. The time passed pleasantly. A few London papers poked fun at our bluejackets, some of whom appeared on the streets in uniform wearing spectacles and some with kid gloves. Otherwise the criticisms and comments were not unfriendly.

On the night of the fleet's arrival at Portland, Adm. Sir William May, commander in chief of the channel squadron, gave a dinner on board the squadron tender *Surprise* to Admiral Schroeder and the captains of the American ships. It had been agreed by the admirals to have no speeches except Admiral May's welcome and Admiral Schroeder's reply. When Admiral May had finished speaking, his flag lieutenant signaled to the band master, stationed outside the cabin, and the band struck up "God Save the King".

"Stop that!" shouted the admiral. "The fellow has gone off half-cocked."

The flag lieutenant rushed from the table to head off the band. The admiral smiled and said, "It's too late."

Of course, the American national air should have been played first, followed by the English. I have heard this question argued both ways. But it seems definitely settled now by Lieutenant Commander Lovette in his excellent *Naval Customs and Traditions,* just issued by the U.S. Naval Institute.

Admiral May's dinner was a stag affair, but Admiral Sturdee entertained the American officers at a dinner on board his flagship, the *Invincible,* at which there were ladies. I took in to dinner the beautiful Lady Napier, wife of Capt. Sir Trevelyan Napier and daughter of Adm. Sir Michael Culme Seymour. Among the other ladies present were Admiral Schroeder's wife and two daughters.

Also at the dinner was Capt.—afterwards Adm.—Mark Kerr, who it was said had more autographs of royalty than any officer in the navy. He was the great-nephew of that General Maitland who, on Lord Raglan's staff during the Crimean War, sent the order for the famous charge to Lord Lucan, who transmitted it to Lord Cardigan.

I remembered that one of the buglers of Balaclava, a man who claimed to have sounded the charge, was with me in the *Hartford* in 1877. Captain Kerr told me that his great-grandmother was the Duchess of Richmond who had given the famous ball at Brussels the night before the battle of Waterloo. I think it was at this dinner that I met Captain Anson, the great-great-grandson of the famous admiral. A few years later the *Invincible,* while flying the flag of Admiral Sturdee, fought Admiral von Spee at the Falkland Islands.

At a reception at the ambassador's I met an American woman whose English husband had been formerly in the navy but was then in parliament. This lady was so critical of everything American, that I asked her if she were English, but she acknowledged she was not. She said our sailors were hirelings and if we went to war with Japan—which she predicted—would not fight. I said I believed that was the common impression in Europe in 1898, but did not know it still existed.

This is only mentioned to show how thoroughly persons can become weaned from their own country. On another occasion I had the good fortune to meet an American of a very different type—Mrs. Ronalds, a leader in London and the president of the Maine Relief Society in the Boer Wars. She had lived in Northern Africa and in younger days had turned the head of a nation by her beauty at an official ball in the late 1860s at one of the continental capitals.

A delightful entertainment was given to the admiral and officers at Sunder Place by the Duchess of Marlborough at which there were many interesting people.

It was a disappointment that I could not accept an invitation of Mr. Thomas Hardy to tea at Max Gate and on the Sunday he was to have been my guest on board the *North Dakota,* the channel weather was at its worst. He wrote a pleasant note saying, "I will try to get to you, according to your kind invitation, on Sunday, weather permitting (I believe one postulates that in all matters marine)." And then, "to my disappointment I could not get to you Sunday, but here was a dense fog and I feared it was still denser at Weymouth."

I was most fortunate when I went as the guest of Mr. and Mrs. Bankes to tea at Wolfton House near Dorchester, not far from Max Gate. The house dates from the reign of Henry VII and has an interesting history. It is the scene of one of Thomas Hardy's stories in *A Group of Noble Dames*. Our hosts entertained us royally and took the greatest interest in showing us the house and telling us of its legends—of Lady Trenchard's ghost, of the Roman Catholic priest who was held as a political prisoner there and afterwards executed in the High Street of Dorset, of the visit of the king of Aragon in the 16th century, and of George III in the 18th. The visit was a memorable one to us.

With Commander Belknap, the executive officer, and Lt. Ralston Holmes, I took advantage of our stay at Portland to make our annual physical test which the president had ordered for all officers of the navy and army on the active list. The test was to walk 52 miles in less than three consecutive days—or there was a bicycle test of 90 miles or a horseback test of 100 miles.

We walked from Weymouth over the hills to Dorchester and beyond at the rate of three miles an hour. Holmes did this in much better time. The next day Ensign Kidd joined us and the walk to Dorchester was repeated. On the return we lunched on cold mutton and ale at the King's Arms. It was Sunday and raining hard. As I watched the people going home from church, I thought of Washington Irving's "A Rainy Day at a Country Inn."

The outstanding reception of the officers of the fleet was given at the guild hall on December 2 by the lord mayor. Preceded by city trumpeters, the reception committees, sheriffs and aldermen, and the sword and mace, the officers were conducted to the dais and presented to the lord mayor and the lady mayoress. From the beginning it was an interesting occasion, and the after dinner speeches by the lord mayor and Admiral Murdock were—to say the least—harmless.

The next day, however, when the city entertained the bluejackets in the same historic banquet hall, Captain Sims added a page to the history of our relations with England which, like the shot at Concord, was heard around the world and stirred up a vertiable hornet's nest in the Wilhelm Strasse.

Sims assured the lord mayor if England ever needed assistance the United States would be ready to shed every drop of our blood to come to the rescue. Ordinarily not overmuch attention is given to postprandial oratory, but this time there was no misfire and President Taft issued a mild reprimand. The following spring Admiral Badger with a squadron was sent to Kiel on a "good will" visit to show the kaiser there was no hard feeling against him.

On the morning of December 8 our division sailed for Cherbourg. In mid-channel we passed Admiral Vreeland's division on the way to Portland harbor. The weather was bad with heavy seas and rain. At 3 p.m. we moored in Cherbourg behind the breakwater.

Our visit to France was a repetition of our stay in England, although necessarily there was lacking the personal element. The French officers were assiduous in their attention and hospitality; but it is always heavy weather trying to speak another language—the accents are so funny and the grammar laughable. Professor Sabine of Harvard College has written "never again will I be caught in the humiliating position of visiting a country of which I am unable to speak the language."

This is a good rule provided one's profession is not visiting foreign countries. However, there were fair linguists in both fleets. Admiral Schroeder spoke beautiful French, having lived abroad many years when a boy, and his flag lieutenant, Drace White, was also an excellent French scholar.

The country around Cherbourg is beautiful and attractive, tempting long walks in the ravines and along the banks of the river. There are several old chateaus nearby, wonderfully situated, especially Tourlaville.

For the greater part of our visit the weather was as cold and bleak as only channel weather can be on the northwest coast of France during the winter. The rain and gales were almost incessant and were said to be the worst in many years.

Admiral Berryer was in command afloat at Brest and was the prefect at Cherbourg. At Admiral Kiessel's official dinner at the prefecture, Admiral Schroeder made a speech in French which was a classic, but at the mayor's dinner in the Hotel de Ville he spoke in lighter vein and surprised his own officers by an unsuspected sense of humor. In toasting the city of Cherbourg he said, "Mt. St. Michel has its omelette, Marseilles its bouillabaisse, and Cherbourg has its bread [alluding to a well-known tradition] and when I ask the good God to give me my daily bread, I add, and may it be from Cherbourg."

In concluding his speech he requested his "adjoints" to join in drinking the health of our hosts "rubis sur l'ongle," which prompted my neighbor, the French Admiral Gros, to say to me, "Your admiral not only speaks classical French, but he even knows our argot."

Unfortunately there was no official entertainment in Paris. Mr. Bacon, our ambassador, accompanied by Comdr. Frederick Chapin, the naval attache, visited the squadron at Cherbourg and extended a cordial invitation to the admiral and officers to be his guests in Paris, but for some reason our admiral declined, much to the disappointment of all hands.

On December 31 we sailed for the fleet rendezvous off Ushant. The next night there was the usual New Year's jubilation with whistles, sirens and bells, and the commander in chief wirelessed his felicitations. At dinner our thoughtful and punctilious executive, Lieutenant Commander Belknap, proposed my health—the first of January being my birthday—and a cake with eleven candles was lighted on the wardroom table. Why eleven candles I never knew—presumably that was all that was in the purser's store. Lieutenant Osterhaus read a clever poem in my honor.

The run across the Atlantic was through heavy seas and the usual rain in the tropics, but personally I was more concerned with the excessive coal consumption of the *North Dakota* which caused the fleet to reduce speed. We did not reach Guantanamo until 13 January 1911.

It is a common saying on board ship that there is only one thing worse than getting to leeward of the "old man" and that is getting to windward of him. After leaving France the admiral signaled the fleet to exercise at deep sea sounding and to report as soon as 100 fathoms of wire was run out.

In due course the *North Dakota* was the first to report and hoisted the signal, "numeral 600".

Flagship signaled, "Do not understand."

This was repeated two or three times. Finally she signaled, "How did you obtain 600 fathoms?"

North Dakota replied, "We signaled 100 fathoms as the signal book directs soundings to be reported in *feet*."

Then there were practically no signals until sunset, which was ominous. I remarked to Reggie Belknap, "We shall hear from this before tomorrow is over."

And we did! Next day my diary records: "A day of hammering from the flagship!"

On the way across the ocean we had a search problem with Admiral Staunton's cruiser division from the Atlantic coast, and at Guantanamo the fleet drilled in battle exercises, day and night, and did not return north until the middle of March after three months of rigorous training.

The following November I was detached from the *North Dakota* and ordered to report for duty as commandant of the second naval district from near Boston to near New York with headquarters at Coasters Harbor Island in Narragansett Bay.

On 11 November, 1911, on the quarterdeck of the *North Dakota* in Newport harbor, I read to the officers and crew the navy department's order. The officers were at the side to say good-bye and the crew on the bridges, turrets and upper decks. All hands cheered three times as I went down the gangway. The marine guard paraded on the quarterdeck and the band played "Auld Lang Syne" unmindful of the rain. I heard the music long after Goat Island had shut out the view of the ship.

It is against the regulations to cheer when officers are detached from the ship or, for that matter, when the crew leave.

In this connection I am reminded of a story Admiral Clark told me of an old fireman who had served with him on the *Monocacy*. The fireman was transferred to another ship on the station. When he went over the side, a number of officers were on the quarterdeck, to each of whom Murphy waved his hat and said "good-bye and God bless you" until he came to Mr. Clark—with whom he had had some trouble on board. Then he stopped and not wishing to leave out anybody said, "And God bless you too, Mr. Clark—that is to a certain extent."

14 The Coming of the War

As these recollections are mainly of life on board ship, the years between leaving the *North Dakota* and joining the *Utah* are passed lightly over, although that period was full of personal interest in command of the second naval district at Newport and of the navy yard at New York. During the time I was commandant at New York the trouble with Mexico occurred. This was followed by preliminary preparations for the war with Germany.

In the autumn of 1914 I was assigned, at my request for sea duty, to the command of the battleship *Utah* in the home fleet. My cruise in her was brief and uneventful. In October 1915 I was promoted to rear admiral and soon afterwards relieved Rear Admiral Sims of the command of the destroyer flotilla operating with the fleet.

His flagship was the cruiser *Birmingham* and at the time was in Boston preparing for the usual winter cruise in the West Indies. On November 22 I broke the twin stars at the masthead and began a service afloat which did not end until February 1921, when the stars had increased to four.

The *Birmingham* was a small cruiser commanded by Captain Sellers, an officer highly esteemed for his professional ability, who eventually commanded the United States fleet. She was entirely unfit to be a flagship, not having proper quarters for a flag officer. Consequently the captain was crowded into a tiny improvised cabin built in the stern. It was an uncomfortable arrangement, but in threatening times it was not ours to complain but to bide better fortunes.

Captain Sellers was not so much concerned as his cruise was nearly over. I had my eye on the *Washington*—a 16,000 ton vessel. Although refused at first by the navy department, she was eventually assigned as flagship to my force which at the time consisted of 30 destroyers and a repair ship. In her name was changed to *Seattle,* as a cruiser of the second line.

I found the flotilla in excellent condition and admirably organized. There was one outstanding job, however, that had never been completed—that of oiling the destroyers at sea. I turned the problem over to Lt. A. L. Bristol and Lt. F. M. Perkins of the staff. They eventually worked out a scheme so successfully that when war came, the "short legged" boats—so called because they did not carry oil enough to cross the Atlantic—were fueled from the *Maumee* stationed in mid-ocean on the route of the first convoy to wait for the ships of the first expeditionary force.

The distinguishing marks of the destroyers at this time were short yards carried in various combinations at the mastheads. As new vessels were joining up all the time, it was evident that some other method was necessary. All the suggestions received were unsatisfactory.

One day while walking down Washington Street in Boston with Lt. C. B. Mayo, my flag lieutenant, we saw a book displayed conspicuously in a shop window called *Germany's Fighting Machine*. We went in to examine the book and turning over the leaves I found on page 86 the solution of our problem. The large numbers painted on the bow of the torpedo boat 71 suggested that our torpedo craft might be treated in the same way—the numbers taking the place of the "chicken coops"—as the sailors termed the combinations of yards.

The suggestion was approved by Admiral Fletcher, the commander in chief, and was accordingly adopted after experiments to determine the proper size of the figures. This system has now been extended to tugs, submarine tenders and other vessels.

During our stay in Boston I walked a great deal, averaging ten to twelve miles daily. One day my flag secretary, A. L. Bristol, Lieutenant Mayo and I walked to Lexington—twelve miles in four hours—which is better time than Paul Revere, according to Longfellow, did on horseback.

In January 1916 the flotilla joined the fleet at Hampton Roads, worked out a tactical problem and then sailed for the West Indies and operated there with the commander in chief. We had target practice with guns and torpedoes daily and accomplished much good work. It was an ideal place for torpedo practice both day and night. As usual, there were disturbances among the Cubans and at Santa Cruz one was reported that threatened to become serious.

In order to ascertain the actual truth of the report I sent Lt. Kenneth Whiting to make an air reconnaissance. This was the first naval employment of an airplane in our service for military purposes. Whiting reported having seen a number of men under arms marching through the streets of the town, but no evidence of riot or disturbance. Whiting was a bold and fearless aviator and did excellent pioneer work in the development of naval aviation. He was the first officer to be catapulted from a man-of-war in a plane. This required nerve of high order. It was equal to his daring exploit of being ejected from a submerged torpedo tube.

The flotilla remained in the West Indies until late spring and when the fleet returned north accompanied it. We were in Newport in the autumn of 1916 preparing for the winter's cruise. The war news from Europe was getting more ominous and it seemed as if Mr. Wilson could not hold out the olive branch longer. Foreign relations were strained, and the duty and necessity of our joining the war were advocated in and out of congress. In the fleet we felt it to be a matter of only a short time before we should get into the game.

A long step toward it was made in October 1916. The U-53 entered Newport harbor and anchored a few hundred yards from the *Birmingham*. It happened I was having a luncheon party on board at our anchorage off Goat Island, given to Rear Admiral Knight who was in command of the station. When the deck officer reported to me that a German submarine, flying the man-of-war flag, was entering the harbor, it seemed incredible. We hurried on deck and there just astern of us was a smart looking sub flying the imperial double eagle on the black and white colors. Knight excused himself and immediately returned to his headquarters.

The usual calls of ceremony were made and the German commander, Hans Rose, sent word to me by our boarding officer that he would be obliged if I would lend him a boat to make his call on Admiral Knight and myself. I was glad to do so, but cautioned the young officer in charge of the boat to permit no German colors to be displayed in the boat.

When Captain Rose came on board the *Birmingham* he was received with the same ceremonies as any other foreign officer of his rank, for we were not at war. A young man of pleasing personality and attractive manners, Captain Rose remained on board a quarter of an hour or so and informed me he was going to sea in a few hours. Of course, there were no restrictions on his communicating with shore, but he said he did not wish to purchase stores or grant liberty to his crew.

On my way to Jamestown, in citizen's dress, about five o'clock I stopped alongside the U-53 and went on board to have a good look at her interior. The officers were most courteous and seemed anxious to show us everything. I observed, however, that while Rose and his officers were polite, the sailors were notably surly in their looks and even in manner. When Rose took me into the torpedo room he opened the door of the bow torpedo tube which was loaded and said, "All ready for firing but nothing to shoot at."

Shortly after I left the sub, he went to sea. Early the following morning I received a radio, intercepted from the British ship *Westpoint* twelve miles SSE of Nantucket lightship, giving the first news of the sinkings by the U-53.

I immediately sent out all the destroyers in port—a total of 17—to the rescue of the survivors. About eleven o'clock while at church, I received a note from Admiral Knight that the American ship *Kansas* had been held up.

These operations of Captain Hans Rose which took place outside the marine league created the greatest excitement in the United States and provoked angry comment in England. Enemies of the administration made the most of the incident to force the president to aggressive action against Germany for an alleged violation of neutrality by the U-53. In the House of Lords, Admiral Beresford and Baron Sydenham were both severely critical, not to say bitter.

The navy department wired asking for reports, not only from me but from all the commanders "on the spot". After a careful examination of our replies the assistant secretary of the navy, Mr. F. D. Roosevelt, issued a statement declaring the operations of all our naval vessels had been conducted in "strict compliance with the dictates of humanity and with the recognized requirements of international law and absolute neutrality"—and characterized the handling of the destroyers as brilliant, as did also the assistant secretary of state, Mr. Frank Polk.

Colonel Roosevelt wrote a similar letter from Osyter Bay to the New York *Times*. These comments were especially gratifying to the flotilla, for there was much criticism loosed by one wing of the daily press. Mr. Page, our ambassador, took up the matter unofficialy with Lord Beresford who replied, "The matter is quite cleared up and I shall endeavor to bring it before the House of Lords next session."

After this affair the entire fleet went south as usual and remained until March. Feeling convinced of the probabilities of a break with Germany, I wrote a letter to the commander in chief recommending that certain destroyers in need of repairs be sent north immediately to be put in "condition for distant service". The letter was prepared by my chief of staff, Capt. DeWitt Blamer, as follows:

Gulf of Guacanayabo, Cuba
21 February 1917

From: Commander, Destroyer Force
To: Commander in Chief

Subject: Preparation for War

Reference: (a) Alnav Availability report C.D.F.R.9-5 of Feb. 4, 1917.
Reference: (b) Opnav radiogram 1102 0 of 20 February, 1917.

1. The Commander, Destroyer Froce estimates that the present situation demands that all destroyers be put in thorough readiness immediately for service on the high seas.

2. When war is declared there will doubtless be an immediate demand for destroyers and cruisers, which will probably be met by releasing destroyers from duty with the Fleet, and by immediately placing in full commission all destoyers and cruisers.

3. My availability report, reference (a) shows that all destroyers are not materially ready for distant service.

4. It is recommended that all destroyers not materially ready be immediately sent to Navy yards for repairs, and that their duties of preserving neutraility, etc., be taken over by destroyers now ready for distant service, keeping with the Fleet only such destroyers as are absolutely necessary for its safety.

5. It is recommended that the following destroyers, now with the Fleet, be sent to Navy Yards immediately:

CASSIN and *CUMMINGS*—Complete repairs to maneuvring valves
JARVIS, MCCALL and *WAINWRIGHT*—Repairs to condensers
FANNING—Installation of blower
ALWYN and *DRAYTON*—Repair damages by collision
DUNCAN, CUSHING and *TUCKER* (Fore River Boats)—Thrust bearings
ERICSSON—Circulating Pump
McDOUGAL, WILKES—Evaporators

6. It is recommended that all destroyers of flotillas one and two be sent to navy yards to fit out for full commission and be put in thorough readiness for distant service.

7. It is recommended that all complements of all destroyers be filled.

8. It is further recommended that no officer who has not had experience

on a destroyer, and who is below the rank of lieutenant be ordered to command any destroyer, and that such orders as may be necessary to put this recommendation into effect be immediately promulgated.

Albert Gleaves

This letter was so strong that it was forwarded by Admiral Mayo by despatch to Washington and was there approved. The action of the department on these recommendations enabled Commander Taussig to report on his arrival in English waters, "We are ready now."

The recommendations for repairs were approved in toto, as I recall, except for the *Wainright.* On the passage across, she was the only one to break down—in submarine waters—but fortunately she was not attacked. It was most gratifying that Admiral Mayo after the war included my preparation of the destroyers for war in my citation for the Distinguished Service Medal.

Captain Blamer who succeeded Captain Sellers in the *Birmingham* (when the renamed *Seattle* was made my flagship), had come with me as chief of staff. He was an officer of marked ability as executive and navigator, and as an organizer had no superior in the service. His gift of foresight was unusually keen. He was a conscientious student of his profession and while at the war college several years afterwards, prepared the plans for the annual war problem which was worked out by the navy and army in the Pacific. I owe much to him and have always deeply regretted his premature retirement as a loss to the service and the country.

When the fleet returned north in the latter part of March, war was in sight. As a matter of fact it was declared at three in the morning, Good Friday, April 6. During the debate of the war resolution by the House, my wife and daughter, Evelina, were in the Speaker's Gallery for 13 hours. One member, who was opposed to war, Jeannette Rankin, got the floor near midnight and shouted, "Remember tomorrow is Good Friday, the day on which our Lord arose from the dead and said, 'Peace on earth good will to men.'"

It was announced that French and English commissioners would visit the country to arrange for our participation in the hostilities. Marshal Joffre and Mons. Viviani would come in men-of-war while Vice Adm. Sir Montague Browning, the commander in chief of the British north Atlantic station, would come to Hampton Roads in his flagship, the *Leviathan*—which must not be confused with our great vessel taken from the Germans and given that name later.

On April 22 Admiral Mayo sent me with the *Seattle* and six destroyers to meet the French men-of-war, *Lorraine* and *Jean Bart,* with the French commissioners. The weather was thick, but we had no difficulty in picking up the French ships and passed with them inside the Capes at eight in the morning. By agreement no salutes were fired; but we dressed ship with French colors at the masthead.

When we anchored off Old Point, I went with Admiral Mayo to call on the commissioners and was agreeably impressed by their appearance and manners. Viviani was youngish looking, but his face sad and serious. He looked not unlike an American, but spoke no English. Marshal Joffre was a big, burly man—about five feet ten or eleven inches—with an abundance of blonde hair, white mustache and blue eyes. His face was full, with a free, determined mouth, but with an expression of amiability rather than force. He talked at some length with me and asked many questions about our navy. Lieutenant Colonel Cosby of the U.S. Army was the interpreter.

Joffre was complimentary to the destroyers for finding him so quickly in the heavy fog, and said he thought it fine work. Soon the *Mayflower* came in and Mayo and I went on board to call on the assistant secretary of the navy, Mr. F. D. Roosevelt. It made me homesick to be in my old ship again. With Mr. Roosevelt were assembled officials from Washington who came down to escort the marshal and Viviani to Washington.

I do not remember when the H.M.S *Leviathan* arrived off Old Point, but it was from her officers we had the first authentic news of what really happened at Jutland. Some of them had been in the battle.

Comdr. R. Drace White, executive officer of the *Seattle,* accompanied Vice Admiral Grasset—commanding the French naval force—as liaison officer. On his return to the *Seattle* he gave me a detailed account of the discussion in Admiral Benson's office when he and Admiral Browning were trying to come to some conclusion regarding the naval force to be sent over by us.

At first the secretary of the navy would consent to sending only one division of destroyers. The English admiral said diplomatically that he had expected more but would take one rather than none—the thing was to show our flag on the sea on the other side. The one division was conceded and orders accordingly issued.

About this time Mr. Balfour arrived and went at once to the White House. After a conference with the president on May 7, it was decided to send all 36 destroyers and the *Melville*. Thus at the beginning of the war I lost my force! I had a talk with Mr. Daniels and then went to Mr. Roosevelt's residence to talk with him, but with no results—except that I had the satisfaction, such as it was, of expressing my own views—which clearly did not make the impression I was seeking.

15 Jeopardy in High Sea

Note: This chapter is written by the editor to the original manuscript, Waldron Kintzing Post (see Appendix I), with the aid of official reports, the logs and "War Diaries" of ships; Gleaves' History of the Transport Service *and his personal journal, but not in his own words except when quoted. Post reports Macaulay would have found Gleaves' story of his own achievements less impassioned than the Sixth Book of Euclid.*

At the beginning of the war, Gleaves was left on the beach. His destroyers, over which he had worked so hard, had almost all been taken from him and sent overseas to add new pages to the history of the navy. The credit for those shining pages is due largely to his preparation. Of their future he felt confident.

On his return to Yorkstown, Gleaves attended a luncheon on board the *Pennsylvania,* flagship of the Atlantic fleet, in honor of President Wilson. After lunch Admiral Benson, chief of operations, took Gleaves into one of the small cabins and in strict confidence told him that a division of the army was to be sent to France as soon as transports could be assembled. He asked if Gleaves would accept command to the convoy.

On May 29 Gleaves received his formal orders to organize the first convoy. He was appointed commander of convoy operations in the Atlantic, in addition to the now rather empty designation of commander of the destroyer force. As soon as possible he went to New York in the armored cruiser *Seattle.*

The chiefs of the German navy, in their plea for unrestricted and merciless submarine warfare, had assured their government that the United States need not be considered. Because of the excellent destruction of all German ships in American ports and the lack of others—not to mention the submarines—very few, if any, American troops could be brought to Europe.

When Gleaves took stock of his new command he found good grounds for that assurance. The navy had then but three vessels available for transports: the *Hancock* and *Henderson*—regular marine transports—and the *Dekalb*—a German ship, formerly the *Prinz Eitel Friedrich,* which had been seized after the declaration of war in April but had not been as badly sabotaged as the others, so had been sufficiently repaired. The army had a few regular transports but none suitable and ready for a transatlantic voyage. Privately owned ships had to be commandeered from the scanty merchant marine or acquired from foreign owners and altered for carrying troops.

Altogether, 17 ships, including the three above mentioned, were assembled early in June, with an aggregate gross tonnage of less than 130,000 tons. In the limited time, everything possible was done to put them in proper shape, but this fell far short of perfection—especially as to watertight bulkheads. In the *History of the Transport Service* Gleaves says,

> The somewhat motley assemblage of ships finally gathered together for the first expedition did not long survive the duty imposed upon them. Some were torpedoed, others relegated to carry cargo and cattle, and some were subsequently wrecked or dropped out altogether because of unseaworthiness.
>
> Looking back to the first expedition of June 1917, it seems indeed that the hand of Providence must have been held over these 'arks' or the task never could have been accomplished. Who would have dreamed at that time that we were laying the foundation of the greatest transport fleet in history?

The term convoy is used to signify the entire fleet of troop or cargo ships, together with their guardian men-of-war. The former are called the train, the latter the escort. In this particular convoy all the escort, except the destroyers, also carried troops. The two regular navy transports—the *Hancock* and *Dekalb*—better armed than the other troopships, acted with the escort. Beside their crews, nearly 14,000 men and their equipment, horses and mules, practically all of the First Division except its engineer and artillery regiments, and the Fifth Marines were crowded into all the vessels that could take any of them. The ships were arranged in four groups, according to their respective speed, in order to avoid congestion at the terminal, and—still more important—to have the eggs in four baskets.

The sailing date had been set for June 9, but was postponed to the 14th, partly for the time needed for preparation but mainly to approach the coast of France during the dark of the moon. Two of the groups were assembled in the North River, the other two off Staten Island, at Tompkinsville. On June 14, day broke, or tried to break, through one of the densest fogs that ever shrouded the harbor.

The fourth group was held by the department for belated stores and despatches. The other three at dawn, such as it was, got underway for the rendezvous at Ambrose Channel Lightship. By extraordinary seamanship in that fog—through the narrow, tide swept, netted and mined channel—all arrived at the lightship without mishap, except the destroyer *Terry*.

In avoiding collision with an overtaking transport, she was forced by the tide into a net and had to return to the navy yard for repairs to her propeller. Her vigilant captain, Lt. Comdr. J. F. Shafroth, Jr., shortly before sailing had reported that in his opinion the nets in New York harbor were not likely to stop any determined submarine commander from entering. He arrived at the office of the commandant of the district with his request for repairs at about the same time as his report. Whether or not the nets were adequate protection against submarines, they had stopped a destroyer in a fog. Shafroth managed to get his repairs in time to sail with the fourth group on June 17.

The best protection against submarines was always the fast, quick turning destroyers—the light cavalry of the sea. To cross the Atlantic, however, under their own power, even the newest and largest of the oil burners had to be refueled once on the way over. The old "short legged" ones of 750 tons and the coal burners could not go even halfway across. The refueling method that Gleaves and his staff had developed had been used by the first destroyers that went over in May with great success, in half a gale.

It was arranged that four divisions of the destroyers that had gone to Ireland—six in each—should meet the four groups of the convoy at the edge of the so-called danger zone. But it was all a danger zone. Large German U-boats could log 15 to 17 knots on the surface, showing no smoke from their diesel engines. They could easily, by day, trail or keep abreast of a convoy of less speed than 14 knots, and then submerge and attack if there was a bright moon. In a smooth sea they could attack in the dark, awash with conning towers open.

In spite of the greatest efforts at secrecy, it was certain that the enemy would be advised of the sailing of the convoy soon after its departure. On that point there was no illusion. Our secret naval code at that time was far from impregnable and the censorship of the cables far from rigid. Comdr. W. R. Sayles, our naval attache in Paris, in a confidential report said:

To show how closely guarded military secrets were kept in the United States, I have only to state that the first knowledge I received that the first convoy had actually sailed was in the course of a social conversation with a woman. Col., then Capt., B———, Gen.———'s personal and confidential aid, was present. As soon as we could draw aside to talk together, I never will forget the words he first said. The expression was classic. Undoubtedly, the woman's husband's business friends in New York had cabled him the news in some sort of a business code. I never pursued the subject further. But if one realizes that at that time the security in France against enemy agents was in the hands of M. Malvy, minister of the interior, since tried and banished for criminal neglect of duty, and that the then head of the secret police and the chief assistant to the prefect of police are both now serving jail sentences for intercourse with the enemy, the necessity for more than ever guarding such a secret will be apparent. Due primarily to inexperience, and secondly, to the fact that three different general staffs were attempting to fix a rendezvous a few days before the first convoy was due, there was still considerable confusion in the French ministry of marine as to just what was to happen, and where it was to happen, when our ships approached the coast.

The admiral in command of the troop convoy had been told in Washington that he would be met by French destroyers, etc., and, as a matter of fact, they didn't exist. Like a great many other matters, it seemed impossible to make the navy department in Washington believe to what desperate straits the French naval forces had been reduced. They had only five destroyers on the West Coast and on the night of 21 May 1917, I had personally seen four of them put out of action for weeks or months to come, in a destroyer fight off Dunkirk.

Now that it is all over, and we have won, and so many big historical events have happened since, we are prone to forget the importance and what was at stake on a successful outcome of this expedition. If even one transport had been sunk, it might have resulted in disaster to the Allied cause.

It is not yet understood generally what Admiral Gleaves and his officers accomplished; it will be years before what it meant psychologically to the Allied cause will be fully appreciated.

Where the submarines might lie in wait and how many there would be were utterly unknown. The British and French naval intelligence services had reported greatest hostile activity east of longitude 20° W and within a 500 miles radius of the Azores. Later it was learned that two days after the first three groups had sailed, a submarine appeared west of that longitude and, during the next six days, had cruised more than 240 miles further west. There was well-founded suspicion of a secret submarine base in the Azores, from which a radius of 500 miles would extend westward more than halfway to our coast.

The enemy was also expected to fringe the coast of Europe as liberally as possible with mines wherever the convoy might come. Not the least of the dangers was the handling of the convoy without lights in every sort of weather.

The first group, theoretically capable of 15 knots, the second of 14, the third of 13, started at intervals of two hours. The actual speed of each group was more than two knots less throughout most of the voyage, being necessarily limited to that of the slowest ship for the time being. The number of miles covered on the base course was further reduced by zigzagging.

On the 20th the first group met the *Maumee*. While the destroyers refueled two at a time, steaming the while at seven knots, the rest of the group engaged in target practice. This took less than two hours per group. The operation was repeated for each of the groups about 24 hours apart. In the fourth group was an oil ship, the *Kanawha,* which refueled some of the destroyers in that group partly because one of her tanks was leaky and leaving a trail.

On June 22 the first group was proceeding in two columns, 1200 yards apart, at twelve knots, all zigzagging. That night the sky was overcast and very dark, but the water was extremely phosphorescent. A stiff northwest breeze was making whitecaps. At 9:56 p.m. the *Seattle*'s rudder jammed hard right and swung her out of line to starboard. The whistle was blown according to the prescribed signal to indicate her shear. By backing the port engine for about two minutes, she cleared the rudder and resumed her place in the line.

A few minutes later, Captain Blamer, Lt. Comdr. Drace White, officer of the deck, and Lt. F. H. Roberts of the admiral's staff, were on the *Seattle*'s bridge. Suddenly Roberts noticed a wake two points on the starboard bow, some 400 yards distant and moving toward the ship's course at right angles to it. He pointed it out to White and the captain. It crossed the bow about 50 yards ahead, which must have been less than a minute after Roberts first saw it, for the ship was making 12 knots. As they crossed the streak it seemed fully 12 feet wide. The ship was swing off 90° to starboard.

Night and day the guns were always manned on every ship. The admiral, napping in the bridge chart house, was called and ordered a general alarm. Before it was sounded, while they were discussing whether the wake was that of a submarine, a torpedo or a fish, they heard a gun from the *Dekalb* and six blasts of her siren—the signal of an attack. Her captain, Walter Gherardi, a torpedo expert, had seen the straight, bubbling, unmistakable wake of a torpedo crossing his bow about 30 yards ahead from port to starboard as he was turning in his zigzag. He immediately fired shots from his port battery in the direction from which the torpedo had come and blew six blasts on the siren. Less than ten minutes later, the wake of a second torpedo crossing astern was reported by the after lookouts.

Immediately upon the signals from the flagship and the *Dekalb,* the train turned 90° to starboard and separated according to orders in case of attack from the port side, while the two destroyers circled in search of the enemy.

Shortly after this the *Havana*'s master, Captain O'Keefe, fired on an object, about one point off the starboard bow "moving through the water very fast and leaving a distinct wake." He had seen the trail in phosphorescent water of many a fish in his day, but this, he reported afterwards, was too straight and fast for any kind of a fish and quite different from anything he had ever seen before.

From the reports, it would seem that the torpedoes were fired from two U-boats. That the attack was made on a dark night, instead of waiting for daylight, can be explained by the *Seattle*'s whistle when her helm jammed being mistaken for an alarm.

The *Wilkes,* on the starboard bow of the *Seattle,* at the alarm from the *Dekalb* turned in that direction, endeavoring to pass ahead of the flagship, but had to turn away at full speed to avoid collision. She was equipped with an oscillator—a recent device for listening under water. Having seen and passed over the wake that crossed the bow of the *Seattle,* she returned to hunt for its cause.

Lieutenant Van Metre and the radio operator heard through the oscillator several times what both thought to be sounds of a submerged submarine. The *Wilkes* endeavored to bring these sounds ahead and to get above the enemy, but without success and finally the sounds died away. The oscillator had not been perfected at that time and was practically useless with the engines running.

In an hour the entire group reassembled and was again on its base course. This maneuver was accomplished without the use of search lights or any kind of signals, but by following previous orders—a rather extraordinary achievement, evidence of the skill in the planning and execution of the orders. The first engagement had been met. The enemy had been dodged and chased off without loss.

The next feat was meeting up with the six destroyers promised for the next day. The time and place had been set. Would they miss contact? The radio could be used with only the greatest caution. Any message from the destroyers to the flagship might be picked up by the lurking enemy. In training his destroyer captains before the war, Gleaves had drilled them again and again in search problems and rendezvous at sea. How well now would they prove themselves in coming to the flag of their old commander?

At eleven p.m. the flagship received a brief radio in code from the *Cushing,* flagship of the approaching destroyer division, giving a spot to the eastward of the one first appointed. This was not communicated to the other vessels whose duty was only to follow the flag, unless separated. They cracked on all speed possible. At about 8:30 a.m. on the 23rd everyone heard the joyful, "Smoke on the port bow."

Up from the sea rose five gray hulls topped with low stacks. The rendezvous had been made to perfection with only that one radio message, and would have been made without that had the point not been changed after the convoy sailed.

The story is told that Gleaves signaled, "Gentlemen, you are ten minutes late."

When he first heard it, the admiral chuckled and observed that he knew just how that yarn must have started: "Some young rascal said that was what the old man would say. The next version was that I did say it, and the final edition, that I signaled it."

On the 25th, smoke was sighted to the northward. The *O'Brien* was sent to reconnoiter, and came back in company with two small French vessels, the *Regulus* and *Oise*—a reception committee. Commander Sayles, U.S. naval attache at Paris, was on board the former. At three p.m. Belle Isle was sighted along with two French airplanes and a dirigible coming from the land (a most welcome addition to the escort for their ability to spot submarines).

Now came the most dangerous period of the whole voyage. The port of destination and the route had been chosen by Gleaves with his aides, Lt. Comdr. F. M. Perkins and Lt. Comdr. A. L. Bristol. Not even Admiral Benson, chief of operations, knew the actual routing, for when Gleaves proposed submitting it to him, he said he preferred to be ignorant of it in order to be able to say so to any inquirer.

Such absolute secrecy, however, could not be maintained in France where preparations had been entrusted to Commander Sayles. He made elaborate plans and preparations for Brest, the nearest and most convenient French port to our coast. As expected, the Germans got wind of this and mined the entrance to that harbor. St. Nazaire had really been chosen and preparations there were purposely insignificant. The Americans brought stevedores with them and used their sailors and soldiers, as well, in unloading.

Teutonic thoroughness, however, did not limit itself wholly to Brest, but added plentifully to the French mines off every possible terminal including the mouth of the Loire. While passing to the southward of Belle Isle at eight p.m. on the 25th, Gleaves received a radio from Brest that two submarines had been sighted 30 miles southward of his position at that time. Since now there were eight destroyers on hand besides the French light craft, there was less reason to worry. Word had also been received of new German mines, and for this the whole group had to slow down well outside of Croisic Bay to take on pilots. So much time was lost in waiting for them, it became necessary to anchor all the large ships in the open roadstead and wait for daylight.

Except for the screen of circling destroyers, the enemy had a perfect opportunity. Why no attack was attempted on the anchored ships will probably never be known—either the Germans did not know of their presence or else they feared the guardians. The following night they mined the channel used by this first group, but that was too late. The succeeding groups used another channel.

On June 26 at 6:45 a.m. the first group dropped anchor in the Loire off the town of St. Nazaire. The first basket had come through without cracking an egg.

The second group encountered a submarine about a hundred miles from the French coast. Neal in the *Cummings* spotted the periscope, made for it at 25 knots as it submerged, and dropped a depth bomb and a buoy to mark the spot. Sometimes Germans threw out oil and debris to play opossum, but there was enough evidence to win from the very conservative British Admiralty and government a decoration for Lietuenant Commander Neal. On June 27, at 5:50 a.m. they arrived safely at St. Nazaire—another basket with every egg whole.

The third group did not come in contact with the enemy and arrived at St. Nazaire on June 28 at 10:30 a.m.

The slow fourth group, like the first, ran the gauntlet. Two torpedoes were shot at the convoy. One went wide, but the other was headed straight for the cargo ship, *Luckenbach,* which fortunately managed to change course just in time. She carried 5,000 tons of ammunition and a deck load of gasoline, hay, motor oil and oxyacetylene tanks. Her commanding officer, Lt. Comdr. A. C. Pickens, expressed himself as "just as well satisfied that the torpedo missed."

After this excitement the convoy soon returned to regular formation and sighted the welcome destroyers from Queenstown on time and on the spot, as usual.

Gleaves' intensive training of his destroyer force had brought its reward. Not only in picking up the four groups of the first convoy, but in similar duty throughout the rest of the war, they astonished the British and French. On the evening of July 1 the fourth group anchored in Quiberon Bay for pilots through the mine fields, and at four the next morning, they arrived at St. Nazaire.

The task was done. Not one ship lost and not one man, even by sickness. As one officer reported, "We lost nothing but one horse and that was a mule."

It was a memorable Fourth of July as news of the safe arrival of the whole convoy was officially announced to the nation.

Albert Gleaves

Midshipman 4th Class

Midshipman 1st Class

USS *Cushing* commanded by Lt. Albert Gleaves
during the Spanish-American War

St. Nazaire Monument, France commemorating the 1917 Convoy (destroyed by Germany during World War II)

Cover of French news magazine

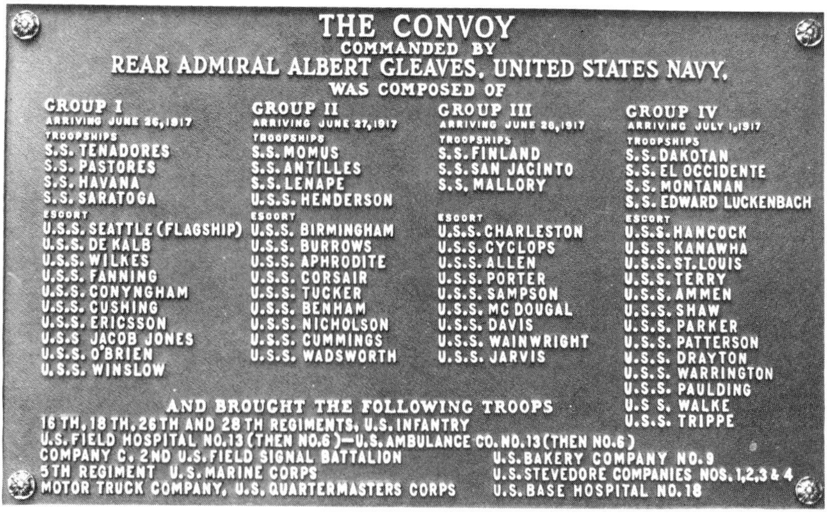

English memorial bronze tablet on seawall at St. Nazaire

Admiral Gleaves with President and Mrs. Wilson in New York City parade on way to League of Nations

Albert Gleaves, Admiral, USN, Commander in Chief
of the Asiatic Fleet

Albert Gleaves and Staff, Vladivostok, 1920

Albert Gleaves and Staff, Asiatic Fleet, 1920

Evelina Gleaves Cohen in Mrs. Chen's ceremonial dress, p. 190.

Admiral and Mrs. Gleaves in Beach Haven, NJ, 1936, with daughter Anne Van Metre and grandsons, Albert Cohen, Albert Van Metre, Thomas Van Metre (*l. to r.*)

USS *Gleaves* after launching at Bath, Maine, on 9 December 1939

USS *Gleaves* christened by granddaughters Clotilda Cohen MacDonald and Evelina Van Metre Thompson (*l. to r.*)

Family members and dignitaries at the launching of the USS *Gleaves*

16 In France

After the *Seattle* and the first group of the convoy arrived off St. Nazaire, General Sibert came on board to offer his congratulations. He was followed by the captain of the port, Captain Gilley of the French navy, General Doyen in command of the marines on board the U.S.S. *Hancock,* Capt. Asher Baker, U.S.N., and all the commanding officers of Group I.

Troop disembarkation began without delay. While the officers were in my cabin General Doyen asked if the marines might land first. It was a splendid spirit and one that has made the Marine Corps what it is. General Sibert also claimed the honor, and I settled what might have proved an unpleasant situation by directing that the marines and soldiers land simultaneously—thus dividing the baby, like Solomon.

When General Pershing came on board to bid us welcome at St. Nazaire, I gave him a luncheon on the *Seattle,* after which a number of newspaper men from Paris came on board. I made a brief speech to them in which I spoke of the services of the French fleet under Admiral de Grasse in the Chesapeake which made possible Washington's victory at Yorktown in 1781. My remarks were brief and entirely extempore, but got a lot of kudos from extensive quotation in papers in Europe and at home.

Henri Lavedan, in an article in *L'Illustration,* referred to them and then went on:

> Who is this de Grasse, and what decisive role did he play in the War of American Independence that, 136 years later, the first salute of Gleaves' soul and sword at that moment, one of the grandest and one of the most solemn of the present and future history of our two countries, should have been a public homage rendered to this French sailor, with such emphasis, and such enthusiastic gratitude? Today the formidable United States for whom he prepared and secured, so long ago, alliance and aid are now returning to him here his visit, and that is why Gleaves, the American admiral of 1917, arriving directly from Virginia and landing on our soil, desired to salute, before the entire world, de Grasse, the French admiral of 1781.

Does it not seem strange that up to the time of that landing of our troops in France the name of de Grasse was so little known to the people not only in America but in his own France? Since then a life of Admiral de Grasse has been written by Canon Max Caron of Versailles, and a statue in his honor has been erected in his own country. In the United States there are statues to Lafayette and Rochambeau and tablets in public places to de Tierney and other Frenchmen who offered their swords to Washington, but there is nothing to commemorate the services of this gallant sailor. Why not a statue of Admiral de Grasse in Washington?

On July 4, I made a visit to Paris, which was *en fete*. The American flag was in evidence everywhere. The day's program in honor of the "Independence Day of the Nations", as M. Ribot put it, was full, including presentation of colors to our 16th Infantry in the courtyard of *Les Invalides* and exercises at the grave of Lafayette across the Seine in the Picpus Cemetery.

At the cemetery were Painleve, Brand Whitlock and General Pershing who all said pleasant things to me about our safe voyage to the Loire with the first troops of the expeditionary force. It was then that someone said, "Lafayette, we are here." Pershing has disclaimed the credit for it and said he "feels sure" it belongs to Colonel Stanton. That is also my recollection.

After a luncheon at the Quai d'Orsay and a reception at our embassy, General Foch entertained General Pershing and his staff at an elaborate dinner at which the minister of war sat opposite Foch. I was on the minister's right and Pershing on the right of Foch. The speeches were short and snappy. I think there were only two. Pershing spoke in French. M. Painleve told me that bringing the troops across the Atlantic was worth more than winning a naval battle, for at that time there was general despondency throughout France and never in history did aid come to a distressed country at a more timely moment.

One morning while in Paris, my flag secretary, Lt. A. L. Bristol, brought me the New York papers with the "story" of the convoy and said, "Listen to this, Admiral." From one of them he read, after enormous headlines, a lurid account of a fierce battle in which "hell broke loose" on all of our ships. It was amusing, but irritating since all of the ships had behaved exactly as ordered in the event of attack and there had been no unnecessary firing or confusion whatever.

I made a short visit to the front, going first to the headquarters of General Michelet, commanding the II Army, with whom we lunched.

The night before, the villa which he occupied with his staff had been under fire from the German batteries, in evidence of which there was a six-inch shell which had not exploded and which had been picked up, cleaned and placed on the general's desk!

The general suggested that we go to the front line rather than to Rheims, where he said "the tourists go, and besides Rheims looks outwardly as it did before the War."

We went to the front line of trenches and heard the shells passing over and also saw one German airplane which attracted the fire of a battery of 75s near our own position. On the other side of no-man's-land we could see plainly the houses of Craconne and Berri-au-Bac on the Chemin-des-Dames. From the latter a German battery was firing on the French lines in our vicinity, to which the French apparently paid no attention, except a concealed battery of 75s, which drove the airplane back to the German lines.

As fast as the ships could be unloaded and prepared for the homeward voyage they sailed in groups under destroyer escort for 600 miles, then dispersed and went on each for itself. When the last had left I sailed in the *Seattle* on July 14, arriving at New York on July 24. On July 16, I had been detached from titular command of the destroyer force (of which very few had been left to me) and had been appointed to the command of the cruiser and transport force of the Atlantic fleet which included also the destroyers not assigned to duty in European waters, and cooperated of necessity with the latter.

On the return of the first ships from St. Nazaire began the operation of the "Bridge Across the Atlantic," so well described by Adm. Yates Stirling in his article.* Most of the ships at first available were old arks and it was only the hand of God that enabled us in those first few weeks to get our stride in the new business of transporting troops and supplies to France.

As the task developed, it was apparent that I could not retain so important a ship as a big armored cruiser for my flagship in view of the fact that I had to remain in one central position. Weekly conferences were held with the captains of the cruisers regarding the readiness of the ships for transport service. Therefore I shifted my headquarters first from the *Seattle* to a specially-constructed building on the dock at 96th Street and North River, and later to the Stenech Building at Hoboken, which we called the Stone Frigate.

*Volume 51, Number 9. *Proceedings of the Naval Institute*, September, 1925.

All during the summer of 1917 the navy yards and private yards were busy night and day fitting out our merchant ships as fast as they could be obtained, and also the 20 German merchantmen that had been in our ports when war was declared. These ships, as Stirling says, were the pioneers of the transport service.

Laid up since August 1914—most of them with machinery wrecked as far as possible by their crews—they were in wretched condition and had been turned over to the shipping board Admiral Benson put the question of repairs to me and I told him that if he would give the ships to me as is, I would ready them for sea. This was done mainly by means of electric welding. The last and biggest of them, the *Vaterland* rechristened *Leviathan,* sailed from New York about 15 December 1917.

Our possession of the *Leviathan* at first was a mixed blessing. The British, on account of her tremendous tonnage, did not want her at Liverpool nor at Southampton. In this emergency it was proposed by some that she be used as a hospital ship. I strongly opposed this as it was practically throwing away the services of the largest ship afloat which could and should be used as a transport. Fortunately my view was adopted by the navy department. The *Leviathan* was brought into regular service as a transport and before the war was over was carrying to Europe a maximum of 14,000 troops each trip. In fact, after the war on her last homeward voyage she carried 17,000.

At Hoboken—designated as the army transportation headquarters—I first met Maj. Gen. David C. Shanks, who was in command, and for many months was associated with him in the duty of getting the troops overseas. Shanks was a man direct in method, affable and courteous in manner, big of body and of heart, and wedded to his uniform. His marked efficiency in handling people, his tact in dealing with diverse business interests, and his firmness made him the ideal person for the position. It was his tragedy that he never got overseas to the front. At the last he was ordered to organize a division forming in the West, but the armistice came and he returned to Hoboken to demobilize the post of which he had made such a great success.

After our experience together in Hoboken it can never again be said that the army and navy cannot work together harmoniously.

The winter of 1917-18 was unusually severe. At times the Hudson River was filled with ice and the Atlantic was raging. On December

30 the thermometer dropped to 12° below zero, making rough going for the cruisers and convoys from Halifax. After driving through a gale in below zero weather these ships became so covered with ice that they looked like veritable icebergs. Naturally they all were constantly in my thoughts during that memorable winter. On Christmas Day I sent out a radio to my command: "A Merry Christmas to all, especially to those at sea."

One of the captains told me long afterwards that when he read this, in the midst of a howling gale, he said to the executive officer, "We are not forgotten. Post this on all bulletin boards. I want every man in the ship's company to read it."

The transports sailed, some under convoy from Halifax and occasionally from Boston, but principally from New York and Old Point. The division at Old Point was commanded by Rear Adm. Hilary P. Jones, my former executive in the *Mayflower*.

Jones and I were very close in all our relations. I had regretted his detachment from the *Mayflower* and now I rejoiced that in far more important duties he was to serve with me again. He was a Virginian of Virginians, and one day at a dinner at the Union League Club, Colonel Appleton ("Dan of the gallant Seventh") was speaking to me of Jones admiringly and when I said, "He is a great-grandson of Chief Justice Marshall," the colonel said, "And he looks the part."

The ships on the northern routes had the worst of it, but I never heard a single complaint of any kind—and everyone knows that growling is a sailor's prerogative. Sometimes the cruisers did not even sight land on the eastern end, but turned their convoys over to the American escorts from England and France and hastened back to the United States to coal and replenish and start out again with another convoy.

It became a matter of keen competition to rush the turnarounds, and it was astonishing what was accomplished by such big ships as the *Leviathan, America* (ex-*George Washington), Agamemnon,* and *Mount Vernon*—to mention only a few of the greatest coal capacity. On one occasion the *Leviathan* got on board 6,500 tons of coal and 8,500 troops with stores and equipment and sailed again in four days. The slogan was "Run 'em till they break down," for Haig had said he was fighting with his back to the wall and must have more men. America was in the war to give them to him at all hazards.

My duty in New York Harbor brought me in daily contact with such personalities as Mr. P. A. S. Franklin, president of the

International Line of Steamships; Mayor Mitchell; Mr. Louis Wiley, manager of the New York *Times;* Mr. C. H. Sabin, president of the New York Chamber of Commerce; Comdr. R. A. C. Smith, dock commissioner; among others. All were eager and helpful in cooperating with us.

On the sea there were Admiral Grout, of the French navy, and his division of cruisers which—while attached to my command for assignment—remained for all disciplinary purposes under its own commander. I was indeed fortunate in having such a coadjutor with me as Admiral Grout, who had all the graciousness and willingness to serve and do his part.

Of the officers of the British navy I saw but little except when I went to Washington. I rarely saw Vice Admiral Grant who had relieved Admiral Browning and had established his offices in Washington. Commodore Welles, in charge of the British ships, had an office in New York and by permission of the navy department, himself routed the British cruisers and transports sailing from New York. I objected to this, but was overruled in a conference at the navy department with Admiral Benson and Vice Admiral Grant.

I did not come in contact with Vice Adm. Sir Montague Browning as much as I would have liked. He had a charm of personality and a presence which was most attractive. Like Captain Cuttle, he wore a silver hook in place of a missing left hand, which was decidedly picturesque. Ex-president Roosevelt took a great fancy to him, and I have an idea was much fascinated by the hook.

Although my force suffered the loss of four big ships during the summer of 1918, the transportation of troops continued with increased speed, shuttling across the ocean eastward and westward until the numbers *daily* leaving United States ports in August 1918—the peak month—were 10,000.

Many amusing stories drifted into me from the transports and cruisers. Once a big transport was making her berth at Newport News on a return trip. She was entering a blind dock, pointed fair and going at slow speed. When the captain gave the order to the young officer at the annunciator, "Full speed astern," the youngster got gallied and put the lever "full speed ahead". After the wreckage was cleared up and the ship secured, the captain—though not especially noted for patience and mildness— put his hand on the youngster's shoulder and said quietly, "I think you have done all you can for us; now you may leave your station." The story is well told by a reserve officer in the *Atlantic Monthly* who concludes,"If I should have to go to sea again, which God forbid, I know whom I would like to have for my skipper."

When the *Vaterland,* in her pre-*Leviathan* days made her epochal first visit to New York in May 1913, the Hamburg American Line gave a luncheon deluxe on board to which several hundred guests were invited. It so happened that I sat next to one of the officers of the company who was eager to answer my many questions. I particularly wanted to know the ship's troop capacity. He replied, "7,000—and we built her to bring them over here." Of course, he smiled as he said it. Remembering Kipling's story of "The Man Who Was," I replied, "And when they come we shall be happy to meet them."

The tricks of Fortune, or the ways of Providence, are past finding out. Four years later I was fitting out that same ship to take 14,000 of our men to the battlefields of France.

Once in the last summer of the war I had a luncheon on board of her in honor of Admiral Browning. It was given in the suite that had been intended for the kaiser. As we sat at table, overlooking the Hudson River, someone said, "What would the kaiser say if he could see this party—an American admiral, a British ambassador and a group of American and British officers in his own private apartment."

Sometime afterwards I met the archbishop of Canterbury at dinner at Bishop Manning's house in Washington Square. The archbishop told the story of the first luncheon on the *Vaterland*, adding that he did not know the name of the officer who had made the retort. As we left the dining room he asked, "Do you know who that officer was?" When I told him that I was the offender he said, "At first I didn't know the name of the ship. Now I know both the ship and the man who said it."

October 27, 1918, is stamped in my recollections as being the last time I saw Colonel Roosevelt. It was his last birthday and there was a small party at Sagamore Hill. He was in his best form, but looked much older than the year before. He spoke to me of seeing von Tirpitz in Berlin, and of his opinion about our not declaring war against Turkey, of President Wilson's appeal to the country, and of his Fourteen Points. I recall his saying, "The president wants disarmament—this means to scrap our army and navy and rely upon a gendarmerie or constabulary."

The end of hostilities was approaching by October 1918.

Restrictions on routing coastwise vessels were removed and running lights were permitted. On November 2 it was decided to discontinue sending troops and for the first time a group sailed without them, taking only cargoes. On the 11th came the news of Germany's surrender.

I cannot close this chapter on the most important command I ever had without a tribute to the men who carried me through so loyally. The full narrative of their labors, achievements and exploits fills a volume—which has already been published: *The History of the Transport Service.**

In the preface of that book written in 1919, I said:

> There seems no excuse for offering the public another book of personal Memoirs of the Great War; but so much has been written about all the different phases of preparation and action, and so little of the actual transportation of the troops, which made the fighting possible, that I have yielded to the persuasion of friends and shipmates to add my contribution to the daily increasing stories of the events of 1917-18. I do this because in a measure I may be able to show my appreciation of the hard work done by the officers and men of the American Transports, and my admiration for their unsurpassed skill and endeavor in the performance of their duties. At sea almost constantly, in the severest weather that has swept the Atlantic Ocean for many years, these Master Mariners of the United States lived up to the highest traditions of the sea, and brought credit to their country. For the most part this story is told by them, in their own words, and so far as possible taken from their official reports.

Admiral Yates Stirling, in his above-mentioned article, has written what seems to me the best professional account of the salvage of the German ships and other features of the story. Secretary Daniels also, in *Our Navy at War,* has told it very well and in far more detail than the limits of this book permit, as has Thomas Frothingham in *Naval History of the World War.*

The summary of what was accomplished is briefly this:

From the small beginning of the first convoy in June 1917, the cruiser and transport force was built up to 24 cruisers and 42 transports with 3,000 officers and 42,000 men in their crews. That is exclusive of the many cargo ships and troop ships that were not United States Navy Transports.

*New York: George H. Doran Co., 1921.

It has been often said that out of the 1,720,360 soldiers escorted by our men-of-war, not one was lost by enemy attack or the perils of the sea—which were enormously increased by the necessity of navigation without lights and zigzagging. Almost unbelievable as that record may seem, it is true of our navy troopships, but not of all others. It's very perfection of success may give a wrong impression of the dangers faced and overcome.

On December 4, 1918, I received notification of my appointment as vice admiral—unfortunately only a temporary appointment and not "by and with the advice and consent of the Senate," although signed by the president.

After a visit to Tennessee to receive a sword presented by the mothers of Nashville, I went to Europe in the *George Washington.* While in France, I visited the battlefields and saw the plane of Quentin Roosevelt on a grassy hillside where he fell—and where he was buried by the Germans with military honors. A recollection of 17 years before, on board the *Dolphin,* came to me of a little boy in the arms of his mother who was singing to him, "There is a green hill far away." I thought this is *his* green hill.

In the village of Chamery, nearby, Mrs. Roosevelt has erected a fountain in his memory with the inscription, "He has outsoared the shadows of our night."

I returned to New York in the latter part of May 1919 and remained there until September, when I received orders to command the China station with the rank (temporary) of full admiral.

17 On the Road West to the Far East

Before leaving the United States in September I lunched with Mr. Frederick Coudert at the Lawyers Club to meet Mr. Willard, whose authoritative opinions on Far Eastern affairs Coudert thought would be of value to me. About the same time I met Mr. Frank Polk on board the *Imperator*. He was on his way to Europe and was most helpful in outlining the situation in eastern Siberia where a detachment of our army was stationed with headquarters at Vladivostok.

The department had assigned to me as flagship the *South Dakota* (afterwards the *Huron*), sister ship of the *Seattle*, commanded by Captain Luby who had the reputation—and lived up to it—of being a fine ship handler. There were several changes made in my personal staff before sailing. Mayo, Bristol, Perkins, Lawson and others were detached. Lawson was replaced by Lieutenant Holcombe.

With the exception of visiting Australia, the secretary of the navy approved my proposed route to Manila, through the canal and the South seas by way of the Galapagos, Society islands and Samoa.

On September 1, 1919, I broke the four star flag of full admiral and assumed command in the North River of the U.S. Asiatic Fleet. Four days later we sailed for the canal. I was glad to get to sea again and into the roaring northeast trade winds which soon blew all the dirt and muck of shore out of the ship.

We had 1,500 souls on board, including green hands of whom we had to make sailors. The wonderful weather compensated somewhat for a dislocated crew. After all, such conditions were natural during demobilization. With our smart officers, the captain's troubles with the men and ship did not last long.

Our stay at the isthmus was brief. I think everyone was eager to get out into the sea pastures and wide rolling prairies of the Pacific—to use Melville's phrase—which I like better than his other one, "the Potter's Field of four continents."

I noticed a curious thing one day at the equator. The sun was practically in the zenith and the navigator was taking the meridian altitude, when suddenly I saw him jump to the opposite side of the deck to catch the sun before it began to descend. I remembered then that when the sun is directly overhead and reaches its highest point it will swing around 180° before you can readjust your sextant.

Although we were in zero latitude, the air was cool and bracing due to the Humboldt current which comes up from the South Polar regions along the coast as far as Peru, turns to the westward and flows for hundreds of miles along the equator towards the South Sea islands. It is a river in the ocean and we turned to the westward with it thereby adding 20 knots to our daily run. Black fish, sea swallows and thousands of flying fish kept with us in the tumbling seas, but not a sail nor smudge of smoke in sight. The *South Dakota* had plenty of sea room and no company.

We came off the Galapagos islands at early daylight, laid to off Dalrymple Rock and sent a boat ashore with the intelligence officer for information. The air was delightfully cool and fragrant, but the views of the coral beach were not especially inviting. We ran down the west coast of Chatham Island and anchored in Wreck Bay near a small Belgian schooner.

After breakfast I went ashore with the captain and flag lieutenant, and walked inland three or four miles towards the village of Progresso—only a few people were visible. It was a rough walk and when we had scrambled over coral and lava and cut our shoes into shreds we returned to the beach.

The captain of the Belgian motor schooner was waiting for us at the pier. He said he had been five months making the voyage from Suva. His eyes were congested from sum and wind. Since April he had bucked the southeast trades and was out of provisions and gasoline. It was lucky for him that our ship met him. We gave him stores and gasoline and reported his arrival by wireless to the Belgian ambassador in Washington. I never heard anything more of him, but I hope his family were not long in getting the news he was alive and well.

He told me he had enlisted in the army at the beginning of the war, but was captured almost immediately—on August 4—and was a prisoner for three years in the Baltic until he escaped and got to sea. On his voyage from the Fijis he lost his fore-topmast. As our barge passed close by the little vessel, I noticed her patched and faded colors flapping in the trade winds and a friendly dog running excitedly along the deck. Her crew of a dozen or so men leaned idly over the rail interested in our trim boat and its highly polished fittings—which was in great contrast to their own sea-battered craft.

I was disappointed not to find 300-pound turtles shambling along the beach, as described by Captain Porter in his journal of the cruise of the *Essex*. The only thing resembling was a small tortoise, which the alcalde of Progresso sent me, and which in a few days the steward served for dinner.

A representative of the Ecuadorian government and a few men came on board and were very friendly. The islands would doubtless interest a naturalist, as they did Darwin, but there is not much to attract a sailor. I have often thought the United States should own the group for a coaling station.

At sunset we got under way, turned westward and resumed our voyage laying a course for Nukahiva in the Marquesas Islands, more than 3,000 miles distant. Passing Albemarle Island at eight p.m. we sighted a dull red glow high up, which I first took to be a lighthouse, but neither the sailing directions nor the charts showed any such aid to navigation. As a matter of fact, what we saw was a volcano. Darwin had written of it in 1835, describing "a jet of smoke coiling from one of the craters". It has been known for more than a hundred years, so it was amusing to read in some of the newspapers a number of years after we were there that the volcano was discovered by the Beebe Expedition!

There are some who say it is not hotter on the equator than it is on Long Island Sound in summer. This depends largely on the longitude. I would not speak disrespectfully of the equator, to quote Sidney Smith, but those who believe that pitch oozing out of the seams of the deck is a figment of the imagination should have been with us in the *South Dakota* in the fall of 1919. It was very hot on deck and 137° in the firerooms.

Conrad is right in saying that "the peace of God begins at any point one thousand miles from land. The rest of a long voyage out of sight of land has no equal for those who seek solitude and quiet."

They say that when doctors have exhausted other remedies they prescribe drawing teeth. My prescription is less painful and simpler: Go to sea, if possible to the serene Pacific where the stars shine with a brightness never seen north of the equator and "cast their spears" more frequently.

At times the tradewind blew with "topgallant" force and rough seas rolled and pitched the ship heavily, no longer on a flat ocean. In due course, one Sunday we sighted Nukahiva and not being sure of the chart, we lay to off the two sentinel-like headlands at the entrance to the harbor—the crater of an extinct volcano.

Leaving the ship for the captain to feel his way in, I went ashore in the barge taking with me several officers and enlisted men. We landed at a neat, substantial little pier and were met by the French representative. The scenery was as beautiful and restful as described by Captain Porter.

Our host took us to the Catholic mission not far away and near the beach, and presented us to the mother superior, an attractive old lady who had passed the scriptural limit of age, the greater part spent in the islands. The mission was situated in a coconut grove at the foot of a cascade that came down from the mountain heights immediately behind the mission cottage. This was a scrupulously clean frame building, perfectly plain save for a colored lithograph of Pius X.

The abbess—so she appeared to me, thinking of Tennyson's Abbess—gave me an idol recently found near the mission and hideously carved from lava which she said was supposed to be 500 years old. We accepted a glass of red wine and invited the abbess to have her picture taken with us by the ship's photographer. She took my arm and in an avenue of palm trees looking toward the sea where Captain Luby was bringing the *South Dakota* slowly into an anchorage, the picture was snapped.

At the suggestion of the representative we visited the cottage of monsieur le cure who had been in the islands many years but not as long as the abbess. He gave me a copy of the treaty captain Porter made with the natives after his war with them in 1814. The names of *Essex, Essex Junior,* and Dupetit-Thouars are decipherable, but the remainder of the manuscript is in the Marquesan language, which is understood by only a few.

The cure said that he had once known a chief called Porta who had died ten years before at a great age. There was another chief mentioned named Mouina, and it is interesting to note that Captain Porter's son William had a son named for this chief whom Porter in his journal speaks of as "the brave Mouina".

The cure recalled that exactly five years before the *South Dakota*'s call, Admiral von Spee had brought his ships into the harbor on a Sunday, and that although the German sailors were well behaved, the gallant admiral levied a ransom of 25,000 gold francs. That was on September 28, 1914.

At sunset we passed out of the little harbor, awakening the shrill cries of thousands of gulls that whiten the rocky entrance on both sides. The wireless that day stated that President Wilson had returned to Washington for rest. If I were his physician I would have prescribed the equatorial solitude of the Pacific and a dismantled wireless.

The next day we skirted close to Matahiva, the northwestern-most of the Tuamotu archipelago. Through the opening in the reef we glimpsed the brilliant jade of the water inside and the long white beach beyond—a beautiful sight in the afternoon sun. Several fishing sloops were anchored in the entrance and natives, a nudist colony evidently, were bathing and singing, undisturbed by the appearance of a man-of-war—perhaps they were lotus-eaters!

We took a few soundings off the opening in the reef and found 35 fathoms where the chart shows 800! As we aproached the Low archipelago, I sent a wireless message to the "Governor of the French Establishments in Oceanica" with greetings and felicitations and received a cordial response from him welcoming the ship to Papeete.

The following day—October 1, 1919—we reached Tahiti, and at early dawn made our landfall at Point Venus, so-called by Captain Cook who made his observations there of the transit of Venus more than a century and a half ago. About noon the *South Dakota,* the biggest ship ever to enter the little harbor, nosed her way into the dredged channel with no room to spare—through the reef which is the natural breakwater of Papeete.

The town, which stretches along the beach, was *en fete* with flags of all colors in honor of our coming. The small vessels in the harbor made a brave display of bunting, as did the signal station at Fort Maa-Rahi. As we passed into the channel the usual salutes were fired to the French flag, which we displayed at the masthead, thus making our bow, as it were, to the governor and his people.

Even here the moving picture man was on the job. The ship passed within a few yards of a sand spit on the edge of the reef where he was grinding his machine. Later he made a beautiful picture of the ship when she was tied up stern to the beach. So calm and clear was the water that it was almost impossible to make out where the substance ended and the reflected image of the ship began.

The governor and citizens were profuse in hospitality and during our brief visit did everything in their power both for officers and enlisted men. The governor's dinner to me was a feast of many courses of vegetables and fruit and wine, in abundance rarely seen outside the tropics. The next day the same party lunched on board the *South Dakota.*

In the afternoon, while the officers entertained the citizens on board at a dance, the governor and his wife drove several of us to Point Venus. We stopped at the forest's edge, near a pool cut out of the rocks by a mountain stream. The sight from the pool was magnificent.

Captain Chack, of the French navy—a worthy successor of Pierre Loti—says modestly that it is a sacrilege to attempt to describe Tahiti after Loti, but reminds us that Loti chanted its praises 70 years ago before the missionaries visited it. Tahiti, as it was when the French took it over in 1842, no longer exists and Chack ironically says because "the progress of civilization has fallen upon her." He sadly adds, "and Rarahu is dead." Only the earth and sky have not changed and the sea is immutable.

The road to Point Venus lay through a forest of tall palms, gorgeous flowers, magnificent fruits and trees with trunks covered with ferns and orchids. The air was soft with the perfume of jasmine which pervades the whole island. Jasmine is really the flower of Tahiti. The native men are the "color of tea," to quote Chack again, very large and supple, and the women who greet you with the smile of a child, are of a pure Grecian beauty. One of them, the daughter of a chief, gave me a necklace of small shells, which now adorns the ancient idol of Marguesas on my desk—with a Chinese god of happiness and a little bronze lion from a Peking temple.

Tahiti wrote a half page of her own in the history of the World War. When Count von Spee sailed from Nukahiva to the coast of Chili he passed through the straits between Tahiti and her beautiful sister, Murea Island, in order to look in at Papeete. With him were the armored cruisers, *Scharnhorst* and *Gneisenau.*

Perhaps his intentions were as peaceful as when he called at Nukahiva, but a 100-ton French gunboat, the *Zelee,* was at anchor in the harbor. Before the Germans entered the straits, the commander of the *Zelee,* Lieutenant Destreman, dragged his ship's battery of four 65 mm. and one 100 mm. to the signal station. When the Germans came within range, he loosed off three salvos and telephoned the *Zelee* to open her sea valves. It was unwise, for it was neither magnificent nor war, and invited the destruction of Papeete. The result was that the gallant *Zelee* soon lay on the coral bottom, a rendezvous for fishes. The bombardment that followed was brief, but several houses were destroyed and the government coal pile set on fire.

The inhabitants of Papeete love to tell how they sent relief to the *Sea-Adler* when she was wrecked on Mopelia Island, 200 miles to the westward. The *Sea-Adler* was commanded by Count von Luckner and her cruising was as much of a mystery as the *Enden*'s. She was reported as many times as the *Flying Dutchman* but, as a matter of fact, was never seen except by the ships she captured. It is said her track chart shows she was never in sight of land, except that on which she was wrecked.

When the *Seattle* left France in 1917, after taking over the first American expedition, I was informed that I might expect to encounter the *Sea-Adler* on the voyage to New York. A rough sketch of her was given to me at St. Nazaire by Captain Gilley, the captain of the port. On the July 14, a few days out, we sighted ahead a small brig under motor power standing to the westward which seemed to answer the description of the raider. This was our chance! But the stranger proved to be a Nova Scotian, and less than a week later the *Sea Adler* was a wreck in the South Pacific. So much for what strategists call *Securite et Information*!

Tahiti lies off the trade routes of the Pacific halfway between New Zealand and the Panama Canal and may justly be called the Pearl of the South Pacific, just as Cuba is called by the Spaniards the Pearl of the Antilles. It was in Papeete that ships of the Old World refitted and refreshed, and its name is linked with those of Wallis and Byron, LaPerouse and James Cook.

Captain Cook, afterwards murdered by the natives of Hawaii, here observed the transit of Venus in 1762 with an accuracy that modern instruments have verified. Bligh of the *Bounty* sailed from Papeete on his last cruise before the mutiny. Vancouver came there and later Wilkes, of our own navy, put into Papeete on his exploring expedition (1838-42). Bougainville of the French navy, the first French officer to circumnavigate the globe, also refitted there.

Bougainville gave his name to the most gorgeous flower of the tropics and is immortalized by its imperial bloom. He had a varied life before he became a sailor. First a lawyer, then a soldier, he was sent by Montcalm to France to insist upon reinforcements and to urge upon the king that unless reinforced, Canada would be lost to the English. To this appeal the ministers of Louis XVI replied, "Quand le maison est en feu, on ne peut pas faire l'attention a l'ecurie." Thus was a phrase made and a colony lost. Bougainville was

51 years old when he entered the navy and circumnavigated the globe. He served with deGrasse against Rodeny, became a squadron commander and died in 1811, aged 82.

Of La Perouse Carlyle wrote, "The brave navigator goes and returns not; seekers search seas for him in vain. He has vanished into blue immensity, and only some mournful, mysterious shadow of him hovers long in all heads and hearts." Long after those memorable words were written, a French ship discovered a few remains of La Perouse's ship which are now in the naval museum of the Louvre. I saw them there with Captain Chack who obtained special permission for me to see them.

But to return to my own voyage in the Pacific to the Far East. From Papeete the course was shaped for the Samoan Islands. The route lay close to Mopelia, and it was my intention to lay to there and have a look at the bones of the famous sea raider, but the weather and sea made it advisable to keep on our voyage.

Between the isthmus and Samoa we crossed the equator twice—the first time near the Galapagos and again between the Gilbert and Solomon islands. Off the Galapagos the decks were so filled with coal that the usual ceremonies of crossing the line were postponed. When we came up from the southward the green hands were in better condition for the mysteries and waited impatiently for the event. It was celebrated in due form, but the chaplain's shoulder was almost dislocated when he was thrown into a shallow tank of water rigged between the booms on the forecastle.

We ran close enough to the harbor of Apia to see plainly where the great storm of 1889 had destroyed the German and American squadrons and from which the British man-of-war *Calliope* alone escaped to the open sea with great credit to herself and her engines. It was off Apia also that Admiral von Spee made the fatal mistake of informing the world where he was when he wirelessed to the station on shore. Until that time, after leaving China, he had disappeared into the vastness of the Pacific while the British and Japanese were frantically "searching far seas in vain". No one has ever ventured an explanation or understood the move, for von Spee was a most capable sea commander.

After a run of three weeks, the *South Dakota* entered the landlocked harbor of Tutuila in American Samoa, our southernmost possession in the world—until Admiral Byrd gave us "Little America". Until recently the governor of Samoa was an officer of the navy, but the island has been handed over now to politicians just as the Virgin Islands were. No one seems to want Guam—not even the army—which in the same manner lost the really big plums: Cuba, the Philippines, Porto Rico and Hawaii.

When the *South Dakota* was at Tutuila, the governor was Captain Terhune—a splendid representative whose administration was impeccable notwithstanding a futile attempt to disparage it. Like all tropical countries, the charm of Samoa lies in its fruits and flowers and wonderful climate. Captain Terhune invited the chief of staff and myself to live at government house, which is built on the side of a mountain spur and overlooks the harbor on one side and the sea on the other.

At night the trade winds rustle the palm leaves and the coconut trees against the screens of the veranda and blow through the open windows and doors the tropic odors which Thackeray says "soothe and allay like poppy and mandragora and all the drowsy syrups of the East."

One afternoon the natives gave dances in honor of the admiral.

They came by dozens from neighboring villages in native dress of sharks teeth, feathers, and flowers—bringing their customary presents of chickens, coconuts, papayas and bananas. The piece de resistance was the siva-siva, a native dance much modified by missionaries from the old days and which on this occasion was danced by the chief's daughter and other maidens from the villages.

The dance is considered the most graceful of those of the South seas, and the dress is just within the law of Eden—a fringe of banana leaves around the waist, the naked bodies covered with coconut oil and a necklace of hibiscus and tiny shells compose the costume de rigueur. The girls' figures, beautifully formed, are like bronzed nymphs. Before the dance all the guests and dancers drink kava from the bowl in the center of the hut, first scattering a few drops on the ground to propitiate the lower gods. After the dance there were speeches, following the American custom of postprandial oratory.

Years ago when our relations with the Samoans were not so pleasant as at present, Lt. Philip Lansdale, a classmate of mine at the Naval Academy, was killed by the natives on the island of Upolu near Apia. As I was anxious to know all the details from a priest then living in Tutuila who had been in Apia at that time, Governor Terhune requested him to come up to government house and tell me the story of Lansdale's death.

Brother Felipe had been in the island more than 30 years and had been fond of Lansdale . He also had close ties to Lansdale's next in command, Ens. John Robert Monahan, a Catholic. On the day of the fatal expedition, Brother Felipe went to Lansdale's quarters in Apia to ask for a general pass through the lines instead of receiving an individual pass. Lansdale was shaving at the time and told the priest he would gladly arrange it for him on his return from an expedition on which he was leaving in an hour.

A reconnaissance mission was to be made by United States sailors and marines in command of Lieutenant Lansdale accompanied by Ensign Monahan and in cooperation with a landing party from a British man-of-war in command of Lt. A. H. Freeman. R.N. Surgeon Long and Li. C. M. Perkins of the marines were also with Lansdale. The plan was to march about ten miles from Apia and return.

The party was accompanied by a guide—an American who had lived in Samoa for many years and was thoroughly familiar with the habits and customs of the natives. Before starting he insisted that no guns should be fired and nothing done to provoke an attack by the natives, assuring Lansdale that if such precautions were taken the natives would not molest him.

Everything went well until the return trip when one of the sailors in the party, seeing a native in a coconut tree, fired his rifle at him as a joke, with no intention to hit him or provoke disorder. At the time they were about two miles from the beach on a road that lay through heavy undergrowth, in which it proved the natives were concealed. The firing of a gun was a signal for the natives to attack, which they did, completely surprising the landing party.

An attempt was made to turn the only machine gun on them, but the gun jammed and became useless. The men had their unloaded rifles slung across their backs. The result was a wild scramble for the beach. Some ran into barbed wire fences and were caught there, while others were shot down. Lansdale was desperately wounded alongside the machine gun. Monahan gallantly came to his rescue but was ordered by Lansdale to leave. He refused and died with his commanding officer. The British Lieutenant Freeman was killed along with two British and two American sailors.

When the party returned to the ship and reported what had occurred, the American and English ships commenced a desulatory bombardment of the island which continued for several days. Little harm was done, but six natives were killed. The bodies of the officers and men were recovered—those of the sailors were found untouched, but the officers' bodies had been mutilated.

After leaving Samoa we received a cordial wireless from Viscount Jellico on board the *New Zealand* regretting that he could not meet us during his stay in the Pacific and another message from Captain Terhune wishing us, on behalf of the naval station, "a safe and happy voyage to the Asiatic Station".

We approached the equator on a NW by W½W course. The trade winds died out and the ship steamed through a flat, grey sea and a dead calm. Heavy nimbus clouds banked along the horizon and then spread up across the sky while the rain poured in torrents in every squall that burst. There were many waterspouts sighted, but none near the ship.

On 14 October we crossed the 180th meridian in latitude 12° 30% south and dropped a day from our calendar. Our track lay straight to San Bernardino Straits, passing within three miles of the Pelew Islands in the Japanese mandate. The Japanese are "mining phospates" there and the three steamers in the harbor and the derricks on shore indicated busy times. We reached Manila October 27, completing a voyage of over 12,500 miles in 52 days.

Amiel in his journal writes, "The calm sea says more to the thoughtful soul than the same sea in storm and tumult."

The weeks of smooth weather afforded ample leisure for reflection. As we shortened the miles to Manila my thoughts naturally turned back to 1 May 1898 when Dewey fought his battle with Montojo. Speaking one day to me of the Sampson-Schley Inquiry, which was then in session, he said that when he wrote his report of the battle he was determined that there should be no back-fires, denials, discussions or repercussions, so he called all the captains on board the *Olympia* and read them his report. Then he said, "Gentlemen, if you have any corrections to suggest, make them now or forever after hold your peace."

18 In Manila and the Southern Islands

We remained six weeks in Manila and the islands. Burton Harrison was the governor-general and I have never met anyone with a more charming personality. The story goes that when he was told at the state department that the president had decided to send him to the Philippines, the secretary of state said, "Harrison, you are the only man who has wanted that job who has not asked first what the salary is."

Brigadier General French was in command of the army in the Philippines; Col. Richmond Pearson Davis commanded at Corregdor. Rear Adm. Casey B. Morgan was in command of Olongapo. Morgan was a fine officer in every way—full of energy, efficient, and thoroughly dependable—a man who considered loyalty to his commanding officer his first duty.

At the time of our arrival Manila was very hot. After the customary exchange of official calls and dinners with the governor at Malacanan Palace in the city, I went to Baguio with my family, having first shifted my flag to the ex-Spanish gunboat *Alava,* tender to the flagship.

Baguio, 5,200 feet above sea level in the mountains back of Manila, is the health-cure of the navy and army, and affords relief to the sick and wounded of both services. The government reservation there has golf links, tennis courts and comfortable cottages for officers. Outside the reservation is the service club. The cottage assigned to the naval commander in chief was built on a crag overlooking a valley between two thickly wooded mountains which afforded a beautiful view. At night, 2,000 feet below the cottage, a single bright reddish light shined above the treetops and the mists and reminded me of Miss Murfee's story, *The Star in the Valley*. It never varied from dusk to dawn. Like the star in the Tennessee mountains, I first saw it in the twilight of a close October evening, "an answering gleam to the earliest planet in the sky," and I never tired of looking at it.

There is a fine hotel under the management of the army for the use of officers and their families who are not housekeeping. It is a bit startling, yet picturesque, to be served at the table by native boys wearing only a white jacket and not another blessed stitch except a red sash serving as a G-string.

Over these mountains there are drives and good military roads made by the army engineers. When Mr. Taft was there he used to ride for miles. One day he covered so much distance that he proudly cabled his achievement to Mr. Root who replied, "Congratulations. How is the horse?"

Our party rode on donkeys to Mount Thomas, the highest peak in the vicinity of Manila—7,000 feet above the sea. The road lay through forests of tropical growth, across hogbacks, up steep inclines and along narrow trails skirting edges of precipices. We slept in rude shacks at the summit to wait for the sunrise. Our supper was a ragout of monkey, or dog—I do not know which—provided by the "Christian" natives. Dog meat is a favorite food of the Filipinos, and one of the most pathetic sights in the world is the dog market in Baguio where the natives bring their dogs to sell for food after fattening them with rice. When the dogs arrive at the market they are so thin they can scarcely walk off the mountain.

The sunrise, that we had traveled so far to see, owing to the fog was not as beautiful as one we had seen a few days before from the deck of the *Alava* in Dingalan Bay, where truly "the dawn came up like thunder". When we returned to Baguio the flag-lieutenant saw a telegram to the commanding officer of the station from General French requesting him to do everything to make us comfortable, and he did.

General French was daily expecting his orders home as he was in poor health. After he left the islands, we heard of his death at home a few weeks later. He was a fine West Pointer, and it was a matter of regret to the services in the Philippines when he returned to the United States.

About this time I decided to have a look at the southern portion of "my domains"—at least as much of it as could be encompassed before the time to go north. On account of the depth of the water, it was decided to use the *Alava*—a good sea boat, but a small one. First we went to Olongapo, about 60 miles from Manila.

The drydock *Dewey*, which cost hundreds of thousands of dollars and no end of worry to tow from the United States, was in the berth where she has lain for many years—a source of anxiety during rumors of war, and of doubtful utility at other times. Whether the question has ever been settled by the strategists to hold on to Olongapo in time of war or to fall back on Cavite dragging along the

Dewey, I do not know, but it was a burning question for many years and afforded the naval general board in Washington many discussions.

After passing Corregidor we ran into rain, wind and heavy seas, and had to anchor during the night. A typhoon was blowing in the Pacific and its effect and backwash were felt in the inland waters, delaying the *Alava*'s arrival at the wharf at Cebu several hours. Although informed by wireless that the ship would be delayed, the citizens and welcoming committee waited on the pier with unfailing patience and courtesy and had cars to take us sightseeing.

First we saw the wooden image of Christ brought there by Magellan. It is a black Nino and is kept in the church, but we were permitted to photograph it. After lunch at the club, the governor of Cebu took us to see the cockfight. It was Sunday—always a gala day in Spanish countries. The shack where the cocks fought was crowded with noisy natives, and for 20 miles the roads leading to it were crowded with farmers and peasants bringing their birds—each cock armed with glistening steel spurs. It was a bloody fight and judging from the enthusiasm of the audience must have been a great success.

After a visit to Dean Worcester's Visayan oil mills on the island opposite Cebu where Magellan was murdered by the natives, the *Alava* got underway for Mindanao. Before sailing I purchased two pearls from a native. I was not at all sure that the man who sold them to me for a mere song—and swore by the prophet that they were the real thing—was telling the truth until a Boston jeweler cracked one in testing it. Returning to the ship at sunset a small crocodile slowly crossed the road ahead of our car and escaped by rolling down the embankment into the sea.

No where in the world are there sunsets quite like in the trade wind regions at sea—so marvelous in light and color—especially as seen from the Lunetta at Manila. I wonder when these islands will give the world some great painter of the going down of the sun in its flaming colors. I once heard a famous general at a meeting of the Society of the Cincinnati in Newport allude to the wonderful sunsets "in the celestial skies of the Philippines"—by which he probably meant *cerulean,* I suppose.

Before we sailed from Manila the quartermaster of the islands, Colonel Bellinger, had prepared a schedule which would insure our seeing as much as possible in a limited time and had written to various officials of our coming. At Camp Overton Governor Coveston of

Mindanao met us with cars and we headed at once up a fine mountain road for Camp Keithly on Lake Lanao. We were on the lookout for monkeys and orchids, according to schedule, but saw only one of each.

At the camp the aged dato, head of the Mohammedans in that region, presented us to his two wives and showed us two gold-headed canes—one given to him by General Pershing, the other by the Spanish General Blanco. The beauty of the women was disfigured by their teeth, blackened by the use of betel nut and lime. Perhaps it is only a question of time before this custom is copied by foreign women, just as they have adopted the henna discoloration of the nails!

The breeze was fresh and Lake Lanao rough. The governor's launch was lively, but the lunch was good and bountiful for those who did not mind the motion. Our destination was the so-called "brass-works"—really only a pit where the Moros melt their brass in which they are skillful workers. As the weather became threatening, we prepared to return to the boat—but too late to escape the downpour.

Governor Coveston pointed out the scene of General Baldwin's fight near the lake, and the place where Johnston won his spurs. He also showed us the tree which they still call the "Alice Roosevelt tree" because Miss Roosevelt smoked a cigarette in its shade—more of a novelty when Mr. Taft's party was at the camp than it would be now.

While the rain was still falling, as it can fall only in the tropics, we started back for Camp Overton at speed, because the governor's car had no lights and we had to do the 36 kilometers downgrade 2,200 feet in the hour remaining before dark.

After our return from the lake, the hospitable governor drove the entire party to his house for refreshments where I touched my lips with Tennessee "Cascade"—and felt that a bit of home had crept into my heart. The governor presented me with two large handsome chow bowls made by the Moros of copper inlaid with silver wire.

Upon going on board the *Alava* I received a cable from the secretary of the navy approving our itinerary but directing me to be in Vladivostok by the first of the year. A radio message also informed us that Omsk had been evacuated and that Vladivostok was occupied by Cossacks. All the party with us during the day dined with me on board the *Alava*, then we said good-bye to Governor Coveston and sailed on the next leg of our voyage to Zamboanga—which is as beautiful and interesting as its name is musical.

Governor Pasedos accompanied by the colonel and captain of constabulary came on board as soon as the *Alava* was tied up at the dock. The usual round of sight-seeing began. Our first stop was the government prison where we listened to an orchestra concert performed by inmates who make their own instruments. On Basilan Island we saw a famous old Vauban fort and visited a rubber plantation, watching the interesting process of extracting rubber from the trees.

Sailing from Zamboanga we crossed the Sulu Sea to the sultanate of Sulu, whose capital is Jolo—the smallest walled town in the world. The native officials and the American Governor Rogers met us at the pier to drive us around the island and gave us an invitation from the sultan to a reception at the palace in the afternoon.

The island of Jolo is one of the most beautiful of the Philippines and the American engineers have crossed it with military roads of best construction. At Mainbum is a girls' school, one of whose teachers is the daughter of a dato and who distinguished herselt at 16 by her part in the fighting against the American troops during our quarrel with Aguinaldo.

The sultan's reception was crowded. His niece, the Princess Daing-Daing—an attractive young woman educated in the United States—acted as hostess. The sultan—an exceedingly diminutive person—is a protege of both the United States and England and receives an allowance from both governments, an arrangement agreed to when the boundaries of the islands of Panay and Iloilo were established.

I asked the sultan (through an interpreter for he speaks no English) to translate an inscription on my seal ring. The sultan decided after careful examination that it said "nyzam"—an Arabic title of honor. Several years afterwards I met a traveler in Naples who said it meant "good luck". Later on I consulted the curator of the Boulak Museum in Cairo who said it meant "Lizzie"—the name of my wife's mother to whom the ring had been given by her husband in Tunis. This confirmed a tradition in the family and I therefore accepted it as correct. The ring was given me by my wife "as my first decoration" on my return from the first convoy.

From Jolo the course to Sandakan on the north tip of Borneo lay about ten miles off the coast. During the night I awoke suddenly out of a sound sleep and went on deck in my pajamas to look around. The moon was shining through heavy cumulus clouds, the air was misty and the sea flat. Looking to the south I saw the palm fringed beach distinctly not more than five miles distant. Soundings put us in 30 fathoms when we should have been in 60. As a matter of fact, the ship had been set in shore by the current. A serious misadventure was avoided. As the chart gave no information regarding the currents, except that they were variable, strong and uncertain, I deemed it prudent to anchor until daylight. We had been set nearly 20 miles to southward of our line and were too close for comfort.

Later in the cruise I had a similar experience in the Gulf of Chihli—the sudden awakening by a near danger. Three times in my sea experience I have been so warned. I have told in the Naval Institute of the first time this occurred on the coast of California. The third time will be spoken of in the account of the *Alava's* run from Tientsin to Chefoo.

About noon we anchored in the harbor of Sandakan and fired a salute of 21 guns with the British flag at the main, which was promptly returned. The acting governor, called the resident, came on board accompanied by the harbor master and the sub-commandant. The resident provided two cars for our sight-seeing and we tried to get to the dense and luxuriant jungle only 15 miles away where there were elephants, both domesticated and wild. Owing to the heavy rains the roads were too bad for the cars, and we missed seeing the elephants piling teak, much to my wife's disappointment.

Returning to the ship I found a radio from Colonel Bellinger that he had reservations for our party on a transport sailing for Japan on the 26th. This meant cutting Iloilo from our itinerary. Sandakan was our farthest south. From there we steamed northward for Manila passing close to the once-disputed Banggi Islands where the Chinese obtain the edible nests used in making the famous bird's nest soup.

I was much pleased with the captain of the *Alava.* Lineally Ponto was a lieutenant and before the war was an enlisted man. He was naturally a seaman and by study had become a fine navigator. I never saw a man who could better hand, reef and steer than Lieutenant Ponto, and he never lost his head in an emergency.

The day after leaving Borneo we ran into a succession of heavy rains as we headed northward for the coast of Panay. After making our landfall the weather cleared and the sea fell smooth, but only for 24 hours when it became restless again and tossed the little *Alava* most uncomfortably. During the following night we passed through the unlighted channels west of Panay, which was taking less risk than with the shoals outside.

After a stormy day at sea we came to the entrance of Manila Harbor. The curious shaped El Fraile, looking like a battleship moored head and stern, is the most conspicuous object of all the island chain about which a legend is woven. The picturesque rocks on Corregidor serve as natural foundations for fortitications that would not stand much battering by modern heavy artillery, but which appear threatening.

On Halloween we went to the cemetery to see the vigils and the illuminations of the graves. In Catholic countries there is a custom of burning lights at shrines in honor of the dead on Halloween. At Manila on All Souls' night, devotees watch and pray at the graves of their departed—over which are placed candles or electric bulbs according to the means of the mourner. The tombs and vaults surrounding the cemetery are also lighted.

We were late in getting to the cemetery and the rain was falling dismally. The candles, for the most part, were either burnt-out or flickering in the holders and many of the watchers were asleep on the wet ground or in chairs. Under such discouraging circumstances their devotion seemed very real, to remain from sunset to dawn. As I watched the candles dimly burning over the graves I thought of Rossetti's lines, slightly amended:

> The souls mounting up to God
> Went by like thin flames.

Before electricity, when only candles or lamps were used, the scene must have been even more impressive.

19 First Visit to Japan

At noon on 29 November 1919 the *South Dakota* got underway bound for Yokohama. A moderate northeast monsoon was raising a heavy sea. The coal was bad and this with head sea and wind reduced the speed to 15 knots.

At sea I received from the department the list of the annual recommendations for promotion to the grade of rear admiral by the selection board. It so happened that all the selections that year were in accordance with seniority and no one was passed over.

Our method of promotion has always seemed to me unjust and cruel because it destroys seniority of those not selected and yet retains them on the active list. It is useless here to argue against it, since it is res adjudicata. Once I was pleading with a secretary of the navy in behalf of a brilliant officer who had been passed over by the board. I was told coldly, "That is not the opinion of the service, is it?"

To which I replied. "I cannot answer for the service, but I have discussed the question with many officers, and have found none who disagrees with me."

"I presume all you have said to me you will write officially, if you have not already done so."

I assured him, "All that I have said is in the official reports the department required of the senior officers on our method of selection of the grade of admiral, but the trouble is no one has seen them."

We carried boisterous wind and sea up to the coast of Japan. As the men dug deeper into the bunkers the coal got worse. The decks were covered with a thick layer of cinders and smudge penetrated every crack of the skylights and worked through into the quarters below. Off the Loo-Choo Islands our speed was down to 13 knots, and we were burning 189 tons coal per day.

The day before arriving at Yokohama the sea flattened down and the sun came out. Running along the coast of Nippon we had the most beautiful views of Fuji-san, snowcapped with a long smoke-like curl of cloud at the summit. I had waited 35 years for this view. We passed close to the heavy forts at the entrance of the harbor and anchored inside the breakwater.

The naval attache at Yokohama, Capt. Edward Watson, came on

board with a long program of official calls, dinners and tiffins that promised a hectic time during our brief visit. The Japanese officials seemed anxious to be friendly and extended cordial greetings in spite of the strained relations which at that time were said to exist between Tokyo and Washington. Watson told me that my presentation to the emperor was to take place at the palace the following Monday and that my party would assemble at the the embassy in the forenoon.

The night before the presentation we dined with the minister of marines, Admiral Kato—afterwards raised to the peerage as Baron Kato for his services at the Disarmament Conference at Washington in 1921-22. Having been informed that I had been made a Knight of the Sacred Treasure, Admiral Kato suggested that I wear his decoration to the palace, as mine had been sent to Washington. He sent his aide for it and put it on me himself. That was the second time I had been so honored by a foreign minister of marines, Monsieur Legues having done that office for me in Paris when I received the medal of Commander of the Legion of Honor.

On Monday morning we went to Tokyo by train and were met at the station by the embassy automobiles. We called on Ambassador Roland Morris who received me with his staff. The palace was not far from the embassy. Crossing the moat surrounding it, we passed the massive stone wall enclosing the castle grounds. From the top of the walls the stunted, grotesque pines looked down on the lotus flowers in the water beneath. Passing through the gigantic gateway we crossed a second moat, then over another bridge into the imperial grounds, then up a steep curving road to the entrance of the palace.

The master of ceremonies, Count Toda, along with some other officials met us at the entrance and conducted us through many carpeted red corridors to a waiting room where we admired in silence the exquisite woodwork, the sliding screens, the bronzes and cloisonne. In a few minutes the ambassador, myself and staff were taken to the entrance of the audience chamber, leaving the ladies who were to be presented only to the empress.

The ceremony of presentation is simple and is exactly the same as agreed upon between Townsend Harris, our first minister to Japan in 1854, and the mikado—a bow at the entrance, another halfway to the emperor, a third when the emperor is reached. Mr. Harris had objected to approaching on his knees or to removing his shoes.

I watched the ambassador approach the open door, saw him make his first bow and then disappear. Presently the signal was given for me to advance. I found myself at the threshold of a small unornamented room. The emperor in plain brown service uniform was standing at the opposite end, the ambassador on his left, the interpreter on his right and in the rear several of the household officers in brilliant uniforms.

I made my first bow, then the second in the middle of the room, then my third when I reached the presence. The emperor extended his gloved hand and the ambassador said, "Your Majesty, may I have the pleasure of presenting Admiral Gleaves, the commander in chief of the United States Asiatic Station."

My information was that court etiquette forbade speaking to the emperor unless he spoke. He said he was glad to see me in Japan and asked several questions: Was I enjoying my visit? Did I have a fine voyage? Then he said he hoped I would enjoy the duck catch he had ordered for me the next day.

I replied to these and added a little speech of my own, saying that I appreciated all that was being done for me, and knew my government would be greatly pleased at my report of it. The emperor extended his hand again and I took position on the ambassador's left. The staff followed in order of rank, but to none of them the emperor either offered his hand or spoke, which was strictly according to the rule.

It is etiquette not to speak above a whisper, so the ceremony was performed in a grave-like silence, broken only by the hammering of our heels on the polished wood floors. It seemed to me as I stood by the side of the ambassador and watched the others come in and back out, that their shoes made as much noise as the sabots of Dutch children on stone pavements in Holland. When the other officers had been presented I approached the emperor, who again gave me his hand, and then I retired.

The next function was the presentation to the empress. We rejoined the ladies and with them were taken to the empress' reception room, called the Peony Hall. It has hardwood floors, beautiful carvings and—like the Phoenix Hall of the emperor—no furniture, pictures or rugs. The empress was accompanied by a lady-in-waiting who spoke English and interpreted. This was Madame Matsudaira. We knew her later in Washington when her husband came to America as ambassador.

The ceremonies were practically the same as for the emperor. The empress asked me several questions similar to those asked by the emperor. She was dressed in a plain morning gown and impressed me by her sweet, cordial manner and her comely appearance. Mrs. Gleaves was presented next and the empress was very gracious to her, asking her several questions. My daughter Evelina was presented last—and never looked prettier. Her inclusion was an unusual compliment, for we were told that she was the only unmarried woman ever presented.

Such was our meeting with the Son of Heaven—heir of 2,500 years of direct descent from the sun goddess.

After leaving the palace a message was received from the emperor inviting us to a duck "catch" the following morning at nine o'clock. Civilian sack suits or sport clothes were prescribed. The pursuit of the ducks was not to be with guns—forbidden inside the palace walls since the days of the shoguns—but with nets on the end of long bamboo poles, like butterfly nets. The ducks are decoyed into ditches, from which they attempt to escape. The sportsmen concealed on the banks try to catch them in the nets as they rise above the water.

It is a high honor to participate in a duck catch and we were told that the Duke of Connaught and his suite were the only other foreigners who had been so favored. It is also considered a royal sport in Japan—the emperor takes great interest in it and requires a report of each catch be made to him. We acquitted ourselves creditably, our total bag being 27, of which Admiral Takeshita caught eleven, my wife two, my daughter Evelina one, Colonel Burnett six, Captain Blamer four and I caught three.

We lunched in a beautiful and picturesque teahouse built over a lake within the palace grounds. These must be very beautiful in cherry blossom time but were then bleak and cold, although the sun was shining brightly. Count Toda, who is the last of the shoguns, was the master of ceremonies and represented the emperor.

After leaving the palace we returned to the hotel, shifted into uniform and drove to the various residences of imperial princes to sign their visitor's books. This takes the place of the formal calls and is acknowledged by cards. In the evening Naval Attache and Mrs. Edward Howe Watson entertained at an informal, but official, dinner, at which were many interesting people—among them General Woodruff of the British embassy (one of the famous "Contemptibles"), the Russian naval attache, the naval attache of Italy and a Japanese officer.

The following day we lunched at the official residence of the minister of foreign affairs, Baron Uchida. Madame Uchida is a graduate of Bryn Mawr College and speaks beautiful English. I think all the prominent people in official life in Tokyo were there and it was a beautifully arranged and interesting luncheon. I had a talk with Viscount Uchida and also the vice minister of foreign affairs, Mr. Hanrihara, whom I used to know in Washington.

After the luncheon at the foreign office, Vice Admiral Takeshita took us out to Sheiba Park to the Beuten Temple and from there to a Geisha dance at the Maple Club. In the evening we dined with the chief of the naval general staff, Admiral Shimamura, at the Peer's Club where we met practically the same people we had met at the foreign minister's. There was a clever sleight of hand entertainment after dinner, but being due at nine to address the American Society at the Tokyo Club, I could not remain, it having previously been arranged that I should be excused at that time.

At the Tokyo Club I was introduced to the society by the ambassador, and was afterwards presented by him to the individual members of the club. The dinner given by the ambassador in honor of the commander in chief at our embassy was notable for the presence not only of the large number of Japanese high officials, but also of ranking foreign diplomats in Tokyo.

One afternoon with the flag lieutenant I called, by appointment, on Admiral Togo—the world's greatest sailor since Nelson and Farragut. He lives in a typical Japanese house where he received us with exquisite courtesy. I had met him at dinner at Admiral Leutze's residence in the navy yard at New York in 1915 where I sat next to him at the table. At that time he avoided reportorial interviews by pleading his inability to speak English, but in Tokyo he spoke enough to us to make his welcome a memorable event and a highlight of our visit.

Before leaving Yokohama, Captain Blamer and I drove to Kamakura to see Old Diabetes—as the famous Buddha is irreverently called by the sailors—and the neighboring temples. Undoubtedly the Diabutsu is the most impressive statue in the world and one can never forget its awful sublimity, loneliness and serenity. A light snow was falling and I felt that under this veil was embodied "the soul of all the East". It was simply unforgettable and to me "the keynote of Japan".

We sailed from Yokohama for Shanghai, passing through the Inland Sea and the Shimonoseki Straits. Arriving in Shanghai, Dr. May, our alert fleet surgeon, reported a suspicious case of smallpox in the crew which meant that the whole ship's company had to be vaccinated.

20 Visit to Peking

For some reason the winter season had brought many tourists to Shanghai and we found the hotels crowded. Had it not been for our friends, Mr. and Mrs. Doremus and Dr. Findley, we should have been much embarrassed for accommodations onshore. We arrived just in time for dinner—which was delicious—and the attendants made us feel thoroughly at home. Outside the streets were cold, wet and bleak, making the blazing coal fires in the grates all the more comfortable at 87 rue Vallon.

The ladies in the party had arrived in the transport *Logan* from Manila in time to join up in Shanghai. We were all to leave for Peking the following morning, Sunday, December 21. After an early breakfast the automobiles were reported ready and the servants all came out to see us safely and comfortably embarked for the North Station where a guard of honor was paraded.

The special envoy and the foreign minister of the province, Admiral Lang, and various secretaries were at the station to see us off. The guard was composed of two companies of infantry and a band. This station several years later was destroyed by Japanese gunfire during the invasion in 1932. The envoy told me that the gaurd of honor belonged to the 27th Regiment which he had personally commanded three years before when it defeated 34,000 rebels at the Shanghai arsenal.

Every arrangement was made for our comfort on the train. Two Chinese naval officers, Commander Wong and Lieutenant Commander Huang, had been detailed as personal aides. Wong is now a rear admiral commanding the Nanking Squadron. By direction of the president of China a special car had been provided and he had ordered every attention to be shown us on the journey to the capital. An invitation from him had been transmitted to me unofficially—but through official channels—to extend our visit beyond New Year. As this would conflict with the navy department's orders to Vladivostok, I felt it necessary to wire Washington for a modification, which was granted promptly.

On the way to Peking we had to cross the river at Nanking. A guard of honor from the gunboats in the river met us at the station and escorted us across the river, which at this point is 3¼ miles wide. The gunboats fired an admiral's salute as we passed them and the tuchun of the Nanking province, General Li, came on board the car to drink our health in champagne. He was most distinghished looking and we conversed with the help of our consul general, Mr. Davis, who was to distinguish himself greatly some years later. General Li was a remarkably handsome man and evidently one of culture and high breeding. We dined with him on our return from Peking. Unfortunately he met an untimely death shortly afterwards.

At Tientsin, the west station, there was an escort of American troops under Col. William Morrow of the 15th U.S. Infantry, and Japanese, Chinese and Italian troops. There were also a number of civil and military officials to greet us. A representative of Admiral Sah, the minister of marine, presented my wife with a bouquet of chrysanthemums.

Leaving, Tientsin, Commander Hutchins, the American naval attache, and Colonel Gullick, U.S. Marine Corps, boarded our car with Lieutenant Chu of the Chinese navy who had been appointed my aide during our visit to Peking. Chu brought his bride of three months to meet my wife.

We reached Peking at eight in the evening and were greeted at the station by troops, bands, a committee, the charge d'affaires, Dr. Tenny, and other American officials. Admiral Sah sent a detachment of sailors to escort us to the Hotel Wagon-Lits which had been selected for our headquarters. Two elaborately decorated welcome arches were erected, one near the station, the other near the Chien-Men gate—the historic gate in the southern wall of the city which saw severe fighting in the Boxer Rebellion.

We were in time for a dance at the Peking Club—a pleasant affair given by Major & Mrs. Hubert of the U.S. Marine Corps. Here we met Miss Carl, who painted the portrait of the Empress Dowager which is now in Washington, also Mr. Putnam-Weale, whose real name is Simpson—author of *Indiscreet Letters from Peking*—as well as Madame la Rue, whose book *Peking* is just out.

Of all the Chinese officials with whom I was closely associated in Peking, Admiral Sah was *facile princeps*. At that time he was the minister of marine but soon afterwards was made premier in addition—a worthy appointment for this honest, able and efficient old sailor.

Educated at Purdue, he spoke English fluently and was devoted to

America—a man of charming manners and high culture. He was about my own age and had served in the navy the same length of time. During the Revolution which overthrew the Manchu government, he commanded a squardon of vessels in the Yangtse River, but went over to the Republic and served in high office until his retirement in 1922. He reached the grade of full admiral in 1912.

Since his retirement he has lived in his native province of Fukien near Foochow, occupying himself with raising funds to build houses for thousands of villagers whose homes were burnt down by the banditti. In doing this he has travelled hundreds of miles on rivers and almost impassable roads. The admiral's wife has been dead many years. His son, a civil engineer, was educated at Cornell and his grandson and one granddaughter are being educated in the United States.

Our friendship began when I first visited Peking. From the beginning I realized what a strong and powerful friend we had in him and was soon further attracted by his personal charm and his fine qualities. When I saw the refugees he had sheltered in his own home prostrating themselves before this modest and retiring man, he seemed to be the embodiment of Sir Roger de Coverley.

We had arrived in Peking at the psychological moment. China was outwardly harassed and embarrassed and internally troubled, but she felt the strong friendship of America was her shield. The United States had refused the share of the Boxer indemnity allowed to us, but required that the money should be devoted to the education of Chinese children in the United States. Many years before when Shanghai was parceled out by Europeans, the portion allotted to the United States was marked on the charts as the American Concession, and is still so called. As a matter of fact the United States never accepted a square foot of the territory, although our consulate is erected there.

In the fighting of 1932 in Shanghai and along the Yangtse, we again carefully maintained our policy of noninterference and neutrality. Even when England, France, Italy, Germany and Japan planned naval stations and established themselves on the mainland, the United States refused to be a party to the partition. This is the reason China cherishes her ancient friendship for America. She knows we have no axes to grind. To the extent of his great power and ability, Admiral Sah reflected and cultivated this cordiality of his government.

Out time in Peking was filled with unforgettable social encounters. The admiralty building in Peking is handsome and of modern construction, but the residence of Marshal Tuan was a cheerless place on that cold forenoon in December when I called there with Dr. Tenny. It was barely furnished and there was nothing to indicate his high office or great wealth. Although the marshal was no longer in the army, he was recognized as the head of the military party. He received us in uniform and was exceptionally cordial. Through an interpreter—for he spoke no English—he offered to send me some tea, which he did.

The premier's house, on the contrary, is that of a rich Chinese gentleman, filled with his collections of rare specimens of jade, lacquer, carvings and tables of bamboo and teak. The premier also was no longer in the army, but wore the uniform of a marshal. He later became the secretary of war. His servants brought in cognac, tea and champagne, and he smoked cigarettes inserted in a bamboo reed four feet long.

Admiral Sah's dinner—at the admiralty house—was remarkable in every respect. The decorations were beautiful, artistic and carefully planned. The doors and windows of the buildings were outlined by growing flowers and electric lights. The full guard of honor and the band were paraded and all the naval officers on duty at the admiralty were present. The dinner was elaborate, the table decorated with flowers and the national flags of both countries. The band played the latest Western music, including Sousa's marches, and the food—delicate and delicious—was served in Western style.

There was on the table a most unusual decoration, peculiar to China. Along its length on the linen cloth were not only flowers but also exquisite pictures drawn out in sand of various colors. In letters of sand reaching from the foot to head of the table for all 48 guests to read was "Welcome to Admiral Gleaves and Staff". The scene was like a banquet in the Arabian nights.

Admiral Sah's speech was touching and even pathetic. It is evident to me that the Chinese government relies absolutely upon the United States to protect it from all aggressors. I was surprised by after dinner speeches, as there had been none in Tokyo or at Admiral Lang's dinner in Shanghai. Fortunately I had remembered the advice of Dr. Humphreys at a dinner of the Cincinnati Society at the Waldorf. When I asked him if he was to speak, he said he did not know but that he always carried along a little ammunition. Fortunately I had some prepared ammunition.

After dinner, according to a custom in China, there was an exhibition of some marvelous sleight of hand and juggling. One youth balanced head down on the head of another man and in this inverted position took soup and a glass of water handed him by an assistant.

One morning we left the hotel in automobiles for an excursion to the Summer Palace—several miles from the city, near the ruins of the old Summer Palace destroyed by the French and English in 1860. My celestial Flag Lieutenant Commander Chu was our conductor. While we were getting ready to go, Chu rushed out of the hotel in a most excited manner and said to me, "I want to congratulate you, Sir. Admiral Sah has just telephoned to say that the president has decorated you with the First Class Order of the Weng-Hu (striped Tiger). Admiral Sah himself has only the second class and I have the sixth class, and I am very happy, Sir."

The day was clear and fine and rather mild. Not even in Italy or Florida are the skies bluer or clearer than in China on a cloudless winter day. But the dust from the centuries-old roads is terrific and unsanitary. The present Summer Palace was erected by the "Old Buddha", as she was called—the Empress Tz'u-hsi—at a cost of 200 million dollars. Chu said this was beautiful from an artistic standpoint, but was a "painful reflection for the Chinese officers that the money which should have been expended on our navy was put into this."

We had luncheon at the so-called marble ship, another fad of the empress—a structure which bears no outward semblance of a ship. Someone said, "China wanted a navy but all she got was a marble boat."

The palace is a collection of buildings and temples with wonderful tiled roofs built on the slopes of steep wooded hills, a long terrace or pergola, and the famous hunch-back marble bridge whose single arch is 30 feet high. Miss Bredon in her historical sketch of Peking says truly that "the greatest feature of Yi Ho Yuan is its setting."

From the Old Buddha's dwelling place in her day of prosperity we drove to the western hills by way of the Jade Pagoda and the Jade Fountain. On our return to the city I received by courier the medal of the Order of Weng-Hu with green and red ribbon which the president had awarded me. A handsome souvenir for transmission to posterity!

The weather turned very cold during the night bringing a blizzard from the Mongolian plains with snow and a dust storm. The coolies who gather nightly under the hotel windows kept up a continous coughing, distressing to hear, as well as destructive to sleep. One who has not seen the Chinese coolies cannot know the depths of their poverty.

Our hall boy, who from his appearance must have been 60 or 70, or perhaps even 80, slept underneath the stairs outside our reception room. He was a tiny little man, an old-timer who still wore a queue and resembled a gnome. His costume never changed—blue overalls with trousers bound tightly around his thin legs. He was very attentive and seemed to sleep with one eye open. One night when I returned late from a stag party, he jumped from his bunk under the stairs, greeted me with a smile, and immediately prepared a whisky and soda for me. He had a sense of humor, which most Chinese lack, and reminded me of Barrie's Lob. I would not have been surprised to see him crawl under the table or vanish through the keyhole.

On Christmas we attended service in the English chapel in the British legation compound, the scene of so much tragedy. The trees and ground were white with new fallen snow. The chapel is small but has withstood sieges, assaults and battle. I noticed that the parson did not include the president of the United States in his prayers for rulers and sovereigns.

In the afternoon we all went to the Temple of Heaven. Its groves and altars, like the old Grecian temples, are among the beauty spots of the whole earth. Miss Bredon says they inspire one's "yearning towards something higher, finer and more enduring" than our "ephemeral existence" and "second only to the palaces in splendor, and surpassing them in holiness, is the magnificent temple dedicated to the Worship of Heaven."

The scenery within the enclosure, three miles in circumference, is beautiful beyond description. The trees were white with hoarfrost and snow, and the silence was most impressive. We went to both altars. I remembered the day 35 years before when, eluding the soldiers at the gates, I got into the North Temple when it was forbidden ground. My wife said as she stood in front of the North Altar, "I have heard you talk of the Temple of Heaven ever since I first knew you, but I never expected to be here myself!"

The South Altar, which the Chinese have considered to be the center of the earth, consists of three concentric marble terraces—perfect rings of immaculate whiteness. On the upper terrace the Son of Heaven used to perform the sacrificial ceremonies. The North Altar lies due north from the South Altar and is covered by a tall pagoda visible from every point of the compass in the city and where the sacred tablets are kept.

The two altars are connected by a broad marble causeway, raised several feet above the ground. In 1889 the North Temple was struck by lightning and destroyed, but rebuilt. We did not return to the entrance by the causeway but walked slowly through the groves. The air was absolutely still, not a sound disturbing the silence—which was almost appalling. Occasionally this was broken by the cawing of crows or the shrill call of magpies.

A few days after our visit to the Temple of Heaven, Admiral Sah called at the hotel and brought Mrs. Gleaves some very fine tea cups. She asked, "Admiral, now that you are not only the secretary of the navy, but also the premier, won't you have the grass and weeds removed from the stones of the South Altar?"

He smiled when he replied, "Why, Mrs. Gleaves, I have never been to the Temple of Heaven!"

To use Mr. Maddox Brown's words on a similar remark about London, "Americans will not understand that. Every Londoner will."

I was much impressed by the marvelous changes the whirligig of time had wrought in China since my first visit there. In 1885 it was death to any foreigner who entered the Forbidden City. When Colonel Denby, our minister, asked the president of the Yung-li-Yamen if he thought it possible he would ever be presented to the emperor, the reply was, "If you remain here long enough." All that is changed, and the grounds and palaces are no longer open only to native officials, nor have they been so restricted since the French troops camped in the grounds of the Temple of Heaven during the Boxer Rebellion.

On the day after Christmas, 1919, we visited the Forbidden City by appointment. At the gate we were met by Admiral Tsai, the assistant master of ceremonies. The weather continued extremely cold. The trees and ground were covered with hoarfrost and again the awful silence of China was awe-inspiring. We rode in rickshas from palace to palace and did not return to the hotel until noon.

That afternoon I was presented by Dr. Tenny to the president of China in the old cabinet building, accompanied by my staff and members of the legation. There was no military display except a guard of honor, but the audience was of the most cordial and friendly character. The president welcomed me to the city and said he hoped everything would be done to make my visit pleasant.

At Dr. Tenny's dinner at the legation, on the same evening, the Bristish minister, Sir John Jordan, the dean of the diplomatic corps, was present. He is a veteran diplomat and I was curious to know what his reaction would be to Dr. Tenny's speech which expressed hope that in the current political crisis there would be hearty cooperation between England, China and the United States. This was a fine opportunity to put his cards on the table! The premier made a lengthy talk expressing the same sentiments, then everybody waited for Sir John. He stood pat! One never gets into trouble if you don't talk.

Admiral Sah's tiffin for Mrs. Gleaves at the Oriental Hotel in the Chinese City was an outstanding event of our visit to Peking. Several Chinese ladies who spoke English or French were among the guests. The food was Chinese but cooked in Western style—bird's nest soup and shark fins from Sandakan were the first courses. Three kinds of Chinese wine were served—Shansi wine, a Chefoo wine and a greenish wine, very heavy, called In-Cheng, 95 percent alcohol and much like vodka. The Shansi wine I think is a cultivated taste.

After the tiffin the ladies of the party were received at the residence of the president by Madame President, who presented Mrs. Gleaves with two handsomely embroidered silk cushions and lacquer boxes of fine tea.

One night at the legation I met Putnam-Weale whose views on the situation differed materially from those of nearly everyone else in Peking. When I remarked that, he replied, "You have probably talked with men who sit at their desks. I take a broader view. I was born in China, speak Chinese, and go everywhere among them, in their cafes, and they all know me and treat me as one of their own. So I hear and see things from a different and wider viewpoint."

I have always thought he was right. Ten years later when he was acting as commissioner of customs at Tientsin, Mr. Simpson—to use his real name—was murdered by Manchurian gunmen.

The government invited us to make a journey to the Great Wall at Nankow Pass. Since the president's private car had blown out a steam pipe the night before, we were given a special coach. The sky was clear, but a half-gale of wind was blowing and the thermometer was down to 15°. From the car windows we saw the never-ending stream of camels loaded with merchandise for Peking merchants coming down from beyond the Great Wall. It was a long, rough and hard climb from the railroad station to the wall and the wind was too strong and the weather too intensely cold to remain long. The following spring we all had the good fortune to make the journey again.

On the night of our return from the wall, Marshal Tuan gave a stag dinner of 24 covers. As it is a Chinese custom for guests to leave immediately after coffee, I got back to the hotel at a reasonable hour.

At an afternoon tea given by the wife of Commander Chen of the navy, we met Madame Tze—the mother of the "Pearl Concubine" who had been put to death by order of the Old Buddha. The latter is said to have been the one true love of the Emperor Kuan-hsi the father by her of the present emperor of Manchukuo. At that time the child was known as the Boy Emperor and was living in retirement in the Forbidden City under the care of an English tutor. The old lady, who was as commanding as the Old Buddha, was followed around the rooms by a little boy who carried her pipe, not at all like our pipes, but an elaborate affair with a silver bowl containing water. The pipe itself held only enough substance for two or three puffs.

Madame Tze was a personage and a character. Her daughter had lived in the palace with the Empress Dowager, and being bright and precocious, had heard more than she should have and seen more than she should have. At times she even ventured to correct the Old Buddha. The result was that the Pearl Concubine met her death by falling into a well, accidently, of course, so it was given out. With the Madame Tze was her daughter-in-law, the Princess Yu.

The party—while not especially gay—was still interesting as it gave us a glimpse of Chinese home life. Mrs. Chen's two small daughters, dressed a la chinois, danced a two-step to Victrola music, and did it remarkably well. Mrs. Chen showed the ladies her wedding trousseau of beautiful embroidery and insisted that my daughter dress up in some of them. Afterwards she sent some of the garments to our hotel so Evelina could put them on for a photograph, which was taken by an English photographer in the legation quarter.

A few nights after the visit to Madame Chen, Madame Tze and the princess invited Mrs. Gleaves to dinner. In the party besides my wife and daughter were Mrs. Poe and Mrs. Horton. My daughter's account of the dinner follows:

> We were greeted by the "Old Lady", her son and his numerous wives. The

latest, a singsong girl, was a great contrast in her gay silk trousers and jacket, with flowers in her hair and vivid makeup, to the other wives all dressed in blue denim trousers and jackets.

They were all very interested in our clothes. My feather fan was passed around for each to see and a great many questions asked about my tulle evening dress and earrings. The singsong girl even lifted my hair on the side to see if I had ears!

A young Chinese girl, who was a teacher and spoke excellent English, was the only other guest outside of the family and she acted as interpreter, as none of the others spoke any English.

We were taken to tea in the courtyard and were shown the goldfish—great tubs of them, all rare specimens. Then the "Old Lady" with great pride showed us several scrolls of Chinese characters written for and presented to her by the Empress Dowager who had caused her daughter to be put to death. Apparently there was no ill feeling!

When we went out to dinner only the No. 1 wife was allowed to sit at the table. The others waited on us. We had the traditional 40 courses, the only one I can recall by name being fried chicken liver. We ate, or attempted to eat, with chopsticks, but it was a difficult task.

The "Old Lady's" son was the only man present.

A dinner at the foreign office included 50 guests with a number of Chinese ladies present. The vice-minister who presided assured everyone that it was entirely social and unofficial. He punctuated his speech with quotations from the Chinese classics and dwelt upon the cordial relations and friendship that China was desirous of cultivating with the United States at that critical time. As a special compliment to Mrs. Gleaves, the wife of the vice-minister attended the dinner.

My Chinese flag lieutenant had been kept busy night and day with his new duties, and this night had followed a hard day. In the big reception room he was plied with questions by the American officers and finally when someone asked the name of a portrait, he raised his heavy lids and said, "Don't know. Too damn tired."

When our Nordic ancestors were wandering in forests 3,000 years ago, wearing skins of wild animals and eating nuts and roots, the Chinese were reading and studying the classics. They were painters of exquisite scenery and the carvers of delicate traceries in ivory which have never been equaled. Their best work (or what the "civilized" Allies left of it after the destruction of the palace in 1860 and the looting of Peking during the Boxer Rebellion in 1900) we saw in the museum in the Forbidden City—works of art, some 3,000 years old, such as ivories and jade, porcelains and manuscripts, bewildering in their marvelous workmanship—all handwork of a people whom we of the West call heathen!

We drove back to the hotel through Central Park, bleak and unattractive in the intense cold, thickly grown with fir trees but the ground bare and void of vegetation of any kind. At the entrance to the park is a simple arch in honor of President Wilson which cost about $100,000 and bears the inscription, "Right makes might". The arch was made from the stones of Baron von Kettler's monument, taken down after the World War.

The premier's dinner at his private residence was purely an official affair. Hearing some noise outside after the dinner, I looked through the partly closed blinds and saw the house was surrounded by an armed guard of soldiers. A significant sign of the times! The premier is famous for his collection of manuscripts and jade. Being also minister of war, several Chinese army officers were guests, two of whom were division commanders. I noted that, just as it was 40 years before, the same people are usually invited to all the parties. The social set in Peking is limited!

On New Year's Day the president, Gen. Shih-ch'ang Hsu, received me and my staff in private audience accompanied by the charge d'affaires and the interpreter, Mr. Peck. The presentations were made in the audience chamber of the emperor's palace, called the Throne Hall of Purple Effulgence—the approach to which is impressive and even thrilling. The hall itself is a vast apartment with a lofty ceiling supported by columns but is extremely simple in its furnishings.

As we were to be the last presented, we were assigned a place apart—in a sort of alcove from which we saw the ceremony. The president entered from his private room and shook hands with the minister of each nation, beginning with the British minister, Sir John Jordan, the dean of the diplomatic corps who was resplendent in gold lace. He was of striking presence, tall and thin, white haired with an inscrutable sphinx-like face. Next in seniority was Mr. Obata, the Japanese minister, and his suite—in red and gold. He it was who had presented the famous 21 demands and it was especially interesting to watch the meeting between the president and the minister, but the face of each was like carved bronze.

After the diplomats were dismissed, the Roman Catholic archbishop of north China and vicar apostolic of Peking, and two priests were received in private audience which lasted only two or three minutes. The white haired prelate wore a loose, purple robe and, saving the lack of his teeth, would have been most distinguished in appearance.

The president, surrounded by a group of brilliantly uniformed officers and soldiers, received us with marked cordiality. The ceremonies were in all respect similar to those at Tokyo. I was escorted by the grand master of ceremonies on one side and on the other by Vice Admiral Tsai. The American officers—who at that time had been deprived of chapeau, epaulets, etc., by order of the secretary of the navy—contrasted sharply with their escorts in their gold trappings. A bow on entering was followed by a second and a third as we approached the president. He held my hand while speaking, congratulated me on my birthday (January 1) and said the beautiful weather was a happy augury of future happiness during the year. This concluded our presentation.

In the evening of the same day the Imperial City and the Chinese city were illuminated with thousands of paper lanterns in honor of the day. The Chinese had recently adopted the Gregorian calendar, which is strictly observed by the officials, but the millions adhere to the lunar year of 13 months.

The day before I left Peking was appointed for the tiffin with the president. Dr. Tenny drove with me to the palace and the others followed. It was enlightening to listen to the aged and charming charge d'affaires, who had known his China thoroughly for 40 years and is most highly esteemed in the diplomatic corps.

We had to park our cars at the palace gates, and transferred to the president's car for the drive to the palace on the Southern Lake. The grand master of ceremonies and Admiral Tsai were in the entrance hall and escorted us through the audience chamber, past troops and music, to a smaller room where the president was waiting. He wore the conventional costume of brocade silk and was most cordial. The general was a tall, spare man in his early 60s highly thought of by his people. We drank tea until some other guests arrived. Among them I noticed Captain Blamer, Captain Luby and Lieutenant Holcombe—all wearing the decoration of the Striped Tiger which had just been awarded and accounted for their delay in arriving.

The president then rose and after greeting the officer, led the way with me to luncheon. The arrangements were simple and in perfect taste, the flowers profuse and very beautiful. There were 14 at the table including three cabinet ministers for a most attractively served luncheon with excellent food and wine.

The president was a man of culture and wide education. He was essentially an agriculturist and on that subject was especially informative. After the luncheon he took us into another room past the household guards where he showed us his fine collection of flowers and dwarfed pines. One flower, named the la-mei, is a yellow bud of sweet and pungent fragrance; and he broke off a branch and gave it to me for my wife with his compliments.

My farewell dinner the same night at the Wagon-Lits to the officials was the last function of my visit. Marshal Tuan did not speak. Before the premier spoke, in reply to my remarks, he obtained the marshal's permission—from which I judge that in China arms do not yield to the toga. At the table the marshal told me that he had never been in the hotel but twice—the other time having been when he returned my call.

Our send-off the next morning was in keeping with all that had gone before. At the station the government had erected a temporary arch bearing the words "au revoir". On the platform were Admiral Sah and five other admirals, also one general, several colonels, a representative of the premier and another of Marshal Tuan. There were two bands and two guards of honor. As the train hauled out, the bands played, the guards saluted and the officers waved their caps.

All the attention paid to the American officers at Peking was repeated at Tientsin. Col. William Morrow of the 15th U.S. Infantry, a prince of hosts, drove me in an open car to his headquarters at the far end of the city. The weather was piercingly cold, but clear and windy. A heavy dust storm was in the making. There was an interesting lot of people to meet us at tiffin—a Chinese admiral, the Italian commandant, Colonel Fassini-Camassi, who proved the life of the party, the French Colonel Pasquier, and a number of others. The warm room with its table beautifully decorated with cherry blossoms (artificial, of course) and asparagus was a striking contrast to the bleak landscape of sand and brown dirt visible through the windows.

In the afternoon we called on the governor. He made several observations about Chinese porcelain: the five claw dragon is indicative of imperial reign, not necessarily imperial possession; porcelain which has no hallmarks is not as valuable as that which has, and hallmarks indicate that the porcelain might have been owned by the imperial family; the five claw dragon indicates porcelain made for the imperial family, but not necessarily owned by them; ordinarily the dragon had only four claws.

On the way to Nanking, at Tsinan, the tuchun, General Ni, sent his seventh son to the train as his representative to urgently invite me to remain. It is the custom when an official sends a representative of his family, to send his eldest son. Number seven was the eldest son available and he was careful to explain that his elder brothers were all absent in the country. It was a matter of great regret that I could not accept the invitation which included a visit to the tomb of Confucius.

At Pukow the train was late, but there was time before dark to visit the sepulcher of Chu Yuan-chang, the founder of the Chinese dynasty that bears his name, and to visit the Ming Tombs, across the river in Nanking, which are not as interesting as those near Peking. The streets of the ancient city are narrow and crooked, but our chauffeur drove at breakneck speed showing much skill, but no judgment or regard for pedestrians.

The troops were paraded at General Li's yamen and made a handsome display in the outer court, the three inner courts and up to the steps of the entrance. The streets between the yamen and consulate, a distance of two or three miles, were lined with soldiers on both sides. Four soldiers stood on each side of the car on the running boards as a protection to the general—a significant indication of the political situation.

We arrived the following morning at Shanghai, and there were the same ceremonies at the North Station that marked our departure. I was glad to get back on board ship and get a chance to look at the mail before my own luncheon to the foreign officers stationed in Shanghai, which I gave on board the flagship.

The banquet in the evening given by the special envoy for foreign affairs, Cheng Yang, was a brilliant affair and was said to be the most elaborate given in Shanghai in many years. There were 200 guests—civil, military and naval. All the consulates were represented. Opposite the host sat Wang-i-Tang, the famous northern delegate to the Peace Conference in Shanghai, one of the most talked of men of the day in China. A big, fine man, he looked like a pundit.

In front of my chair was suspended an illuminated Chinese character, which the envoy told me meant four blessings as defined by Confucius—health, wealth, honorable offspring and an untarnished name.

21 The *South Dakota* at Vladivostok

On 8 January 1920 while at Shanghai, I received a dispatch from the USS *Albany* at Vladivostok that the American troops had been ordered to evacuate Siberia. As they were supposed to remain until after the Czech troops had been evacuated, this was real news—but not surprising as the China press had published the increasing demands in congress for the withdrawal of our soldiers.

In the afternoon of the same day we dropped down the river and anchored off the Woosung forts to wait for the next tide. At daylight we got underway again and were soon heading north. Shortly after leaving the Yangtze, the captain sighted a Chinese junk displaying signals of distress. We ran down to it, lowered a boat to offer assistance and found they were out of rice, which was all they wanted. We gave them the rice and in return they sent us a quantity of lobsters for all the messes and a cryptogrammic message to the admiral: "If you get ill, put it in the papers." I could only guess that John did not trust the lobsters, but we took a chance.

Two days later we passed through the battle waters of Tsushima Straits. Our track thence lay close to the rocky coast of Korea which was covered with snow down to sea edge.

On the morning of the twelfth the ship arrived off Vladivostok after breaking through the ice floes off Russian Islands. An icebreaker and a tug came out to meet us and to bring our mail. At this time the weather was clear, cold and exhilarating, but the shores, covered with snow, were bleak and treeless and without sign of life of any kind.

At noon we came within sight of the city on the south side of the Golden Horn. Suddenly the wind shifted to the northward, blowing with great violence accompanied by heavy snow, while the thermometer dropped below zero. Entering the harbor we noticed that the wharves were practically deserted. The few merchant ships tied up to them seemed to be abandoned. Further inside the bay were the masts of several American, Japanese and French men-of-war. On shore the Japanese and American flags were displayed everywhere. Over the largest building downtown was a big American ensign, which the pilot said was over the U.S. Army headquarters.

At the head of the dock assigned to the *South Dakota* was a sergeant's guard sent by the Italian high commissioner. Bravely they faced the blizzard at present arms, but the music of their band was blown away over the frozen hills—not a note reaching the ship. I felt relieved when these sons of sunny Italy suddenly broke ranks and scampered up the steep, rocky and completely empty street to their barracks.

So this was Siberia! Snow, ice and blizzards!

The afternoon was taken up in receiving officials, all of the visitors bundled in furs. The first to come on board was the Chinese high commissioner, Mr. Li-kao, a gentleman whom I was to see often. He spoke no English but had an efficient young interpreter, a graduate of Harvard, I believe. The commissioner and his suite lived in a special train on tracks near the shoreline. Commodore Lin, commander of the Chinese squadron, followed and then came the representatives of the other "allies and associates" ashore and afloat, with the exception of the Japanese rear admiral lying a few hundred yards away in his flagship, who sent his aide to say that on account of the weather he would defer his call. This excuse of a hardy sailor man was naive to say the least!

Captain Watts of the *Albany*, who had been in Vladivostok some time, prepared a paper for my information on the political situation. This and the aide-memoire given me by our ambassador at Tokyo outlining the American policy in Japan, Siberia and China were a help in unraveling the tangle of a confused puzzle as it existed in the beginning of 1920.

As is well-known, President Wilson had reluctantly consented to the occupation of Eastern Siberia by American troops and had finally agreed to send 7,000 men. The British, French, Italian and Chinese sent much smaller contingents, but the Japanese sent 72,000 which spread over the country as far west as Lake Baikal and to the south along the Amur and Ussuri rivers. Later they overflowed into the strategic island of Sakhalin to the northward.

In the beginning of 1920 the Czecho-Slovak troops were on their trek to the eastward and the sea, after months of fighting in Siberia from the Ural Mountains to Lake Baikal. The peace had ended their hopes for a successful issue of their ambitions and they were now preparing to withdraw from Siberia and return to Europe in transports provided by Great Britain and the United States. Congress was demanding the speedy evacuation of our troops, but Japanese troops continued to arrive. These newcomers were called "replacements" and were garrisoned in the forts around the city, or sent out into the towns along the railroads.

Mr. Wilson, in answering an inquiry of the senate, had said that our troops were in Siberia to protect the Czecho-Slovaks against hostile armies in their movement to Vladivostok and "to steady any efforts of the Russians at self-defense, in the establishment of law and order in which they might be willing to accept advice, and to protect the Siberian Railway from the Bolsheviks; to protect also the vast quantities of military stores which were lying in the open air, the railroad yards and on the hillside."

These stores were scattered about in the vicinity of Egerscheldt Point, at the eastern end of the harbor. They belonged to the Russians and were estimated to be worth one billion dollars.

When the *South Dakota* arrived at Vladivostok the dominant military figure in the city was General Oi, commander in chief of the Japanese forces in Siberia, whose headquarters were in a handsome building on a hill in rear of the Svetlanskaya, the main street of the city. His chief of staff was Lieutenant General Inagaki. The headquarters at all times swarmed like a beehive with Japanese soldiers.

Rear Admiral Kawahara, commanding a Japanese special naval division, was flying his flag in H.I.J.U.S. *Hizen,* originally *Retvizan,* built for the Russians and captured by the Japanese at Tsushima. The fact of sending this ship to do duty in a Russian harbor and her presence there, were constant sources of irritation to the Russians—and fairly illustrates the Japanese psychology.

Practically all the Allied troops had been withdrawn at this time, except the Americans and the Japanese. Only a handful of the others remained on guard duty at the foreign missions.

About 600 Chinese troops were in barracks on the western end of the Golden Horn, and about 3,000 Czecho-Slovakian troops in process of evacuation were also in barracks not far from the Chinese. The Czechs were commanded by a brilliant young major general, Stanislau Cecek, who had taken part in most of the fighting with the Bolsheviks since his troops had started on their long march through Siberia to the Pacific coast. About 3,000 American troops remained in the Vladivostok area, the others were distributed along the Siberian railroad as far west as Lake Baikal.

General Janin was the chief of the French military commission and

General Lavergne commanded the French base at Vladivostok. Besides these and Mr. Li, the other diplomatic representatives with whom I was associated, included the Japanese high commissioner, Mr. Tsuneo Matsudaira, afterwards ambassador to the U.S.; and Dr. V. Kirsa, chief of the Czecho diplomatic mission. These were the chief dramatis personae when, to use Mr. Putnam-Weale's expression, Siberia "was slipped on the green baize."

General Oi's rank as a full general was junior by five or six weeks to my corresponding rank of full admiral, although his was permanent and mine, by the grace of congress, only temporary. As it is an international agreement for the naval officer, whatever his rank, on entering port to make the first call on the military commander, I called by appointment on the Japanese general at his headquarters.

He was a short, rotund man, about my own age, with an impassive face, of course, and while coldly polite was meticulously observant of all the courtesies. He spoke no English, but General Inagaki, who had studied in Europe, knew English well. I could not fathom what was in the air, because the last time I was at the admiralty in Tokyo, Admiral Kato told me he had specially written to Admiral Kawahara directing him to offer his services for anything I might need. That a curtain had been let down was evident.

The Russians at Vladivostok kept very much to themselves. Lieutenant General Rozanoff was in command of the district, Major General Verigo was in command of the fortress and Rear Admiral Fedorovich commanded the Russian naval forces in the Far East. The notorious Semenoff and Kalmakoff were frequently heard of as operating in the Priamur district, but were not seen in Vladivostok while we were there. I met the admiral only once and that was when he came on board and demanded that the United States wireless station on Russian Island be turned over to him as the representative of the Russian government! I declined and when I returned his call he was "out"!

Everywhere the Japanese troops were the most conspicuous by the red facings on their uniforms and their odd-shaped fur caps. They invariably carried their rifles and full cartridge belts. The Japanese staff officers were fond of dashing through the streets in automobiles. General Oi always displayed his four star red flag in his car, when like Jehu—the son of Nimshi—he "drove furiously" as was his wont on the Svetlanskaya accompanied by his personal aides.

The city remained quiet until the end of the month. Daily the grapevine hummed with rumors, but little happened except every night there was desultory firing in the streets and along the waterfront, to which little attention was paid. As the streets were badly lighted, and for the most part ill-paved, few people remained out after night fall. It was considered dangerous to go abroad after dark.

During the last week in January events speeded up and it was evident that a crisis was at hand. One afternoon I received a call from an American, the wife of a Russian naval captain bearing the name of a famous family that is legendary in Russia. As she entered my cabin she exclaimed, "We are beaten, we have lost everything!" She asked if I would take charge of two small black handbags and gave me a letter addressed to her mother in New York, to be delivered to our ambassador in Tokyo in case she was murdered. She seemed unduly alarmed and thought me frivolous for asking if the bags contained the crown jewels.

Opening a small reticule to get a handkerchief, she took out an automatic and laid it on the table. "Do you know how to use that?" I asked.

"Oh, rather," she said. Then she requested asylum for herself and her husband on board the *South Dakota*, which, of course, I refused as neither was in danger of life. She remained to tea and I never saw her again as she left Vladivostok with the Russians in the *Orel*. Later I received a scolding letter from her in Shanghai.

The same day the director of the Russian naval school at the arsenal requested me by letter to advise him as to the propriety of his leaving Vladivostok. It was a pathetic sort of letter, but of course I declined to advise him. However, I had information that the cadets of the school had been already transferred to the Russian naval yacht, *Orel*, lying at a dock close to the *South Dakota*.

I then received information that the Bolsheviks (partisans) under Krakavetski would arrive in three days from Nikolsk and before that time General Rozanoff would probably flee the city. It was not expected that the host of officers or the naval cadets he had with him would seriously resist.

The next evening Consul Macgowan telephoned to say that General Rozanoff had just left the consulate, having requested the consul to ask me if I would request the partisans to give him three days extension on their ultimatum, which was dated January 28, but which he had received only a few minutes before. He also asked the consul if I would grant protection to the Russian officers and their wives.

I replied that I could not comply with his first request because that would be interference in the affairs of the Russian people. Nor could I comply with the second. I took this stand temporarily because I felt that in all probability an assurance to the general of protection for his officers and families might encourage him to offer resistance, which otherwise he might not do.

I told the consul to inform the consuls of all nations not having ships in port that I would afford them the usual protection on board the *South Dakota* and *Albany* and also on board the newly arrived *Woban*, if necessary. At the consul's suggestion, I requested the secretary of the Y.M.C.A. to place his hut, which was very close to the *South Dakota*, at the disposal of the Allied consuls for the protection of such people onshore as might seek refuge, which would be guarded by our army.

The consul had written a letter to the master of the *Woban* telling him to give refuge to any unarmed person who might ask for it. He asked me to place a guard of sailors on board that ship, but I felt this would not be a good move as I would not countenance an attempt to take off the ship any who might come aboard as a political refugee. Therefore offering the ship as a refuge might unnecessarily produce complications in the future.

My journal for 30 January 1920 reads:

The day has been quiet but everyone, at least the officials, are standing by for anything that may happen. The National Democrats, as they call themselves (the same that captured Nikol'sk), are expected to arrive anytime between now and Monday.

The *Orel* is getting ready for sea and is said to have all of the naval cadets on board, as Mr. Hodson, the British high commissioner, told me this morning. There are rumors that General Rozanoff is going in her; also other rumors to the effect that the officers will not take him.

I returned the calls this morning of Rear Admiral Behrens of the Russian navy, the new naval commander, and found him at the admiralty, unshaven and looking very forlorn. The building was filled with Russian refugees, men and women, evidently waiting for interviews. Drove with Blamer to Egerscheldt Station to return the call on General Ilustranoff, the Russian liaison officer, but he was not in his railroad car. The Amur River is frozen over solid and automobiles are crossing on the ice to Russian Island.

5 p.m.: Just returned from a long drive to Second River. There are more

soldiers than usual in the streets, but everybody seemed to be going about their lawful duties: children coasting or coming from school, the shops are open and the Svetlanskaya has its usual busy crowd of people.

General Oi today denies positively that he intended to stop the Bolsheviks outside the town, as he does not propose to interfere with them unless they create disorder in the city.

Rozanoff has had an interview with General Oi. He told General Oi that he had less than 100 men he could trust. General Oi explained his view of the situation and it is hoped that Rozanoff will offer no resistance. He also asked for an interview with American Consul Macgowan at six o'clock. It is expected that he will leave town tonight.

The Czechs have declined to assist in the patrol of the city as they say they have no men for the purpose. This is their official reason, but as a matter of fact they are not cooperating because they consider they were treated unfairly at the time of Gaida's "revolution" last November when he was prevented from pulling off his coup by the action of the Allies who established a cordon at the railroad station, not only confining the fighting to a restricted area but also preventing reinforcements.

I shall land 400 men in the morning who are assigned to patrol the residential and business portion of the city. Captain Watts is in charge of the landing party, but in accordance with regulations when our sailors and marines get onshore they will be under the orders of the army. Major Johnson of the U.S. Army will command the combined Allied forces. The Japanese have agreed to send him 16 companies of infantry.

I have just heard that the Bolsheviks are only 21 miles from Vladivostok.

My journal continues:

Saturday, January 31, 1920

At 5:30 a.m. the officer of the deck came into the cabin, awoke me and reported that the *Orel* was leaving the harbor. At seven o'clock a few stray shots were heard onshore near the ship. As Rozanoff has been informed that the ultimatum would expire at nine in the morning, it was supposed that the revolution, if any, would begin at that time. About 8:45 the discharge of a field piece was heard, and also a machine gun in the direction of the consulate.

Lieutenant Holcombe went to investigate and on his return reported a number of Bolshevik troops around Rozanoff's house, which was not far from the American consulate. The field piece had been fired at his residence, but the shell struck the ground and exploded in front of the house. There was not much excitement, and he had also been up to the consulate with the consul.

In the meantime, I had seen from my airport with my glasses the irregular troops straggling through the cut in the road leading from Second River—several hundred of them. Holcombe brought back the request of Major Johnson to land the patrol, which was done immediately. They got off in good shape from both ships.

Nine o'clock passed without any unusual disturbances and at a quarter to ten my car came. With Blamer and Holcombe I drove up the Svetlanskaya as far as Rozanoff's house, stopping a few minutes at the consulate. I passed a number of partisans, Bolsheviks, National Democrats, or whatever they might be, in the streets—infantry, cavalry, artillery—all well-equipped, fine-looking and for the most part quite young.

The streets at this time were crowded with people—men, women and children. Everybody seemed orderly, no excitement. It seemed more like a parade of troops in peacetime than the capture of a city, but there was an unusual display of red flags.

Mr. Macgowan told me that General Rozanoff had been arrested by the cossacks and taken to General Oi's apartment, on the top floor of our own consulate building, directly over tie consul's private apartment. While I was standing at the window in the consul's office looking into the street, he pointed to the household effects of General Rozanoff—bedding, etc.—that had just been brought into the compound.

The partisans have established a guard at the railroad station.

General Oi in a proclamation yesterday stated that the Japanese army, with a view of maintaining peace and also not to hinder the line of communications, would not permit fighting in the city. In this he acted independently of the other Allies, who had agreed not to interfere with the internal affairs of the Russians.

This morning, when the partisans were coming down the road into the town, a machine gun was fired from the roof of General Oi's apartment over the American consulate. General Inagaki stepped in front of the field battery of the partisans, raised his hands, and told them that the Allies would not permit them to fire in the streets.

Colonel Eichelberger of the American staff heard this interpreted, and disclaimed it at once, telling the partisan leader that it was the Japanese and not the Allies who stated there would be no street fighting. In spite of this, however, the troops did enter but there was no street fighting.

Rozanoff was taken by the Japanese, in a Japanese uniform, from Oi's apartment to Japanese headquarters. Major Johnson recognized

Rozanoff as he entered the headquarters and Rozanoff tried to pull his cap down over his face, but it was too small, so he turned the collar up around his neck.

While this was going on, news came that Major Clark of the Inter-Allied Railroad Commission had just telephoned because he had received a message from the partisan leader at the 21-Verst Station saying the Japanese guards were interfering with the passage of their trains and if they did not stop, the partisans would tear up the track between Nikol'sk and Vladivostok.

As this would seriously affect the evacuation by our own troops and the Czechs, this was protested. General Oi, who said he knew nothing about it, promised to look into the matter at once.

February came in with snow and gales, but the weather was not colder than New York or Boston.

Three armored trains arrived at First River with 1,000 partisan troops on board from Nikol'sk. The partisans ousted the zemstors and made themselves disagreeably felt.

Colonel Krakavetski (someone said his name sounded like a machine gun) called on board the *South Dakota*. He was a typical revolutionist in appearance—tall and slender, keen brown eyes and a noticeably firm mouth and jaw. His uniform was neat and well-fitted. He wore no insignia of rank but, of course, the inevitable splash of red on the standing collar of his tunic. He said the partisans wanted the new Far Eastern Republic modeled on American lines.

He had had an interesting career, but was a stormy petrel. In the Gaida revolution he was one of the directorate of three appointed to select temporary members of the Siberian Constituent Assembly. When the meeting was raided, Krakavetski escaped and found asylum at the American headquarters, but fled again and was not seen in Vladivostok until the so-called coup d'etat of January 31 when he returned at the head of the partisan troops.

It was not expected that his government in the city would be stablized, so the shopkeepers were keeping their shutters closed. Even the Hong Kong and Shanghai Bank—which had a large amount of gold—asked me if I thought it safe to retain so much treasure. If not, would I take it on board ship?

Gradually quiet prevailed. Japanese troops continued to arrive from Japan—Japanese officers still called them replacements. They were put in barracks built by the Russians at First and Second Rivers. The paper ruble dropped to 350, and it was impossible to buy a gold one at any price.

On the 13th, H.M.S. *Cairo* arrived flying the flag of Rear Admiral Borrett. A significant incident occurred: I signaled to him as he steamed into the Golden Horn that it had been agreed by the Allies to waive all gun salutes on account of the disturbed conditions onshore.

However, the admiral on nearing the *South Dakota* displayed the American flag and fired 17 guns. As soon as this was returned gun for gun, Commodore Lin continued the motion, followed by that delightful Frenchman, Capt. Jean Hervey, commanding the French cruiser. All the vessels saluted regardless of the oral agreement except the Japanese ship, which was conspicuous by its silence.

The next day the confirmation of Kolchak's death was received in Vladivostok. Kolchak reputedly was on his way to Salonica for the British government when he was recalled from Japan where he then was and went at once to Eastern Siberia. On November 18 (1918) he overthrew the directorate at Omsk and proclaimed himself "Supreme Ruler".

This apparently was a mistake for the Russians were tired of rulers of any sort. On assuming control he pledged himself to call a constituent assembly, but he made concessions to the old regime in order to obtain the allegiance of General Horvath, whom he appointed governor of the Far East. Ataman Semenoff was his obstinate and bitter enemy, as were also the brigand chief Kalmakoff and others. Later Gaida conspired against him.

Forced by these men, Kolchak steadily lost strength, in spite of the fact that he was favored by the United States and Great Britain. It was a singular historical fact that Kolchak was trapped in the Irkutsk station at the very hour that the first Japanese troop train arrived there. Although the Japanese commander made frantic efforts to save him, Kolchak was led away by Bolsheviks who had entered his car in the early morning to arrest him. The train was surrounded by armed troops and "great numbers of machine guns".

"I have only one question to ask," said Kolchak to the Bolshevik in charge. "Does this mean that the Allies have deserted me?" He was told that it did and was shot immediately.

General Janin, when accused of being directly responsible for Kolchak's betrayal, denied this in a long statement. He had been ordered by the Allied high commissioner to give safe transit to the admiral and the gold reserve of 40 million pounds he had with him and declared that he had exerted himself to do so, but had received no support from the high commissioner.

One night I dined on board the Japanese flagship with Admiral Kawahara. After dinner as we sat in the after cabin looking at various photographs, I amused myself watching General Inagaki writing Chinese characters and discussing their similarity to the Japanese with Commodore Lin. Inagaki used a bamboo brush and was deftly writing Chinese with the finesse and delicacy of an engraver.

It was an interesting group—worth remembering—in the cabin of the flagship. Kawahara had participated in the battles between China and Japan in 1904-1905. Admiral Borrett commanded the *Monarch* during the chase of the *Goeben* and *Breslau*, and also was in the battle of Jutland. Commodore Lin was a veteran of the Sino-Japanese wars and fought at the battle of the Yalu. General Inagaki, General Oi's chief of staff, fought in the Manchurian campaign under General Nogi.

Referring to my diary again, I find:

February 20th. Influenza has broken out aboard ship and we have 30 cases which have been transferred to the army hospital.

Vladivostok is so crowded with refugees, soldiers and foreign commissioners that many people are compelled to live in trains on the railroad tracks along the waterfront. The Chinese high commissioner has his special train astern the berth of the *Hai Yung*, the Chinese flagship.

I found him in his car this afternoon. He told me of a cable just received from the supreme council in Paris informing him that armed Japanese troops had crossed the frontier and entered Manchuria and that he had directed the Chinese commanding officer to disarm them.

February 21: My opinion has been asked as to the propriety of recommending closing our consulate here. The facts are the United States is paying over $1,000 a month for the lease of the building. The only other consulate we have now in all Russia is at Chita, the others having been closed—including those at Odessa, Irkutsk, Omsk, etc. I advised closing the consulate temporarily. There are only 40 men and ten women American citizens remaining in Vladivostok, all engaged in more or less nondescript mercantile enterprises and who, as someone remarked, carry their offices in their hats.

The weather continues cold: thermometer "0°". The Golden Horn is frozen solid and the icebreakers have difficulty in keeping a way open for the ships. From Egerscheldt Point the view of the Gulf of Amur is extraordinarily fine, stretching to the limit of visibility under its white cover of snow and ice. Russian Island across the straits looks as bleak as Tierra del

Fuego. Communication with it is easy now by either sled, droshky or automobile.

Commodore Lin gave a small musicale on board the *Hai Yung* this afternoon. There were five pieces in the orchestra and a young Chinese girl who sang well, but never got off one key.

March 1: Consul General Harris gave a large dinner party in his private car. He has in his train, besides the locomotive, six coaches and pays for the outfit about eight dollars gold per day! During the dinner Mr. Harris told a thrilling ghost story of an experience he had when he was consul in Smyrna.

The setting was perfect for such a story, which he said was 80 percent true. There was a light fall of snow on the ground and the moon shining through the clouds cast a weird light from behind the drawn curtains of the diner. Not a sound came from the outside, except that of the ships' bells striking the hour. As the climax of the story approached Mr. Harris, who is a perfect actor, gave imitation of a rising wind, thunder and rain. All the candles were blown out and the car was in darkness while he was spinning the yarn.

The story was of the mysterious murder of a young wife, the opening of her grave at night, the disappearance of her coffin, and later the apparent reappearance of the woman in a streetcar, and a shooting affray at the consulate at midnight in the presence of Harris himself. At this point Harris ended his story by suddenly firing six blank shots through the roof of the car from his own revolver.

When the lights were turned on, Major Lively of the Red Cross astonished everyone by saying, "That story reminds me . . . "

How could anyone have the temerity to tell a story after such a thrilling one?

The major, however, was equal to the occasion and made the car roar with laughter. He said once a man was trying to explain the crucifixion to an ignorant person. He described the harrowing details and when he finished the other man said, "Well, that is a horrible story, Sir, and I hope it ain't true."

3 March 1920: Dined with General Oi in his apartments. There were 20 guests at the table. Besides Oi and Inagaki there were American officers including those just back from one and a half years' campaign with our troops in the interior of Siberia and a number of Japanese army and navy officers.

At the fish course, an enormous but delicate fish imported for the occasion from Japan was placed before the general. He removed the eyes and insisted upon giving me one, he taking the other, saying that in Japan the eyes are considered the best part of the fish. The eye seemed to me to be as big as an oyster and to gaze reproachfully from the edge of the plate, for needless to say I could not eat it. It was a severe physical test to which I did not succumb. The British Captain Carrington sitting opposite me said afterwards, "You handled that eye with tact and diplomacy."

After dinner General Oi said he wanted to discuss the situation in Vladivostok with me and began by saying that it was essential for Japan and the United States to cooperate and work together in harmony. His interpeter—Captain———, a bright army officer—said, "His Excellency says, 'What is your opinion?' "

I spoke slowly, deliberately and at some length. When the general replied he spoke even longer, so I waited with interest for Captain N——— to translate. To my great disappointment he said, "His Excellency says, 'Absolutely'." That was all.

The *Carlisle* is secured on the opposite side of our float. I took Carrington back to his ship in my car and went on board with him for a doch-an-dorrach.

March 4: I called a conference on board the flagship and asked the American representatives for a suggestion of how to get in touch with American citizens here, relative to their attitude in the event of oppressive action by the provisional government and the Soviets (Bolsheviki) if the latter came into power.

It was decided that Mr. Macgowan should consult the principal American business people and ascertain their ideas on the question. (On the 9th Macgowan reported to the conference that the consensus of opinion was to continue on their occasions as long as possible and take their chances, in their hope to establish a permanent and lucrative trade in Vladivostok.)

Two telegrams were received from Mr. Smith in Chita which are considered encouraging in regard to the Czech evacuation. I radioed Washington that conditions continued quiet in Vladivostok and the interior, that I would sail for Japan in a few days and that Captain Watts would remain at Vladivostok in the *Albany*.

The transport *Thomas* has arrived. Evelina is on board with Mrs. Poe and Evelina secunda. Drove with the newcomers around the Golden Horn to Diomedes Bay and Ulysses Bay, to the cathedral in town and to Egerscheldt Point to show them Russian Islands and the frozen Gulf of Amur. The billion dollars' worth of war stores remains undisturbed, although one of the commissioners had proposed to divide them between the Allies.

March 8: The recent storms have covered the mountain roads with snow and ice and rendered them dangerous. After lunch we drove in an army car to Second River to see the old Russian fortifications and the extensive barracks now occupied by Japanese troops. If there is any real fighting near Vladivostok it will be out here.

The roads are cut from the sides of the mountain, in some places entirely unprotected on the outboard side, and parts are bad. Once our car skidded on broken stone to the very edge of a steep declivity. It was a close call.

After passing the summit and beginning the steep descent we turned around to go back to the city. As we swung around a sharp curve on the outer edge of a high cliff, we met a droshky rounding the same curve, but on the wrong side of the road and directly ahead of us. In passing, our steering gear jammed and our car ran off the road and turned over. Its momentum carried it down the side of the mountain until it struck a stump which stopped it.

There were five persons inside the car and on the front seat two soldiers. My daughter Evelina and the flag lieutenant climbed out of the car which was lying on its side, but the other three of us were wedged in on the rear seat and I had to break the glass shield to get out. Gasoline began to leak, but fortunately the chauffeur had shut off the engine. The car was of steel and had no side windows.

Just as the accident occurred, an automobile driven by a Russian and containing a Bolshevik soldier and a Russian woman appeared. After some argument they consented to take my wife, myself and also the soldier guide who was cut on the head and stunned. Holcombe, the chauffeur, Mrs. Poe and my daughter Evelina walked to town over a rough road—a distance of five miles—which they did in two and a half hours.

It was now about five o'clock and the sun was nearly down. With much difficulty I made the Russians understand we wanted to go to the American headquarters where we arrived in about an hour. Obtaining another car, I returned to the scene of the accident. It was now completely dark and on the way we narrowly escaped plunging off a stone bridge which was almost in ruins with only room enough on one side to cross.

I hoped to meet the remainder of the party on their way back, but saw no signs of them. My anxiety was great for we were in a lawless country. Night had fallen and there were no lights on the road. The country was swarming with banditti, who feared neither God, man nor the devil. I had great confidence in Holcombe and the soldier-chauffeur who were both armed, but even they could be easily overwhelmed.

As soon as we found and located our wrecked car I hurried back to the city expecting to find the party on board ship. To my consternation I was told by the officer of the deck that they had not returned. I went into the cabin to tell my wife that my search was unsuccessful and at that moment I heard my daughter's voice in the passageway, "Here we are."

I never was so relieved in my life. They had taken a shortcut through the railroad yards at First River and saved two miles. As both Mrs. Poe and my daughter were wearing thin shoes and the roads and paths were horribly rough with loose stones and snow and ice, it has always been a mystery how they accomplished the distance to the ship at all.

The Macgowans had planned a dinner and dance at the consulate in our honor. We were so late in getting back that I telephoned begging them not to wait, but to go ahead with the dinner and we would be up to the dance later.

They refused, and it was 8:30 when we finally arrived.

The Four Hundred of Vladivostok were at the party, and as the news of our adventure and escape had spread over the city, we were hailed with congratulations. The imperturbable General Oi was particularly polite and sympathetic.

The next day Mrs. Gleaves and her party sailed for Tsugaru in the *Hozan Maru* in a dense fog. The aemstvom official at the steamer made himself disagreeable by insisting the passports were not properly made out. Had it not been for Mr. Macgowan who was on board, he would have been more troublesome. Edgar Poe went in the same vessel as a bearer of dispatches to the ambassador in Tokyo.

There was a noisy mob on the dock alongside the *Hozan* and it was only by using Admiral Kawahara's name that I managed to get on board. One of Kawahara's aides was on board and also Colonel Baldessero, Italian high commissioner, so that I feel my party will be in good care.

March 10: Gave *diner d'adieu* on board the *South Dakota* to General Oi. I showed him a wood carving of a bronze and asked him what he thought it was worth. He said $100 and Commodore Lin said the same. As I had bought it for a mere song from a Russian naval captain I sent it back the following day and told him that he had apparently undervalued it, but he would not accept it.

On March 11 we took our departure. Mr. Li and Mr. Chang came on board at 7:30 a.m. to say good-bye. Mr. Li had secured a handsome house onshore for his residence, so no longer lived on the railroad tracks. Commodore Lin came down to our dock, but too late to get on board. Cast off lines at 8:10. All the foreign men-of-war signaled, "Good-bye, wish you pleasant voyage."

When fairly pointed out, we signaled, "Thank you, good-bye" and played the national anthems of the ships in order of rank.

Commander Fite, the fleet paymaster, dined with me. I found him a most efficient officer who should make a fine paymaster general. While we were at Vladivostok he prepared a paper showing that the officers and men in the fleet were placed at a great disadvantage in the matter of pay by the then rates of exchange and showed how this might be avoided. Mr. Daniels approved this and sent it to congress, but so far as I know, no action was taken.

22 To Nagasaki and Back to Siberia

The ship anchored in the man-of-war anchorage at Nagasaki on March 13, 1920. The governor, Vice Admiral Vanabeta, was in Tokyo. After leaving cards at the government house, our consul, Mr. DeNeill, took me to Mogi in his car. It was good to be in Japan again, that miniature country where everything is as neat as wax, except perhaps some of the narrow streets of Nagasaki.

The drive to Mogi was through beautiful and interesting country. The roads, cut into the hillsides, were fine examples of engineering skill, but some sharp, short curves seemed as inviting to disaster as those roads in the Siberian hills where we had the accident. It is a popular belief that the Japanese are not good aviators. I don't know, but they are fierce drivers of automobiles and revel in high speed.

We seemed to have brought bad weather with us and soon the terraced hills were hidden in fog and rain. Our excursion to Hot Springs, which the Mitsui Co. had planned, was given up on account of rain. Instead we went ashore and bought tortoiseshell combs and toilet sets.

The Japanese admiralty did a gracious thing: On our way through the Inland Sea I received a wireless from Tokyo saying that in appreciation of the cooperation of the American forces at Vladivostok with the Japanese, the government had granted us special permission to use our wireless while in Japanese waters. This was so unusual that I informed the secretary of the navy in Washington of the courtesy.

We made a pilgrimage to Momoyama, considered a sacred place, for not only is the Emperor Meiji buried there but close by his shrine is that of General Nogi, the national hero of the war with Russia—the faithful knight who refused to live when his royal master died. As we arrived at Nogi's tomb a company of Japanese bluejackets under arms, in smart uniforms, was just leaving having performed some formal ceremony in honor of the great soldier.

A haunting anecdote was told me of General Nogi: After the battle of Port Arthur in the war with Russia, the Japanese losses were so heavy in the capture of 203 Metre Hill that General Nogi sent word to the emperor that he did not feel he had a right to survive himself. This meant, of course, that he intended to commit suicide. He was commanded by the emperor to live, but ten years later when the emperor died, General Nogi and his wife immediately committed hara-kiri. Many Japanese say that while the funeral procession was passing to the tomb at Momoyama the soul of General Nogi hovered over the coffin in the shape of a blue flame.

A light rain was falling and a mist shrouded the tombs and the valley as we returned to Kyoto. I felt keenly what Julian Street calls the mysterious influence of Japan—in fact, one never escapes it whether in the gardens of Kyoto, at Lake Biwa and its picturesque temple overlooking the lake, passing down the rapids of the Juza-Gawa or standing on the sacred bridge at Nikko. It is a benediction from which no one would wish to escape.

From Kyoto we made rather a long visit at Kobe, and thence to Yokohama where we arrived April 1, about the same time that the latest masterpiece of British naval construction, the *Hawkins*, flying the ambassadorial flag of Sir Charles Elliot, entered and took the buoy inside the breakwater. As the ambassador went ashore immediately I did not see him, but we exchanged gun salutes.

When I called at the foreign office, Mr. Uchida said he had just received news of the massacre of Japanese at Nikolayev by the Bolsheviks. The following day Captain Watts cabled me that the Japanese troops were on the loose again in Vladivostok. There had been much firing the night before—no casualties and everything had quieted down quickly. General Oi had taken command of the city. Was the mask off? Were their words only "springes to catch wood-cocks?"

On Easter my wife and I went to service at the English chapel on the bluff. Floral decorations of acacia, jonquils and bamboo trees filled the chancel. The white cherry and plum blossoms were out and the trees in Ueno Park looked as if a deep snow had fallen. Immense crowds thronged the walks, among them many schoolboys who on feast days and holidays were taken to the various war statues and war trophies and told of the deeds of their forebears. Thus the warlike spirit is inculcated from the beginning in the youth of the nation.

We went to Kamakura where, as in the parks in the city, the gardens and temples were thronged with people wandering around old Diabutsu—who looks down upon them imperturbably with a face as impassive as theirs.

Looking seaward from the hotel the view is equally attractive—the green waters of the bay and the two headlands with a white sandy beach curving between. The hotel is kept by a veteran of the Black Watch who gave up soldiering first to become a newspaper man and then went on to become a maitre d'hotel. On the table in the reception room are hundreds of excellent wartime photographs, not for sale, but for the entertainment of the guests.

Admiral Shimamura who had distinguished himself at the battle of Tsushima and who was associated with Admiral Kato at the admiralty, gave a garden party to the officers of the *South Dakota* and their wives at the naval club. The admiral was an unusually big man for a Japanese, cordial and affable, but handicapped as a host by his inability to speak English and by ours to speak Japanese.

The naval club was formerly the residence of one of the old daimio's. It is picturesquely situated in a park adjoining the grounds of the Hama Detached Palace. The admiral and his wife, the latter in Japanese dress, received us standing at the bandstand. Some distance back of the admiral under the trees were grouped at least 200 Japanese naval officers—admirals, captains and commanders. The gold lace and the cherry blossoms made a beautiful combination of color.

There were many booths and refreshment tables scattered through the grounds. An interesting feature of the entertainment was the baking of little pottery jars and platters by hired ceramists for souvenirs. The guests wrote their names on the jars and saucers, which were then baked in portable ovens. There were also several artists who painted fans and cards for souvenirs of the party.

Secured at the seawall of the school was the training ship for the midshipmen fitting out for her annual cruise, her bowsprit reaching over the grounds. The Japanese retain sails for training—the proper school for making sailors—but we have abandoned it, just as England has returned to it.

When Admiral Brownson was a captain he had on the bulkhead of his cabin the series of paintings of men-of-war of the sail period by Admiral Beachy of the Royal Navy. One day at luncheon Captain McCalla, looking at these, asked, "What are these pictures, Brownson? They are very interesting."

"They are Beachy's paintings. I sent to London for them."

"But why do you want them? They are out-of-date. If you are looking for old ships, why not go back to the galley period?"

The poet of our Class of '77 was Commodore Bostwick who made his midshipman cruise in the Orient. He had been taken at that time by an attractive Japanese child in Yokohama and wrote a poem in her praise which for years had a vogue in the Asiatic fleet. It had been published by the Bancrofts in San Francisco and issued in an appropriate binding as a gift book.

I did not know if Oyucha-san, the child, could still be alive, but I did know that 40 years before she had lived with her mother in their teahouse at the top of the One Hundred Steps in Yokohama.

One afternoon my wife and I walked there to inquire if the family was still there. The teahouse was situated on a steep declivity overlooking the harbor and the cherry trees around the house were in full bloom—making me think of the scenery of *Madame Butterfly*. The setting of Puccini's music, I believe, is partially copied from this hilltop.

We were welcomed by three generations—the old mother, Oyucha-san herself and her little son. The women spoke English fluently and showed us an album with photographs and cards of foreign naval officers and people from all over the world. Most of the pictures of naval officers were those of Americans. The grandmother told us that her daughter was the original Oyucha-san and had been a little girl when Bostwick was out there as a midshipman. Their hospitality and graciousness were boundless. They gave us tea and cake and oranges and begged us to stay longer. To the small grandson I gave a coin, whereupon he prostrated himself upon a mat and struck his head on the floor several times as a token of thanks.

It was not long after our visit that the great earthquake came and destroyed that part of Yokohama where this happy and attractive family lived. I have heard that all the bluff in the vicinity of the Hundred Steps caved in completely.

Travel in Japan at this season was a burden. Hotels were crowded and the charges exorbitant even in the inferior inns. A lady from Washington said that at her hotel a room at the end of the hall was screened off, a cot placed in it and the price for one night was $12. Prices everywhere had doubled. Steamers were crowded, both coastwise and overseas, and passages had to be engaged months ahead.

On our previous stop in Tokyo, Admiral Kato had told Mrs. Gleaves that on her return to Japan he would give her a dinner *a la japonaise*. He gave it at the Maple Club in Sheiba Park—a beautiful party never to be forgotten. A number of Japanese officers' wives were there with Madame Kato. I recall Madame Shimamura and

Madame Takeshita. Officers were in Japanese dress, as were the ladies. We sat on spotless mats laid on the floor while geisha girls, flashing in and out like little gaudy butterflies, served from the opposite side of the low tables. During the dinner Admiral Kato was much amused at Mrs. Gleaves' enjoyment of the raw fish—which she had declared was the one thing she could never eat. It was so skillfully prepared that she thought it was rare beef. The tiny saki cups were kept full and after the dinner there was geisha dancing.

May is the flower month of Japan when the gardens are at their loveliest and, as someone has said, the glory of the gardens lies in more than meets the eye. We went to a garden party at Kiyozumi Cho Fukagawaka, the home of Baron Kyoata-Errasaki—the second richest man in Japan. This garden is one of the showplaces of Tokyo and famed for the harmony and beauty of its landscape effects.

Formerly it was the garden of a great daimio. There is a tidewater lake with many fish. The little teahouse where we had refreshments is built over the lake and connected with the garden by an arched bridge. The rocks abounding in the garden were brought from various parts of Japan. The garden is the last word in landscape gardening, but the European house in the grounds, which the baron does not occupy, is French in adornment and furniture—and very like a Parisian villa where I lunched once near St. Cloud.

My flag lieutenant, Holcombe, went with us to Nikko in the mountains where we arrived at the inn in time for dinner. Afterwards Holcombe and I walked to the sacred red lacquered bridge over the Daiya River—which is not a river but a roaring, narrow torrent rushing down from Kegon Falls.

It was getting late and I wanted to go to bed. I told Holcombe I felt sure I would be awakened by a telephone message directing me to return to Vladivostok. So it was. About midnight the bell in my room rang: "Call from Yokohama" came the message from the office.

"What is it?" I asked.

Then I recognized the voice of the chief of staff, who said, "I have a wireless from Washington directing the *South Dakota* to return to Vladivostok.

"Will return to Yokohama on the five o'clock train tomorrow," I replied—and went to bed again.

Thanks to the scarcity of trains, we had enough time to see the beautiful sights of Nikko—the Great Temple, the Hundred Buddhas and the Avenue of Crytomerias.

I wondered if Washington was convinced the Japanese in Siberia had at last taken the buttons off their foils!

My visit to Japan closed with the garden party of the empress in the palace grounds to celebrate the festival of the cherry blossoms, which were on the wane. The weather was a bit chilly and the sky partially overcast. There were some 5,000 persons present wandering through the park. Under the cherry trees there was an informal presentation to the imperial party of those who had not been previously presented. I remained in the ambassadorial group and was not presented again.

Opposite the line of ambassadors were the Japanese officials—Admiral Togo being on the right of the line and taking precedence over all others. The Order of the Chrysanthemum, which he wore on his breast, is the highest of all Japanese decorations. Next to him in line was the prime minister, Mr. Hara, then the admiral of the fleet and further down the line cabinet ministers and field marshalls—among them the celebrated Count Oku and Admiral Kato. At the end of the line on the left was the towering figure of Admiral Shimamura.

After this ceremony the empress and her ladies—in European dress—went to the palace for tea. The ambassadors and their suites followed. I sat with the Swedish ambassador who was very complimentary to my daughter Evelina. He spoke of her popularity in Tokyo and said it was graciousness such as hers that brought countries closer together.

The imperial party consisting of the empress, the crown prince, another prince and two princesses sat apart at a table in the center of the pavilion. The refreshments were very simple—sandwiches, tea, cake and ice cream, claret cup, orangeade, tea and Apollinaris water. After this a liqueur was served.

The following day General Onehara sent his aide on board with invitations for the admiral and staff to a luncheon in the admiral's honor in Tokyo. This was reluctantly declined due to the ship's sailing for Vladivostok.

We sailed via the Tsugaru Strait, April 23, and passed within sight of Hakodate. The weather was damp and cold to the northward in the straits, the hills covered with snow. Soon we entered the everlasting fog belt of the region which shut out our view of the Islands of Mystery.

An incident occurred on this visit to Japan which might have led to complications. All the ships of the Asiatic fleet in the southern portions of the station were by special orders painted white due to climatic conditions. We had been treated with such unusual courtesy and consideration by Japan that although in the north, I decided to paint the *South Dakota* white—a sort of peace offering as it were. This called forth most friendly comments from the Japanese press.

Of course I reported my action to the navy department because the standard color for all men-of-war since 1898 had been lead color. A reply was promptly cabled from the secretary of the navy to resume the standard color. This revocation came at an inappropriate time as the row then on with General Oi's force in Vladivostok had to be straightened out, and to return there in our war paint caused much comment and inquiry. Fortunately it was satisfactorily explained by our diplomatic and efficient naval attache who was held in high esteem at the admiralty.

23 Springtime in Siberia

The next morning the fog cleared and after passing Skripleff Island we entered the Golden Horn in bright sunshine and moored in the *Albany*'s old berth at the docks—the *Albany* being in the stream ready to sail. The *President Grant* was taking her quota of Czech troops at Egerscheldt Point.

Captain Watts came on board and told me the story of the emeute during the night of April 4-5. The Japanese military and naval forces undertook active military operations on a large-scale against the Russian troops, occupying all public buildings, the radio station, telegraph and cable offices, arresting members of the government and numerous others, taking charge of the Russian naval vessels, cutting the telephone wires and opening a heavy fire simultaneously in various parts of the city—with small arms, machine guns and artillery.

Many callers came on board, the first being Admiral Kawahara. When Dr. Girza came with General Cecek and Major Broz, the doctor spoke of his great relief and thankfulness at seeing the flagship "nosing" around the point and entering the harbor for, he added, "When the cat's away, the mice will play."

When I called on General Oi, in speaking of events which prompted the navy department to bring the *South Dakota* back to Vladivostok, he said his idea was that there was a "third party"—name not mentioned—trying to make trouble between the Japanese and Americans and many stories were circulated which he did not believe.

He pointed out that the arrival in Vladivostok of the American flagship in January had been followed by trouble, and that the Gaida revolution in November came close upon the arrival of the *Brooklyn*. He also noted that the coup d'etat of 31 January had occurred shortly after the *South Dakota* had come in. Then the Russians had taken that occasion to overthrow the provisional government. He attributed the recent troubles to the propaganda of agitators fomenting trouble with the Koreans.

The situation became so bad, he said, he deemed it necessary to take precautions. On the night of April 4 about 20 Russians opened fire on Japanese soldiers at their base, General Oi's residence and upon the Japanese garage. Consequently orders were given to disarm all Russians in the city and district. He had directed that the Japanese occupy Vladivostok, but said that he only desired the establishment of a stable government in Siberia. He did not want to interfere in Russian affairs, but wanted the Russian people to resume work and the commerce of Vladivostok to be restored. Since he had disarmed the Russians, there had been many strikes but practically all the workmen had since resumed work.

On April 29 I called on the new British military commissioner, General Blair, whose office was on square opposite the railroad station on the Aleutskaya—the favorite battlefield of opposing factions as attested by the bullet-scarred buildings around it.

The streets were crowded with idlers waiting to see the new Japanese regiment, just landed. About 650 troops marched passed the reviewing officer who was General Oi. They were well set up and equipped, and stepped out briskly with a modified goose step, swinging the left arm in unison.

General Blair was an attractive type of Englishman—tall, fair and thin, with charming manners. His bony face was burned a brick red, and although young—not over 40—he had seen much service in the field.

The Russians had made peace offers to the Japanese which had been rejected.

On May 1 a great parade was held by the Russians in celebration of the Third International in the Aleutskaya and the Stretlanskaya. Hundreds of men, women and children carried red banners, many inscribed "Long Life to the Soviet Republic and the Brotherhood of Man"—also a generous display of the names of Lenin, Trotsky and Viliksky. Few Japanese solders were in sight. The crowds were orderly, but had there been any sign of riot, I am sure the soldiers would have been on the spot instantly.

On May 3 I went to Russian Island in the barge and took with me Major Lively and Major Allen of the Red Cross, Captain Blamer and the fleet surgeon, Dr. May, to visit the Russian children—nearly 1,000—under the care of the Red Cross who were to be sent back to Russia the next month.

These children were living in barracks built during the war for Russian soldiers. There were a great number of these barracks on the island and on the mainland—enormous, well-built, red brick buildings which had cost an immense amount of money. The children were well cared for in every way, but seemed rather forlorn. In ages they ranged from eight to 18. Some of the girls were quite pretty and they did some Russian dances for us and sang Russian songs.

They appeared to be bright and happy in spite of their sad story. During the revolution they had been sent out of Petrograd and distributed among seven towns in western Siberia. When Kolchak's armies fell back, the minister of interior of the ever-changing government appealed to the Red Cross which took charge of the seven groups, and none too soon, for in some of the cities shells were falling as they moved out.

The Red Cross brought them to Vladivostok in 1918 and for two years the children were wards of the Red Cross. They were not altogether lost from their families—many of the older children had a fair idea of where their parents were, or at any rate had been. They were compelled to attend school regularly, education being one of the main objects of their asylum.

Russian Island was at one time strongly fortified, as was Vladivostok, at the cost of millions. Yet the Japanese had come in practically without any opposition and dominated the whole situation. Of course, they had the stiff neutrality of the Allies on their side. The United States maintained a powerful naval radio station in the island and the Japanese had one of less power not far from ours.

Our sailors, quartered in a massive stone building, liked their job—although they were practically in exile. Warrant officers, petty officers and enlisted men all told me they wanted to remain as long as possible. Of course, they were saving all their pay. They had large rooms, well furnished and comfortably heated, and escaped the petty vexations of life on board ship. Besides they liked the ice and snow and the novelty of the duty had not worn off.

The situation in Vladivostok was evidently approaching the point where the Japanese, unless checked by the Allied Powers, would assume all authority in Eastern Siberia. Mr. Charles Smith of the Inter-Allied Committee informed me on May 3 that the Japanese no longer recognized the authority of the Railway Committee. General Hashura had informed him that the Japanese had taken over the Assari Railway for military reasons, but would return it if the Russians would agree to their terms.

Another annoyance came from another direction. Admiral Chernilovsky-Sokol, who came on board frequently to see me, said that a tug with supplies for the lighthouse had been held up by the Japanese and compelled to ask their permission to leave harbor. He asked my advice. I suggested that the provisional government take up the matter at once with the Japanese high command, since an agreement—the terms of which I did not know—had been signed by both parties.

The tide of trouble and unrest continued to run strong and found expression in labor strikes, railroad strikes and revolutionary demonstrations. It was evident that the partisans were losing ground and that the Japanese influence was as steadily gaining. There was an air of possession on the part of the Japanese that fanned the flame of Russian hatred and discontent. Troops were coming weekly from Japan but no one saw any depart, except into the interior.

Under such conditions it was impossible for business to continue. One day the shops would open and the next day barred shutters would give the streets a gloomy and sinister aspect. No one knew when the batteries on Tiger Hill and the other forts commanding the city and bay would open fire. Early in May both the French and British commissioners were withdrawn and the *South Dakota* alone remained of the western fleets.

On May 4 President Medridieff called. There was nothing typically Russian about him, but he had a strong, firm face, somewhat softened by thick, iron gray hair. He handed me a written statement of his version of the affair of April 4-5, which differed materially, of course, from General Oi's statement. I asserted our absolute neutrality yet said that the United States in evacuating our troops had not relinquished its interest in the present and future welfare of the Russian people in Siberia.

Following Mr. Medridieff came General Boldereff, the new commandant of the fortress of Vladivostok. In appearance he was unmistakably Russian, good-looking, soldierly and of medium height. His complexion was ruddy and weather-beaten, his hair *en brosse*. On his khaki uniform he wore the major general's insignia, a Russian war cross on his left breast and a star on the right. He spoke English fairly well and was a very pleasant man with much war service in the field to his credit.

I returned General Boldereff's call at his residence where he gave me a glass of vodka. He lived in the house formerly occupied by General Rozanoff, which was stripped of everything except some tawdry French gilt furniture in the reception room.

Later I called, without sidearms, on Mr. Medridieff at the zemstov building—built of stone and iron, diagonally across the street from where the Japanese had established an armed post. On the night of April 4-5 the Japanese had fired at close range into the zemstov offices and riddled the building with shot and shell.

Although that was a month before, the debris had only been partially cleared and showed the great and wanton destruction of property. One of the commissioner's rooms most exposed to the fire was literally shot to pieces, but a large icon that hung near the ceiling in the corner had escaped injury except for two bullet holes. I obtained from Mr. Medridieff valuable information in regard to the navigation of the approaches to Nikolayevsk, which would have been useful if I had decided to send a ship there.

On May 6 I dined at the British mission with General and Mrs. Blair. The other guests were General Inagaki, Consul General and Mrs. Caldwell, Captain Blamer and a number of British officers. The next day I met the Blairs again at a luncheon at Mr. Brown's of Standard Oil. Our host introduced us to a new combination drink—pale ale and champagne, which he called "velvet".

In the evening the sailors gave a ball at the Y.M.C.A. hut. I led the grand march. Every detail was shipshape. When I arrived eight chief petty officers "attended side" and the boatswain piped me "over". The bugler gave four flourishes and the band played "The Admiral's March". The four star flag was displayed on the wall opposite the admiral's chair. Sailors never do things by halves and they never consider the cost. "Money to come off the books" is their slogan for whatever they want to do. I was surprised to see the number of pretty girls who seemed to enjoy dancing with the sailors as much as the men liked dancing with them. It was a real party.

On May 8 I gave a dinner on board to Dr. Girza, high commissioner of the Czech-Slovaks. The other guests were his aide, Colonel Broz, and General Cecek, General Blair, General Lavergne and his aide, Colonel Renandeau. General Lavergne is the French high commissioner and has been especially kind to me. When our troops left Siberia I had to return the car the army had courteously lent to the ship. General Lavergne saw what was not visible in Washington, namely that transit on foot in Vladivostok was not possible in making official calls. He had several cars and placed one at my disposal.

May 9, being Mother's Day, was celebrated by assembling all

hands on the quarterdeck. The executive read the radiogram from the secretary of the navy on the subject, and our chaplain offered a most appropriate prayer.

At lunch that day with me were our Consul and Mrs. Caldwell, the Belgian consul, Mr. Lang who was an Englishman and had lost an eye at the Dardanelles, Mrs. Lang, and General and Mrs. Blair. After lunch the Blairs and Langs went with me in the motor barge to Russian Island. We went through the canal, passed the Japanese wireless station and landed at what was once the Russian officers' school when the English were instructing them. Here we found a good road along the inlet and walked three miles on the beach. The day was fine with harbingers of spring in the wild flowers covering the hillsides, azaleas, violets, pansies and buttercups. We had tea at the Langs' at the Belgian consulate.

I received a pleasant note from Commodore Lin saying he had been directed by the Chinese government to arrange for Mrs. Gleaves' trip to Hangchow as the guest of the government; that he had telegraphed the navy command in Shanghai requesting an escort to accompany her party to Soochow and Hangchow, and to the minister of foreign affairs to issue instructions to the authorities at those places to afford protection. He enclosed special stamps to use on our letters by courier to Peking. The Chinese are always thoughtful.

At a tea a Russian lady told me this story of an intimate friend of hers who was in love with Admiral Kolchak. She had been divorced from her husband, had followed the admiral to Siberia and was with him when he was executed. She went to prison with him upon his arrest at Irkutsk and begged to be shot at the same time. Her request was not granted, but she was shot later. She was only 24 and my informant said rather naively, I thought, she was "an awfully nice girl".

General Oi gave an elaborate luncheon in his quarters and among the guests were several high commissioners, including Mr. Matsudaira. Afterwards General Oi sent his aide with Captain Blamer and me to Fort No. 6, which was unfinished, but of great magnitude in the first line of defense. The Russians stopped work on it at the beginning of the war and it had become a wreck. From the ramparts is a wonderful view of the Gulf of Amur and of the surrounding country—then green and in full foliage.

General Cecek decorated me with the Military Cross of Czecho-

Slovakia on board the *South Dakota* in recognition of our cooperation with the Czecho-Slovakian forces. The cross has the lime leaves—the lime tree is their sacred tree and the cross with those leaves is the insignia of the highest military order. After the ceremony I reviewed the Slovakian troops onshore. I never saw finer looking soldiers. They wore their tin hats and marched as proudly as possible with the silly goose step. They had been especially selected for the occasion, survivors of the heaviest fighting in Siberia from a regiment that had been almost annihilated.

The *New Orleans'* Captain Larimer arrived from Shanghai and I was so interested in all he said of the news from the Yangtse that I forgot to go to the station to see my good friend, Mr. Li, depart for Peking.

Admiral Chernilovsky-Sokol gave me a small silver tray and a pair of silver candlesnuffers, very old.

Admiral Kawahara's dinner on board the *Hizen*, given to me the night before we sailed for Taku, is worthy of special mention, for it showed entire change of heart on the part of the Japanese authorities toward the Americans from the frigid attitude I had at first encountered from them in Vladivostok.

The decorations of the ship were unique and could only have been designed by an Oriental. The after part of the quarterdeck was screened off and dressed with colored signal flags. At the stern were draped together the national colors of the United States and Japan. Artificial flowers made by the sailors were arranged in the lower rigging and around the rail in profusion. The chef d'oeuvre was a large artificial cherry tree with wide-spreading branches covered with double blossoms. On the starboard side of the deck were rows of chrysanthemums and on the dining table in the cabin the flowers were arranged after the manner of those at Izizi. All of this was lighted by Japanese lanterns and electric lights.

Among the admiral's guests were General Oi, General Inagaki, Mr. Matsudaira, a number of Japanese officers and Captains Blamer and Luby of the *South Dakota*. I never saw Admiral Kawahara in better form or more jolly. He and I danced a waltz together on the quarterdeck, much to the interest of the sailors.

At the table Mr. Matsudaira was on my right. I had an interesting conversation with him on the political situation and was greatly impressed by his fund of information and his generous outlook of affairs in Eastern Siberia. Of course, he was conservative, and to use an expression of his own craft—"made no commitments"—and yet he did not impress me as being overcautious.

As Japanese are not given to postprandial oratory, I was surprised when the admiral proposed a toast with the champagne. The speech went beyond the bounds of the usual conventional banalities and was most cordial. In closing his remarks he said:

> It is my sincere and earnest hope that your excellency will not stint your valuable effort in promoting the understanding and friendship between America and Japan, even as was done by that distinguished American who made his name so distinct, beloved and honorable in the annals of intercourse between the two countries—Commodore Perry.

In thanking the admiral for his cordial sentiments, I said:

> The more we see of each other, the better we shall understand each other, and in such gatherings as this the closest bonds are often formed. It is my firm belief that we shall always have peace, and it certainly shall be my utmost endeavor to do my part in the accomplishment of that great end.

Kawahara gave me a pretty piece of porcelain—a saki bottle—which they call "the Nightingale" on account of the bird like whistle the saki makes when passing through a small aperture inside the bottle.

The day after the dinner on board the *Hizen* was the day of our departure for Taku. The weather was cloudy and cold and the thermometer down to 45°.

Representatives from all the missions came on board to say bon voyage. First, Dr. Girza and his aide, Colonel Broz, and several Czech officers; then General Inagaki, followed by Admiral Kawahara and staff, who made a dashing approach to the gangway in his barge; Commodore Lin and his staff; Mr. Caldwell and the consular officers with General Cecek and staff; and finally General Oi and his staff.

The cabin was well filled when General Oi presented me with a souvenir two-handed sword in a plain wood scabbard, but the blade of finest dark blue steel and so sharp that the general said it could decapitate five men without being resharpened. As M. Prudhomme in the comedy might have said, "Le sabre est le plus beau jour de ma vie."

To a Japanese the sword is no tawdry badge of office, but is the soul of the samurai. It is believed that at the moment of tempering, the soul of the sword takes life from the sword-smith. In appearance this sword looks like stainless steel, but on close examination, reveals a delicate pattern on the blade which is the hallmark of the forger.

General Oi showed me his own sword which had been presented to him by the government for his services in the Sino-Japanese war—a handsome weapon with gold basket hilt and the blade exactly like the one he gave me. I noticed that he handled both swords affectionately and reverently. In former times the final making of the sword, when tempered, was the occasion of a religious ceremony of form and pomp.

At eleven sharp we cast off lines and got underway for Taku. Unusual honors were rendered the ship as she left the harbor. General Cecek paraded his troops on the dock and their band played "The Star-Spangled Banner". The *Hizen* manned her rail as did also the *Hai Yung* and all the ships cheered and signaled, "Good-bye—Pleasant Voyage," to which the *South Dakota* replied, "Thank you. Good-bye."

We were soon hidden in a dense fog. I thought we had seen the last of Vladivostok, but there was still another visit when I returned to investigate the Langdon tragedy the following January.

24 China revisted

We arrived off Chefoo the afternoon of May 22, 1920. A number of vessels of the squadron were in port. After receiving $100,000 from the destroyer *Greer*, we went on to Taku where I transferred to the *Alava* on May 25.

The *General Alava* was a gunboat of 1,100 tons, with a rated speed of ten knots, but an actual speed two knots less. She carried a saluting battery of two-three pounders and was one of Admiral Dewey's prizes captured at Manila. Ever since the fighting in the Philippines she had served as fleet tender. Compared with the yacht, *Alacrity*—the tender to the British flagship—she did not measure up to the requirements, but was a good sea boat, and fairly well fitted out for the use of the commander in chief.

We had a fine run up the Peiko to Tientsin, escorted by a Chinese gunboat. All the honors, of which the Chinese are so meticulous, were tendered to the *Alava* as she went alongside the bund. The personal welcomes from the officials—civil and military—were extremely gratifying. Admiral Sah had sent Commander Chen in a private car to accompany us to Peking.

First they all took me to the Jockey Club where I bet on the races and picked the wrong horses. Then we boarded the train for Peking where, at the Chien Meng gate, we were met by Dr. Tenny and a number of others from the legation.

My younger daughter Evelina was at the station and thrilled me by saying, "Father, I've flown over the Temple of Heaven."

It seemed most interesting that she should have flown over the Temple of Heaven where 35 years before I had avoided the guards and gotten in, when it was forbidden under the death penalty for any foreigner to enter even the sacred enclosure. She had heard the story all her life and was curious to compare her first impressions of the temple with mine, especially as it was her first flight.

Mrs. Gleaves had been delighted with her excursion to Soochow and Hangchow and said it more than compensated her for having missed Korea. The trip had been made in a private car under a military escort. Commander Wong (now rear admiral), who had been with us from Shanghai to Peking the previous winter, had been detailed by Admiral Ling as her aide. His wife was with him and he explained it to be the custom in China that when an officer escorted a lady, his own wife must go with him. Mrs. Gleaves replied the custom was an excellent one and should be adopted by other countries.

Wong seemed proud of his aiguillettes and remarked, "I have been aide to Admiral Sah and to Admiral Gleaves, and now I am aide to Mrs. Gleaves."

The trees were all in leaf and Peking was beautiful. The grass was not only growing in the crevices of the flags on the streets but also between the tiles on the roofs of the temples and pagodas; nevertheless there was a saddening air of decay over it all. We went again to the Temple of Heaven and strolled in the vast enclosure which we decided, however, is more impressive in winter than in summer.

The new premier—Admiral Sah—arranged for an excursion to the Western Tombs about four hours by rail from the capital, Commander Chu in charge. The approach to the Western Tombs where the Manchus are buried is by rail to Liang-ko-Chwong, thence in chairs to the tombs.

The old tombs are ten miles from the station and the chair bearers were quite unequal to the journey. No one can be so provoking as a coolie. At the tombs they rested a half hour. After walking seven minutes they stopped at a walled village for five minutes more. That was their rate of progress. At the village one of them walked off and we did not see him again. They were the only quarrelsome Chinamen we had seen.

Finally we decided to get out and walk—Holcombe, the marine sergeant who had come with us and myself. The clouds gathered heavily but there was no rain. The wind increased and the clouds tumbled over the hills presaging a storm. The beautiful scenery of the hills was the more impressive half veiled, as it was, by the clouds and mist.

The tombs are well preserved and in front of the altar in the temple hung silk draperies of exquisite workmanship, very dirty but not in the least faded. The tomb itself was horseshoe shaped and covered with a forest of small trees, but the top of Kuan-hsi's tomb was perfectly bare. As the site of the Manchu tombs was selected only 200 years ago, the marble bridges are intact, while those at the Ming Tombs are in ruins.

We crossed a bridge over a small stream near an old barrack. A

Chinaman was sitting on his haunches, apparently with perfect ease and comfort. It is their natural position when resting.

The most interesting tomb is that of the little Pearl Concubine whose tragic story I have already told. When the empress dowager's conscience began to trouble her, she issued a decree granting her victim a posthumous title, but the grave of Lady Chen is neglected "with the exception of one lonely poplar growing out of the little tumulus".

A long walk with the sergeant completed my visit to the tombs and temples and at seven o'clock our car was attached to the regular train but we did not arrive in Peking until midnight.

Two days after our visit to the Western Tombs we lunched with Admiral Sah in his home. His son came to the hotel for us and took my wife, daughter Evelina, Holcombe and myself to the admiral's house to a conventional Chinese tiffin. The table was beautifully set and I have no doubt that the food was delicious. My daughter and Holcombe said it was, but I have never learned to enjoy Chinese cooking. I contented myself with bread and roast duck.

After tiffin the admiral took us over his house, a typical Chinese home—a series of stone courts surrounded by one story apartments. The courts are all connected by paneled glass sliding doors. The admiral, like most sailors, is fond of agriculture and flowers. He had trained melon vines over bamboo frames and made a comfortable shade over each court. The leaves were all gone then and only big pendulous melons remained, of which he was very proud.

In a rear building he opened a door. Inside were six famine refugees rescued by the kindhearted admiral from the starving hordes at the North Gate. There were a father, mother, a grown son and three little children. The room was not more than twelve by 14 feet and the ceiling was low.

As we entered and they saw the admiral, they fell on their knees and touched the floor with their foreheads, then straightened up, still kneeling, clasped their hands together and pressed them to their foreheads, then stood up and bowed several times—their movements being almost like a military drill except that it was all so natural. I have never seen such gratitude and reverence as these forlorn creatures exhibited. I asked the admiral where he got them, and he said he sent one of his officers to the North Gate to select six of the starving refugees from the famine district.

My wife was impressed with the fact that the admiral was

unmindful of germs, as he has several little grandchildren living with him. In the front court were two large carved stone bowls of gold fish, of which the admiral is very fond, as are nearly all Chinese. It is a national trait.

Before leaving, the admiral showed us his ceremonial robes which he had worn in the forenoon at a religious ceremony at the Temple of the God of War near the North Gate, celebrating the festival of the harvest moon. At our request, and in spite of his protestations, he allowed a servant to dress him in his robes and hat. The vestments were handsomely embroidered in black silk and gold and of exactly the same pattern worn by his ancestors 3,000 years ago.

Some of the most interesting sights in the world may be seen any day from the wall at the Chien Meng gate. It is a real moving picture show of strange humanity. One afternoon Hutchins and I, leaning over the parapet, watched a funeral pass in the street below. An enormous catafalque borne by 32 men was preceded by banner men and boys carrying make-believe red lions, tigers and other wild animals. The procession was headed by a half dozen priests. There was much noise from tom-toms and similar instruments, but no one seemed to pay attention to it.

Just as the head of the procession was to pass through the gate, two of the banner men started a fight. When it was evident one man was getting the worst of it, another joined up to help him. Then a policeman took a hand in the row and beat the others. About this time the corpse was brought along, as Hutchins said, "to let the dead man see the fight," and the 32 bearers ahead turned back to join the crowd. Finally they all passed. The tom-toms took up their hideous noise and the crowd dispersed.

This corner of the city is big with history. Here it was that during the Boxer troubles military reputations were made and some lost. The gate overlooks the square where the Peking-Tientsin railroad terminates.

On the opposite side of the Tartar Wall the gate commands a view of the American marine barracks. It was the point of attack by the American troops and the gallant Captain Reilly was killed here while trying to force an entrance. Captain Summerall made a name for himself by calmly chalking spots on the heavy gate for his men to fire at. This was done under fire from the Chinese. On top of the wall our marines were having a hot time and my friend and shipmate of *Boston* days, Jack Myers, a major general now, fought until he was badly wounded and had to be carried off. Putnam-Weale speaks of Myers' fight as a "brilliant little affair" and of Myers in the highest terms.

On May 31 arrangements were completed for our visit to the Ming Tombs and the Great Wall. When we arrived at the hotel at Nankow, sedan chairs and donkeys were waiting for the party. The tombs are twelve miles from the hotel. The sun was very hot but there was no dust. The ride was not uninteresting and the tombs are the finest in China, and majestic in their ruins. They are built in a valley and are approached by a long avenue called "The Triumphal Way Leading to the Temples". The magnificent marble archway at the approach is a work of art. It was erected nearly 400 years ago and is the finest in China. On both sides of this road are colossal and grotesque statues of men and animals.

The next morning we completed the journey to the wall and climbed the highest point at Nankow Pass without much difficulty. The air was clear, there was only a light breeze and the view of the Mongolian plains was superb—to which a human touch was given by caravans of camels, nearly all of them ambling northward, a few bound in the opposite direction.

There was a blind and ragged beggar at the Nankow gate, selling curios spread out on a cloth. We bought a small bronze Buddha, very ancient. The old sailor orderly from Admiral Sah who always looked out for me, gave me a star-shaped spike which the Chinese used hundreds of years ago. It has five prongs, so shaped that in whatever position it may be dropped on the ground, one spoike will always point upwards. The spikes are scattered in the rear of retreating soldiers for the purpose of disabling pursuing cavalry. It is said the Germans used them during the World War.

One afternoon back in Peking, my wife and I staged a trip to the observatory on the East Wall to see the famous astronomical instruments—some of them made by Jesuits several hundred years ago and some presented by Louis XIV. After the Boxer Rebellion the Germans took some of these to Potsdam, but were compelled to return them by the Treaty of Versailles.

The evidence of German *schrecklichkeit* is seen wherever their soldiers passed. For instance, in the old days students came to Peking from all parts of China for literary examinations. The cells in which they lived were cubicles in a building near the East Gate. During the Boxer trouble this building was destroyed by the Germans along with priceless Chinese classics.

When we descended from the East Wall, two teachers of the temple invited us to have tea with them, and explained the water clocks which are 400 years old. While with them we heard the drone of an airplane. It passed over our heads high up, and I exclaimed, "I'll wager that Evelina and Mrs. Poe are in that plane!" It was a curious sensation to stand in a Chinese temple and watch our daughter flying over old Peking.

It was now June 1 and the time of our departure from Peking was approaching. The remaining time was taken up with dinners and the leftovers of sight-seeing, of which there was not much.

Our old friend, Commissioner Li, was living in the Peking Hotel—a modern, gilded caravansary, with jazz music and up-to-date decollete paintings on the walls. His dinner to us was elaborate, and—unlike mine—there was no dry champagne. Chateau Yeuem and rare Burgundy flowed like water. Mr. Li was in great form and his toast to Dr. Tenny, who was soon to return to the United States after 40 years service, was flattering and deserved. Tenny responded with much feeling. Admiral Sah made a short speech and then the dinner was closed by Mr. Li again rising and toasting the ladies. He said that a dinner without ladies would be as bare as a dinner table without flowers. This was greeted with loud applause.

After Mr. Li's dinner we left Peking for Tientsin where we remained only a few days—days of luncheons and dinners.

At one function I was told this story by a Chinese general whom we frequently met: He had begun life as an uneducated soldier, but had developed an aptitude for detective work and got an appointment in the customs where his duties were principally those of a spy. There he made many friends and became popular with everyone except the criminal classes, to whom he was a terror.

His successful military career began when he discovered a conspiracy against the life of empress dowager. A certain Englishman, he found out, was going to Peking for the purpose of assassinating her. The general got to Peking ahead of him, and when the Englishman's train arrived, he boarded it and arrested the conspirator who was found to have a bomb in his possession.

For thus saving her life the empress was very grateful and heaped honors, riches and decorations upon him. Thus he was made a general and his breast, when I saw him, was covered with the most varied assortment of medals I had ever seen. It is said that when his mother died he honored her memory with a funeral which cost $200,000.

We boarded the *Alava* at the dock and Colonel Morrow added a touch of color to the rather spectacular send-off by coming down to the ship with all his officers on horseback. Two companies of Chinese troops presented arms and the band played its best and loudest as the lines were cast off and the *Alava* swung around to the tide. Hats and caps were waved and the cheers from ship and shore drowned the music of "Auld Lang Syne". We anchored off Taku to wait for the tide.

The forts at Taku are not formidable, but have played their share of history. The old mud forts which became famous in 1860 when the Allies bombarded them were intact as late as 1886 when they were demolished and the present forts replaced them.

At 4:30 we got underway again and headed out into the shallow, muddy sea against a stiff easterly wind bound for Chefoo. It was on that passage to Chefoo from Taku that I had my third experience of what seems to be clairvoyance.

About four in the morning I awoke suddenly. A few minutes afterwards the engines stopped. Something was wrong. I looked out of the airport and saw that land was close aboard on the starboard hand and we were running parallel to it, which meant that we were steering to the northward instead of to the eastward which was the course through Howki Channel. I hurried on deck, the atmosphere was hazy, and the wind still fresh from the eastward, but being under the lee of the land, the sea was smooth. Looking at the compass I saw we were headed NNE instead of ESE, but no change of course had been reported to me.

This is what happened: At four, just at the time I woke up, Takin Tao Island suddenly loomed up through the mist dead ahead and close aboard. The captain took in the situation instantly. We had been set to the northward and had missed the narrow strait between the islands. He put the helm to starboard and ran to the northward. A few years before the battleship *Oregon* had run ashore attempting to pass through the Howki Channel during the night. We worked around the islands, set the course for Chefoo and arrived there in the afternoon.

We remained at Chefoo a week and then sailed for Nagasaki where we arrived and took a buoy in front of the hotel, convenient for getting onshore.

Adm. C. F. Goodrich, U.S.N., was staying at the guest house of the Mitsui Company. He was on his way home and not well. He had had a distinguished career in the service and this seemed probably the end of it.

Captain LaCombe of the French cruiser *D'estrees* which was in port, invited me on a big game hunt if we were to be in Saigon next winter—elephants, tigers and "les grand cerfs"! At the same time a cable was received from the navy department that it was not "opportune" for the *South Dakota* to visit Australia at this time.

Another Frenchman, Major French-Courtland, came on board who said he had served in the British army and also navy and that he was now in a transport bound for Vladivostok to repatriate the Czechs. He told me he was blown up three times during the war, was wounded once and also gassed. An interesting but not convincing talker.

I gave a dinner on board the *Alava* to our new consul, Mr. Curtice. He pointed out the house on the hill, close to the consulate, where the original Madame Butterfly lived.

Captain Marriott, the British naval attache, was a guest—an interesting man. He was secretary to Admiral Wemyss when the latter represented the English government at the signing of the armistice. He told me that when the English battleship *Russell* was torpedoed off Malta, Admiral Freemantle was on board and had with him a spyglass which had belonged to Lord Nelson. When the ship went down the glass was lost. Captain Marriott gave me a photograph taken on the train in which Foch received the German delegates in the Forest of Compiegne.

The U.S. transport, *Madawaska*, arrived, homeward bound, and my daughter Evelina and Mrs. Poe took passage in her. She was a big ship, and needed naval care and inspection. I found that she was using harbor water, infected with cholera germs, for washing down decks and in the bathrooms. Even in the scullery the same water was used for the washing of the troops' mess gear. As there were several cases of cholera onshore, we changed all that and no serious trouble resulted.

Having been informed of serious riots at Woochow on the Yangtse, I hurried over to Shanghai in the *Alava* to consult with our consul general, Mr. Cunningham, after which I decided to go up the river to Hankow. For this trip I selected the destroyer, *Elliot*, commanded by Lieutenant Gunther. She was in excellent condition and a great credit in every way to the fleet. The trim appearance of ship, officers and crew showed there was a master hand at the helm.

The scenery on both banks of the Yangtse River is attractive—dotted with pagodas and temples. The river is a muddy, deep, swift running stream, and at this time its surface was covered with a multitude of junks. The following morning I communicated with the destroyer, *Rizal*, who reported everything quiet in the river and the campaign over for the summer. I was sorry to hear that the Japanese wireless station at Hankow dominated all communications on the river. On our second day in the river we passed the British gunboat, *Kinsha*, flying the flag of Rear Admiral Borrett. She came within hail and signalled that the admiral had gone to Shanghai.

In some parts of the river we had to reduce our speed from 25 knots to 15 to avoid damage to the sampans tied up at the various villages. At high speeds the *Elliot*'s stern wash is as destructive as a tidal wave. Even at 15 knots I fear we may have done some damage to the small craft on the banks—but I never heard so afterwards.

On July 2 about eleven in the morning we passed Kinkiang, a large city on the south bank. Behind Kinkiang lie the famous Lashan Mountains, 5,000 feet high, and Kuling—a popular summer resort—is located there. After Kinkiang we passed close to a walled city, not as picturesque, however, as the village of Hukow on the brink of the river, back of which runs a portion of the Great Wall extending for many miles over the hills. A pagoda on a nearby hill and many junks sailing along in front of the village completed one of the most characteristic views on the river.

At 6 p.m. we passed Hiwangchow where Kublai Khan crossed the river with his enormous army in the 13th century. An hour later we arrived at Hankow. I went ashore to the club there and hospitable hosts urged us to remain another day, saying they had never had an American admiral in Hankow on the Fourth of July. I declined, being anxious to get over to Woochow where the trouble had been and one missionary killed.

Woochow is only a short distance from Hankow, across the river. We left early in the morning and soon passed a number of junks filled with soldiers. They were the remnants of General Chang's Northern Army in full retreat down the Yangtse—half naked, carrying umbrellas and rifles. The big junks were in tow of small craft and all were loaded with tents and camp equipage. General Chang's "yacht" proved to be an old river steamer, crowded like the junks with soldiers.

At Chenglin we found our gunboat flotilla at anchor and also a Spanish gunboat. We passed on to Yochow, at the entrance of the Tungt'ing Lakes. The weather continued intensely hot and I felt sorry for the people on board the gunboats which have little protection from the sun and the terrible mosquitoes.

In the cool of the afternoon I went ashore to look at the town, which a few days before had been overrun and looted by the northern troops. It was a dreadfully dirty place and the missionaries are out of luck who have to live there. During the recent riots 10,000 noncombatant refugees had been herded like cattle in the compound, under conditions which can be imagined better than described. No one apparently had attempted to improve the situation.

Captain Strother of the U.S. destroyer *Upshur* had done everything necessary to protect the missionaries and proposed to land his men if need arose. It was our row, but he received a heartening message from Admiral Borrett who was a looker-on in the *Kinsha:* "Of course, I cannot take part in this landing, but if you are attacked I will come to your assistance with every gun and every man." Thus he created a phrase which deserves a place in history.

The Fourth of July, falling on Sunday, was duly celebrated on the fifth at the American Club in Shanghai. Our consul general, Mr. Cunningham, made an appropriate and forceful speech and both he and I emphasized Admiral Borrett's fine message to Captain Strother.

The following day we sailed for Chefoo, stopping at Weihaiwei to return the call of my colleague, Vice Admiral Duff, who was there in the *Alacrity*. The admiral asked us all to lunch on board. We then proceeded to Chefoo but hearing from the minister at Peking of a threatened outbreak at Peitaiho, I went at his request to Peking incognito with Lieutenant Holcombe and arrived in time for dinner.

The "critical" situation seemed to be a personal quarrel between Marshal Tuan and his party on one side, and Wu Pei-fu on the other. General Chang Tso-lin, who had been in Peking a few days before, had returned to Mukden, and having stirred up all the row, then proclaimed his neutrality.

I increased the legation guard temporarily by 150 men from the destroyers. There was no principle involved in the Chinese operations and the soldiers did not want to fight—having no desire to die for the ambitions of the tuchuns. There was another change, more serious—

the scarcity of food caused by the interrupted rail communication. The prices of rice and wheat flour had gone beyond the reach of the poor. Rice was $15 a picul, but as a matter of fact the people in the north depend more on wheat flour, but principally on millet.

After dinner we sat out on the broad, vine covered verandah of the legation listening to Mr. Crane's interesting stories of distinguished men whom he had known personally. He had been a worldwide traveller, and his reminiscences of the neglected corners of the earth merit a place on the shelves of the Explorers' Club.

Peking in summer is almost as hot as Aden. I woke up at five o'clock with the sun streaming into the room. Getting up to close the blinds, I looked out of the window at the yellow tiles of the palaces in the Forbidden City rising above the trees, not far away, glistening in the morning light. There was no air stirring and the city lay burning in the sun. I went to sleep again until awakened by military music. My first thought was that it might be the troops, but it was guard mounting of our own marines in the legation compound.

I ordered the *Huron* (the new name of my flagship, formerly the *South Dakota*) to meet me at Chingwangtao. Arriving there in the *Alava*, I anchored near the *Huron*, but due to stormy weather and rough sea ran down to Peitaiho, the summer resort of the foreign colony in Peking.

Captains Blamer and Luby had returned to the United States and Captain Cone had taken over their associated duties. The Cranes and Athertons had adjoining cottages at Peitaiho in a pine and mimosa grove near the beach. The political situation in Peking had improved. Marshal Tuan's forces, I heard, had been defeated outside the walls and were retreating. The *Madawaska* had arrived in San Francisco.

The long white road to Peitaiho sizzles in the terrific heat and glare, but the journey is pleasant in a ricksha. Naked children, donkeys, fruit venders and workmen take shelter under the trees. Fat women toil up the road from the beach where the surf rolls in from a glassy sea. The sweating ricksha men and the naked coolies with their burdens swung from poles on their shoulders are the only signs of life in the blistering rays of the sun.

Life at Peitaiho in peace time is one of sweet idleness, but storm clouds were gathering and from Vladivostok came the news from Captain Larimer that Japanese soldiers had fired on our shore patrol.

A short distance from Peitaiho to the northward is Shanhaikwan where the Great wall comes down to the sea. This is the eastern end of that Wonder of the World's construction which extends 1,200 miles over mountains and hills and across valleys. We anchored in the *Alava* near the Wall. There is no harbor at Shanhaikwan, only an open roadstead, so Holcombe left the ship to find a good landing place. Since there was not much surf and no wind, we had no difficulty in landing on the Ninghai beach. Donkey boys soon appeared and we rode to the city—four or five miles distant. According to the guide books Shanhaikwan rivals Mukden and Tientsin in interest. We did not find it so. It was the scene of fierce fighting several years afterwards with the Japanese.

When we returned to the beach the wind had increased, blowing onshore, the surf heavy. The motor dory was anchored outside the surf, and the dinghy came in to take us off. In doing so, the crew lost control of her and she swamped and we were all thrown into the water and had a hard time to scramble out. It so happened that Mrs. Simpson, wife of Putnam-Weale, was on the beach with her child. She took us to her cottage and gave us dry clothes—my share being a polo coat, a pair of socks and also a bottle of whiskey. Captain Ponto and Lieutenant Holcombe bailed out the boat and pulled out to the ship to get the whale boat to take the women on board.

There were a number of men on the beach near the club but none came to the rescue. The people who helped us were women. One woman, Mrs. Simpson told us, wrung her hands and shrieked, "They will be drowned! Somebody save them. Send for the lifeboat."

When Ponto and Holcombe returned after dark with the boat, they dropped anchor and then veered her into the beach. We embarked without further trouble after a delicious dinner with Mrs. Simpson of rice and curry, cooked as only a Chinese chef can cook it.

After the adventure on the beach at Ninghai we ran down to Port Arthur in the *Alava*. At 9:30 the next morning we stood into the harbor and fired a national salute. I wondered at the delay in returning our salute, but when he came on board the harbor master explained there was no saluting battery on the hill, and they had to haul a gun from one of the forts down to the port. Immediately after returning the national salute, they fired a 17-gun salute to my flag, which was returned gun for gun. After the guns, came the official calls, the automobile excursions, dinners and luncheons.

Port Arthur has been made famous in our own times not only by its baptism of fire and blood in the war between Japan and Russia, but when Admiral Togo taught the world the great lesson of the value of naval preparedness and readiness for war. (I was in Admiral Taylor's office at the navy department the morning the cable was received telling of the surprise attack by the Japanese. I never saw any one more jubilant as he said to Secretary Moody, "This vindicates all our teaching at the War College for preparedness.")

A monument erected by the Japanese to the Russian dead overlooks the harbor and is a conspicuous landmark. It is a tall, cylindrical stone column capped by an enormous stone shell. A curious design, but a beau geste to raise a monument to a defeated foe.

The famous 203 Metre Hill was in plain sight of the ship. Crowned with a small monument in the shape of a shell and cartridge standing on end, it is a long and hard climb to the summit. Here 30,000 Japanese soldiers were killed in the assaults before it was captured. There is probably nothing in history comparable to it except Gallipoli as told in the saga of John Masefield.

It is said that when General Nogi visited the battlefield after the fighting he noticed a mound and a stone marker. When told that his son was buried there, he had the place razed because he said his son's grave was not more entitled to be marked than that of any other soldier who had fallen. The whole place is full of interest and Vice Admiral Matsamura, who is in command, was anxious we should see everything, from the fort where General Kondratenko was killed—blown to pieces by a 42 cm. shell—to the mummies in the museum.

Kondratenko was the outstanding Russian officer at Port Arthur. One cannot read the history of the fights for the forts without being impressed with the great difference between this distinguished soldier and his immediate superior in Port Arthur. When the surrender took place, Stoessel offered a very handsome horse to General Nogi as a personal gift. This was declined, Nogi saying that all surrendered property belonged to his government. Stoessel was among the first of the Russians to quit Port Arthur.

The mummies we saw had been recently found in Tibet and according to the dates on the bricks of the tomb are 1,300 years old but in such a state of preservation as to look human. Two of them are men, the other a woman. Their expressions are almost lifelike. It was a curious experience to look at people who had lived in the reign of the early Mings, 600 years before the days of Kublai Khan.

Admiral Matsumura told me that the governor general had prepared his villa for me and expected me to occupy it. He had written to this effect and the letter was sent to the Japanese consul at Chefoo, who forwarded it to the American consul. There it remained. It was not delivered to me until it was too late for me to accept, as we sailed shortly for Dairen.

The ADC to the admiral took me in a carriage, formerly General Alexieff's, to make a few official calls—one of which was to the general commandant in the house where General Stoessel lived when in command of the fortress during the war. I went also to Governor Yamagata's villa where I was to have visited and which had been made ready for me.

The war museum contains many interesting relics and trophies. Over a small stream a bridge has been constructed, using Russian artillery wheels for the side rails. It contains maps and plans of the forts surrounding Port Arthur, showing them before and after the demolition by gunfire.

As the *Alava's* cabin was very small and the weather was very hot, we rigged a table on the hurricane deck for 21 guests who were to lunch with us. Although the tiffin was of necessity not a conversational affair, we got through with it fairly well and the Japanese officers and their wives seemed to enjoy it.

When our guests had left, we steamed out of the harbor and passed close to the buoys marking the grave of the *Petropavlovsk*, the flagship of Admiral Makaroff which was sunk in 13 fathoms by two mines exploding simultaneously, one on either side. Admiral Matsumara told me that when she was blown up, he was looking at her through his glasses from the bridge of his own ship. It was about nine in the morning and the mines had been dropped the night before.

After exchanging farewell signals with the signal station on Golden Hill we headed for Dairen, a run of only four hours. We anchored outside the breakwater, but not far enough away to escape the vile odors of the offshore breeze.

The following day the polite and attentive American consul at Dairen took us on a long automobile drive and we saw the city from every point. An American lady, Mrs. Kellogg, the widow of a commander in our navy, invited us to dinner. Her son had the distinction of being the only American in the employ of the great banking firm of the Hong Kong-Shanghai Corporation. Our consul, poor chap, was later transferred to the more exalted post at Yokohoma and was there only a short time when he was killed in the great earthquake.

25 Last Visit to Peking

Our visit to the fringes of Manchuria did not last long. I had intended to go to Korea, but the consul at Seoul advised me to postpone my visit on account of an epidemic of smallpox onshore. At the same time I received a pleasant telegram from the famous governor, Baron Saito, expressing his regrets and disappointment that the *Alava*'s visit had to be deferred.

We returned to Chefoo to wait for the finish of target practice by the destroyers. For a month we remained there behind the new breakwater (built by the American engineer, Mr. A. S. Bowers) while the weather blew itself out in heavy rains, accompanied by strong, cold northwest winds. One day I received a request from Mr. Crane to come to Peking if convenient.

Commander Chu met us at Tientsin with oral messages from Admiral Sah. As we were not to start for Peking for several days, Chu arranged for me to call on ex-President Li Yuan-hung and also Mr. Liung Ch'i-chi'ao, two great men of China.

Mr. Liung Ch'i-chi'ao had been the chief of the Chinese delegation at the European conference in Paris and was considered a brilliant scholar. Chu said his royalties from his writings amounted to $20,000 a year. He is strongly anti-Japanese and had rendered great service to China in denouncing the 21 Demands. He had also opposed Yuan Shih-k'ai's imperalistic movement.

I found him very pleasant and remarkably well informed. Chu's praises were not exaggerated. He received us in the library of his handsome house, modern and furnished in Western style. I had a long conversation with him during which he expressed the hope that when the time came for China to reconstruct her navy, the United States would give her counsel. Seeing him surrounded by his books and manuscripts, I recalled what Mr. Li-kao had said to me in Peking, "The Chinese proverb says, 'It is better to be an hour with a learned man, than ten years with books.' "

The ex-president lived in a more pretentious establishment. He was equally cordial and invited up to dinner, and expressed a desire to come on board the *Alava*, which of course I was glad to gratify. As ships cannot fire salutes alongside the bund I could only break the

Chinese flag at the main while he was on board. Li Yuan-hung's dinner was informal but the party was large and included his wife and two daughters, an unusual compliment. The dinner began at 6:30 and at 10 we were back on board ship.

At the club I was given a new drink called a gimlet—a mild affair of gin, lime juice and water. Velvet at Vladivostok, gimlets at Tientsin—names to write in my diary and remember afterwards.

When I went overboard at Ninghai, my wrist atch had been submerged and I took it to Vrard's in Tientsin to be repaired. Coming out of his place we fell in with a group of beggars on the sidewalk, apparently a family. The man had in one of the baskets on the end of a pole a dead baby which he was exposing to excite sympathy and get alms. I have never seen anything more gruesome. He turned back the ragged shirt of the baby and showed his little wrinkled arm and hand like a bird's claw. Evidently the child had died of starvation, although the others of the family seemed well nourished.

The conditions in north China, where the famine was making terrible ravages, were said to be the worst in years. Foreigners were taking up collections to relieve the distress. I cabled to the navy department recommending that supplies of necessary food—principally millet—be sent out if possible from Manila.

On 20 September 1920 I came again to Peking, where the sun was bright and warm and the pomegranates in full bloom. I found the Athertons in their garden at the legation having tiffin. They are omnivorous but eclectic readers and had just received from their bookseller in Shanghai the monthly package of the latest publications. I enjoyed examining them.

Professor Hornbeck of the state department and Dr. and Mrs. John Dewey were in Peking. I met them at dinner at the legation. Before dinner I drove with Commander Hutchins to the Western Hills, the Jade Fountain Pagoda and that other marvel of architecture—the Pa-Li-Chiang Pagoda, said to be the finest of 10,000 once near Peking.

I consulted the minister regarding the relief ship for the famine sufferers. He read me a long cable to be sent to Washington which would cost $1,200 and asked me to block out a paragraph. The gist of this message was for the army transports to bring supplies to Chingwangtao. I suggested another to send relief to the Chinese gunboats in the Amur River before the river should be frozen and navigation stopped by the ice. Mr. Crane said that some of his staff thought his cable too long and that the state department would balk at the tolls.

The Russian legation compound was the oldest foreign-owned property in Peking. The walls were thick enough to stand an artillery attack. It dates back before the days of Peter the Great. The first Chinese diplomatic mission was to the Court of Russia in 1731. The current legation had been built after the Boxer outbreak.

One day I had tiffin there with Mr. Crane. The minister, Prince Kondacheff, had been six years in Washington and a member of the Portsmouth Peace Conference. As he had lived on board the *Mayflower* and had known the Bakhmetieffs, we had many things in common to discuss. The party was informal and *en famille,* the sister of the prince and an attache of the Russian legation being the other guests.

After tiffin General Horvath came in. He was one of the most important men in Far Eastern affairs, and at that time was president of the Chinese Eastern Railroad and had played an important part as well in the political affairs of Eastern Siberia. He was six feet six and wore a long patriarchal white beard. Horvath was one of Kolchak's serious mistakes. As the "Supreme Ruler" he could not be cashiered completely, but to sidetrack him, Kolchak appointed him governor general of the Chinese Eastern Railroad territory. He was regarded by many as a loyal patriot standing for a United Russia in spite of his open acknowledgment that he was a monarchist. He spoke little English, but his manner was gracious and courtly.

Minister Crane's dinner to the Russian minister was noteworthy as being the last official function attended by Prince Kondacheff. On returning to his legation that night after the dinner he found a cable informing him that his services as minister were no longer required and in a few days he and his suite withdrew from the handsome compound that had flown the imperial flag of Russia since July 1861.

We lunched with Admiral Sah at the palace in which the unfortunate Emperor Kuan-hsi was confined by the Dowager Empress for two years before his death. The palace is on a small island, of great beauty, but, as Miss Bredon says, "of melancholy memories." It is here that the Emperor Kuan found his St. Helena. He was strictly guarded by eunuchs. At night the drawbridge was hauled up and he was left to wander through the courts of his palace prison or sit on the terraces overlooking the lotus lake.

At all events it was in this palace he "mounted the dragon and ascended on high." And in the alcove chamber where he died, Admiral Sah had our tiffin. He told us that Kuan-hsi always kept in order the forsaken grave of his predecessor Tung-chih who was treacherously murdered and that this forlorn emperor had at least the comfort of ministering to a kindred spirit.

In October I went to Tsingtao in the *Huron*. General Yui was in command—a genial, pleasant man who organized an excursion for us to Mt. Laighan, a peak on the Shantung Peninsula about 4,000 feet high. It was a hard day's work but worth the labor. The general was living in the administration building, built by the Germans on a lavish scale but criticized by Prince Henry as "not good enough for a German governor".

While we were visiting the battlefields, some of our sailors started a little battle of their own in the town with the Chinese, which did not result in anything more serious than a brief correspondence between the consul and the governor.

At my dinner to General Yui, I expressed regret that I could not give him wine. He said his wife told him she was glad he was going on board an American man-of-war because he couldn't get anything to drink.

Hearing that a sailor who had been with me in the *St. Louis* was in the hospital badly injured by a fall on board ship, I went to see him and found him perfectly helpless. Fortunately I was able to arrange for his transfer to the naval hospital at Cavite.

Our visit to Tsingtao was brief as we had to hurry south, bound for the Philippines. After a cordial farewell to General Yui and his officers we started at midnight for Shanghai.

On October 12 the *Huron* moored off the French bund at Shanghai. It was rumored that the secretary of the navy intended to change the commanders of the various squadrons before he left office, so presumably this would be our last visit to the Yangtse. I was sorry, but it was part of the game.

Chevalier Chen of the foreign office together with Captain Cope, the disbursing U.S. pay officer, arranged for a trip to Hangchow and Soochow. Admiral Ho suggested we make it by moonlight. Moonshine could at least hide the dust and wear of the ages.

One night several gentlemen from the club along with Commander Fite dined with me on board—the principal attraction being the men's smoker and the movies afterwards. The entertainment of the men was always in charge of our chaplain, Witherspoon, who was not only most efficient in his own calling, but belonged to the Church Militant. I called him the Master of Revels.

After this we all went ashore to a dance at the Carleton Hotel. Ataman Semenoff's "friend", Marie, a striking petite brunette about 25 or 26 years old, who been the talk—if not the toast—of three countries in the Far East, was there.The next day on the Szechwan Road I passed close to her ricksha and was amused at her voluble altercations with the bewildered coolie who evidently did not know what to do with this lady of a famous overcoat worth 250,000 rubles, diamonds worth two millions and an emerald valued at 280,000 rubles. It was said she called herself "the present-day Josephine".

The Minister and Mrs. Crane arrived from Peking. He had sent a cable to Washington requesting that the *Huron* take him to Petropavlovsk. He and I had discussed this visit at Peitaiho and I was disappointed that the department did not approve.

26 Hong Kong and Canton and the End

The cruise in north China waters ended in the last part of October 1920 and the ship sailed south for Foochow, Amoy and Formosa. While we were anchored off Wusung waiting for the tide, H.B.M.S. *Alacrity*, flying the flag of Vice Adm. Sir Alexander Duff, came in and lay to under our stern. The admiral came on board to make a personal call and told me that he had expected to be in Shanghai several days with me and was disappointed that the *Huron* was sailing. He had come from Hong Kong for some shooting in the paddy fields between Shanghai and Soochow.

This was to be the last time I would meet my distinguished colleague. In appearance he was an attractive man—over six feet in height and finely proportioned, a very "castle of a man", as was once said of Fenimore Cooper. As he stood on the gangway receiving his salute, I thought I had never seen a handsomer naval picture. With the sun shining brightly on his gold laced uniform and his hand touching the visor of his cap, he made an impression to be remembered.

I am sure that if any questions of policy had arisen, we would have undertaken their solution in a spirit of hearty cooperation. He and Admiral Borrett were well matched, and I was fortunate to have such associates, especially when no one knew when the expected crisis would come.

Duff had distinguished himself in the World War. Admiral Jellicoe had requested his detail as director of the antisubmarine division of the war staff at the admiralty—where according to Jellicoe he did "great work". He was largely responsible for the successful development of the Burney paravane, a device for the protection of ships against mines. In the battle of Jutland he commanded the Fourth Battle Squadron and won the Order of the Bath.

Going on to Foochow I found everything had changed since last seen in 1885—except the beautiful scenery, the centuries old pagoda at the anchorage nine miles from the city, and the Bridge of Ten Thousand Ages. In 1884 there was no shipping on the river except junks and a few small seagoing vessels that never came up to the city. By 1920 ships of respectable tonnage could anchor off the city. The government shipyard at the anchorage had a bustling air unknown in the days before Admiral Courbet destroyed it.

The American consul, Mr. Price, came down from Foochow to call and Vice Admiral Chen also came on board from the arsenal. After tiffin we went to Foochow with Mr. Price to make our official call on the tuchun. A strong ebb tide delayed our arrival at the landing and it was a long drive to the yamen through the ancient city.

The reception was elaborate, but as there was also a reception at the American consulate in the foreign section, we were compelled to turn away from the feast. Our route lay between hundreds of soldiers, bands and banner men and across the Bridge of Ten Thousand Ages. The *Huron*'s band was playing at the consulate and everyone was dancing when we arrived.

On the next day when the genial tuchun returned my call, he brought presents of carved wood, lacquer work and tea. The lacquer of Foochow is the most famous in China but it is said that the secret of its making is now lost.

Arrangements had been made by cable with our consul at Formosa for the *Huron* to pay a visit to Keelung. This was an interesting diversion, but proved not altogether free from unpleasantness due to a misunderstanding. We were unfortunately bidden to come to the island on the mikado's birthday—which was also the 25th anniversay of the occupation of Formosa by the Japanese—but were not told of this until we arrived in the harbor.

At once the *Huron* and her consort, the *New Orleans*, dressed ship in honor of the day and at noon fired a national salute with the Japanese flag at the fore truck. We were cordially greeted by representatives of the military and civil governors and every effort was made by them to conceal the embarrassment caused by the visit of the ship at a time when they were entirely given over to entertaining their royal guest, Prince Kuni.

Our visit to Formosa was doubly interesting as our war ships rarely go there. So in spite of our untimely visit on a national holiday, and during the entertainment of Prince Kuni and the princess, the civil and military governors sent off the usual presents to the ship of flowers, fruits and tobacco, and arranged as far as possible in our short time in port for us to see the sights.

Representatives of the governor met us at the dock in automobiles and drove us to the palace, 20 miles in the interior, where we met the prince at Taihuku. The entire day was spent in sight-seeing. It was an especially interesting experience to meet his highness the prince, who—as one of the officers remarked—should be called "His Lowness" as he was only five feet. There is not much to be seen in Taihuku except the beautiful scenery and the shrine of the prince who was the commander in chief when the island passed into Japanese hands in 1895.

Even though this brief call of the *Huron* was most inopportune as it interrupted not only the celebration of a great conquest, but also the entertainment of a member of the blood royal before whom all other considerations must yield, it was impressed upon me time and time again that both governors greatly regretted that they were unable to give me their personal and undivided attention. The Japanese are certainly gentlemen and they proved it on this occasion.

After an informal dinner we attended a gala performance at the theater in honor of the prince and princess to which 1,000 guests were invited. That finished our call in the Island of Head Hunters and we sailed the next morning for the China coast.

Our next port was the beautiful city of Amoy. The admiral of that port was anxious to do everything for our pleasure and arranged a beautiful lunch at the naval club—bountiful and copious—at which he insisted on "gambai" meaning "no heel taps"—thus imposing a heavy task.

Our visit to Swatow, not far south of Amoy, was also brief. Mr. Major, the British consul, suggested in appearance Thackeray's description of Rawdon Crawley, and when I met him I thought of Colonel Roosevelt's letter to Trevelyan expressing interest in Rawdon because of his namesake, Thackeray's fundamentally good fellow in *Vanity Fair*.

It was only a short distance from Swatow to Hong Kong and it was good to get back. The weather was gorgeous and the harbor with its variegated shipping never appeared to better advantage than when the *Huron* steamed to her buoy.

To elaborate on the gun salutes which are fired by a man-of-war when she enters a foreign port, let me note in detail what happened as we arrived in Hong Kong. As the *Huron* approached the anchorage, we fired a national salute of 21 guns, with the British ensign at the fore truck. This was promptly returned by the signal station on the peak. Then the USS *Helena*, at anchor in the harbor, saluted the four star flag with 17 guns, which was returned with seven guns. Then the British ship *Tamar* fired 17 guns, which was returned by the *Huron*, gun for gun.

It sounds easy, but I know of nothing in the punctilious etiquette of naval service so susceptible of mistakes and misunderstandings. On our way out to China many mistakes were made with the saluting batteries and flags until our green crew were thoroughly indoctrinated.

I was on the bridge before eight o'clock to enjoy the scenery at the entrance of the harbor. The rain which had fallen all night had ceased and the monsoon was not strong. The wind was on the quarter, and while the *Huron* was not affected, the *New Orleans* was making rather heavy weather of it 500 yards astern, rolling in a rough sea.

We passed close to Mir's Bay, put on the map by Admiral Dewey when he took his squadron there after war had been declared against Spain and he had to leave Hong Kong. Captain Cone, who was in the *Baltimore* at the time, told me that when the squadron anchored in Mir's Bay, all the woodwork, chests, tables and bureaus were thrown overboard. Chinese junks and sampans swarmed around the wreckage in hundreds struggling to pick up as much of the furniture as possible.

The following day, a Sunday, I called on the governor, Sir Reginald Stubbs. A company of the Wiltshires and the full regimental band paraded on the dock. On the invitation of the ADC I inspected the company and was impressed by the smart appearance of the men. After this ceremony we were driven to the government house on the hill, a dignified residence surrounded by tropical plants—green and in flower.

The governor, dressed in white uniform with gold embroidered collar, was most cordial. He returned my call before noon. When he came on board I presented Lieutenant Edgar Allan Poe to him, since he had expressed a desire to personally meet the great-great-nephew of the poet, who Govenor Stubbs said was better known in England than any other American author. Such amenities contribute to a pleasant understanding and good feeling and are in accordance with the navy regulations enjoining all of us to "cultivate friendly relations with the inhabitants onshore".

It is a steep climb to the peak and the flag lieutenant and I, after going up to the first station of the funicular, decided that the weather was too hot for climbing. Yet in the days before the railroad all the houses that are on the side of the peak were built of stone and brick brought laboriously up the mountain by men, women and even children. The day was clear and the views from the station were superb all around the coast to Repulse Bay.

In the evening there was a party on board the *Tamar* where I played roulette on the quarterdeck and won a few shillings. In the Royal Navy they do not have shore duty, as we call it, but duty on the guardo amounts to the same thing. These ships, fitted out in the most comfortable fashion for the officers' families, make attractive homes. The rank of the commanding officer is commodore, which is retained in the service for that purpose.

The major general commanding the troops here, although he was on the retired list, paid me a visit. He asked me not to return his call in person, but to send the flag lieutenant "to sign up his book".

At my tiffin to the governor and his wife on board the *Huron*, Miss Duff, the admiral's daughter, acted as hostess. Afterwards we danced on the quarterdeck and then went ashore to the annual cricket match with the Australian team. It is my opinion that while cricket may be interesting to those born to it, compared with baseball it is a parlor game and an indoor sport.

One night our men gave a smoker on board with many British officers, sailors and marines present. The boxing champions were selected from our men and the English sailors—a rather dangerous venture. However, as the honors were about even, everything went off quietly. Once when an Englishman was knocked out, there was a whirlwind of applause from our men which was deftly stopped by Weller, the watertender in charge, who ordered the band to strike up.

I have never understood why, when sailors sing at smokers, they usually strike falsetto notes and sing through their noses. One of the numbers on the program was a recitation of "Mandalay" by the chief master-at-arms. He got very confused and his rendition of "Mandalay" was, to say the least, original and highly entertaining. Weller's speeches and interpretations were also very funny. He constantly referred to the visitors as "our shipmates in the royal navy".

The governor's dinner was formal, but pleasant. I took out Lady Stubbs and Mrs. James, the wife of a captain, RN, sat on my right. Only one toast was drunk—to the king and president. The banquet room at the government house is of handsome proportions. There are large portraits of the king and queen, the former in his coronation robes and wearing the uniform of a full admiral. Around the rooms were the portraits of former governors.

As I was particularly interested in one of them—Sir John Bowring—the governor took me to the billiard room where it hung, and pointed it out. It bore the dates 1854-59. The governor did not know until I told him that Sir John wrote hymns—two of them favorites in the hymnal today: "Watchman, Tell Us of the Night," and "In the Cross of Christ I Glory." The governor remarked that he didn't look as if he wrote hymns and thought he had a wicked face. I replied that on the contrary I thought him very good looking and that perhaps he wrote beautiful hymns only when not dictating orders for the bombardment of Canton or the slaying of smugglers.

During this visit to Hong Kong I took several officers with me to Macao—only four hours run by steamer from Hong Kong. Viewed from seaward, Macao is beautiful. We spent two hours in driving around the island and seeing the sights including Camoes' tomb in the cemetery where several American officers of the "old navy" are buried.

The Camoes' garden and a Chinese private garden are extremely interesting, but not as much as the factory where opium is prepared from the poppy and openly put up for sale. There is also Mr. Sun-tai's gambling house, plainly so marked. It is a curious sight to watch the game of fan-tan which goes on night and day, for the Chinese are the original gamblers. Macao has other attractions which may not enter here. On the return to Hong Kong the captain of the steamer told me that there were 6,000 prostitutes in Macao who paid a tax to the government of $72,000 annually!

There were innumerable war junks anchored in the waterways, nearly all of them presumably pirates. They were armed with old muzzle-loading cannon of small caliber. At one point I counted on one side of the steamer more than 200 junks on the horizon. Their attacks on the coastline shipping are frequent and nearly always accompanied by hard and bloody fighting.

On November 12, I went on board the destroyer *Hart* with Post, Poe and Holcombe of my staff, and several other officers bound for Canton. The waterways were crowded with junks—big and little. These most picturesque craft in the world look awkward to handle, but the Chinese maneuver them with marvelous skill. On the bows of each one are painted eyes, and many have small black and white poles fastened to a cap at the fore truck which are supposed to represent dragon whiskers to appease the water dragon. Chinese are a rare combination of superstition and science. The junkmen of today are the lineal descendants of the inventors of the mariner's compass, double bottoms, and watertight compartments—so Marco Polo tells us.

Many years had passed since I had been on the Shamien, the foreign concession which is the small island directly in front of the city of Canton. It is connected with the city by several bridges, and is the foreign residential section where the consulates are situated. It is a beautiful breathing place in torrid months, and has been a wonderful refuge for foreigners in time of riots and confusion. A small British gunboat was anchored off the bund and there was the usual interchange of courtesies but, on account of disturbed policital conditions, no gun salutes.

Canton is outwardly more changed in the past two decades than any other city on the coast. I recalled an incident of my first visit when the viceroy of the province returned Minister Denby's call and remained to lunch at the consulate. There had been a procession of high officials in sedan chairs followed by banner men, umbrella carriers, tom-tom beaters and all the accessories of a ceremonial march of those days. The viceroy and the mandarins wore handsome gowns of silk, satins and rich sables. Each one also wore enormous tortoiseshell-rimmed spectacles and carried a handsome fan. The West has adopted the horn spectacles and some day perhaps our men of fashion may use fans.

After the ceremonies of the call, lunch was announced. When the meal was half over the consul demanded silence and rising said, "There is a custom in American I always observe when I entertain foreigners. We always have ham and eggs in the middle of the repast."

Everything else was "in due form and technically correct". There was, however, one break when the consul ordered the French windows opened to free the room of tobacco smoke. There was a fresh breeze blowing directly up Pearl River which the consulate faced. The wind blew the smoke back into the room and started everyone coughing so violently, the party broke up. I wondered if this was the consul's strategy to get rid of his guests.

During the few hours of visit to Canton I visited many places familiar from my younger days, then went into the city to buy curios. There was no change there: it was as it had been when the Temple of the Ten Hundred Genii and the Flowery Pagoda were built centuries ago. The pagoda is the most interesting object in Canton and in the garden around it are asters, dahlias, chrysanthemums and cockscombs—red and yellow—all very beautiful.

Our day closed with a very pleasant dinner party given by another consul in the room of the International Banking Corporation.

While in Canton I received a dispatch that the military and political situation in Swatow was bad. I sent the *New Orleans* over to keep communications open and ordered a destroyer from Cavite to take up patrol duty at Hong Kong, pending repairs to the *Wilmington.* Swatow had been captured by northern troops. These disturbances were the rumblings of the work of Sun Yat-sen, a native of Canton who had always lived there. Nothing, however, seemed to disturb the equanimity of the Chinese in the street. There was no outward sign of turmoil but I am quite sure that every foreign soldier and sailor had his hand on his gun.

One afternoon after our return to Hong Kong I went ashore to shop and then in chairs to a reception hall well up on the hill, which is called the King's Clere. All the American colony was there—about 200 probably—and I saw them all again on board the *Huron* before we sailed for Manila.

Our visit to Hong Kong was unusually pleasant. Great cordiality had been shown—quite different from the atmosphere encountered in the earlier days of intercourse with the officials, but that was before our war with Spain.

On 18 November 1920 we sailed from Hong Kong at 10 a.m. The thick weather of the past night cleared, fog and wind decreased and outside the Heads a fresh NE monsoon which had been blowing died down. Suddenly the wind shifted to SE in a heavy rainsquall which blew itself out in a few hours, leaving a clear sky and a flat sea—which we carried in to Manila.

Admiral Morgan had arranged for our quarters in the hotel. We had a desirable northern and western exposure, but the lizards kept up a continuous rattling in the ceilings and between the walls. We heard them, but never saw them. The weather was very hot and I decided to go to Baguio. General Kernan had placed an army automobile at my disposal and Senator Quezon sent us up to the mountains in the private car of the president of the Manila railroad, attached to a special train. We went by train as far as Dormitos, thence by the army automobile to Baguio, a two-hour drive.

Captain McDowell who arrived from the United States to command the destroyers on this station, told me I was to be relieved of the command of the Asiatic station about Christmas.

I met Senator Quezon on the golf course and thanked him for his courtesy for the special train which brought us to Baguio. He is now the president of the Philippine Islands, and one of the few men I know who has realized his ambitions.

Our bungalow was a delightful and restful haven and down in the valley beneath it, my "star" still glowed through the mists like a yellow topaz. The month of December was passed at Baguio with golf and driving in the mountains. The autumn scenery was beautiful and there was much gaiety on the reservation. On January 1, my birthday, Governor Harrison sent me a case of champagne and the occasion was celebrated at the admiral's cottage by a party to the army officers and their wives.

We returned to Manila a week later and began preparations for our departure in the *Empress of Russia*, which was to sail from Hong Kong for Vancouver. Before sailing I made another visit to Olongapo and Corregidor. While at Olongapo I received a radio from the *Albany* that Lieutenant Langdon of that ship had been shot by a Japanese sentry in the streets of Vladivostok. He died shortly afterwards. At once I decided to return to Vladivistok and personally investigate the shooting and to take the destroyer, *Elliot*. with the chief of staff, Captain Cone, Lieutenant Commander Lowe and Major Fortsam of the marines.

Before sailing for the north, Mr. Stanley Hornbeck of the state department and young Mr. Crane, the minister's son, came on board to dine with us. They were bound for the southern islands and Siam.

As Lieutenant Holcombe had a serious crash in his airplane, I decided to leave him at Manila. He begged to go to Vladivostok, but was too badly shaken up to go. His plane had a narrow escape. First they ran into an air pocket and dropped into the water near Cavite. Holcombe, who is a fine swimmer, said he thought he was never coming up. A second accident occurred several hours afterwards when they started for Olongapo and the engine suddenly stopped. The plane fell from 3000 feet to 200 feet above the sea when the pilot managed to bring the plane down to the water—which was rough. They succeeded in taxiing into a cave and were found there by the *Hart*.

On the morning of January 16 we got underway for Shanghai. A strong wind was blowing outside and the sea was so heavy that we slowed from 25 knots to 20 knots off the northern end of Luzon, when the motion became so violent that it was difficult to set the table for dinner. As all the airports had to be closed and the hatches battened down, the atmosphere was, to say the least, oppresive—as the artificial ventilation proved defective.

Captain Gunther of the *Elliot* was a sportsman as well as a prime sailor and had four dogs on board—a pointer, an airedale and two little chows. None of them seemed to mind the conditions, except the pointer who looked forlorn.

During the night the weather moderated. There were six flying fish found on deck in the morning and the captain had one for breakfast and said it was good. In the Formosa Channel we passed a number of small craft—their hulls were black, about 20 feet long, and each carried a big mast and a small sail in the bow. I do not know what purpose it served. The men in the boats were evidently unmindful of rough weather.

Overhead it was bright and clear. The distant shores of Formosa reminded me of the low approaches to New York on the Jersey coast. Stormy weather continued all day and the speed was reduced to 15 knots. I received a message from the *Alava* that Holcombe's injuries, though painful, were not serious.

When the Saddles were sighted I radioed to Captain Owens in the *New Orleans* to select a good lee in the islands and we would join him there and shift my flag. This would save 40 or 50 miles in the destroyer—whose water in the tanks had become unpalatable after our shaking up during the rough weather.

The sea flattened down in the lee of the islands and about four p.m. I transferred to the *New Orleans* off Balfour Island, not far from the Argon lighthouse. The *Elliot* then proceeded to Shanghai, and the *New Orleans* headed for Vladivostok passing to the southward of Quelpart Island.

fter the tumbling about in the destroyer, the steadiness of the *New Orleans* was a relief. This ship was built in England for Brazil at the beginning of the war with Spain and her cabin fittings were comfortable and ample—and not very different from the equipment of our own ships.

The Shanghai papers brought to me by Captain Owens had many dispatches regarding the shooting of Lieutenant Langdon at Vladivostok—with favorable comments on the proposed investigation by the American commander in chief in person. I radioed Captain Richardson in the *Albany* at Vladivostok to have coal ready for us and to notify the consul I would remain as short a time as possible. The Chinese coal is bad stuff and the *New Orleans* was burning 140 tons per day to make 14 knots.

On the morning of the 21st, after crossing the Gulf of Korea, we picked up rugged weather again—skies overcast, wind fresh and seas so heavy that even the *New Orleans'* 3,500 tons found it a lively seaway to negotiate. About ten o'clock we sighted a small open boat with five men in it making signals of distress. We stood down to it and found Koreans suffering from exposure, and the boat in bad shape. After getting the castaways on board the *New Orleans*, we cut their boat adrift and shortly after saw it sink.

We hugged the coast the remainder of the day steaming within two or three miles of the shore rising precipitately from the sea to a height of 300 or 400 feet—covered with snow, very rugged and desolate, not a sign of life of any kind.

The next day we arrived at Vladivostok. It was early morning when we entered the floe ice and passed through two large fields of it. I was awakened by the ice crunching against the ship's side with a force that would have pierced the thin plates of a destroyer. Although all the radiators were turned on, the cabin was very cold. At 8:20 we passed the abandoned Russian church on Scripleff Island, which had become a familiar landmark to us. Shortly afterwards the pilot came on board from the icebreaker, and it was not long before we were backing into our snug berth alongside the *Albany*. The harbor was filled with ice, and the hills around the Golden Horn were sprinkled with snow.

Captain Richardson came on board immediately to report, and was, as to be expected, extremely interesting. General Oi sent his aid with his compliments and his welcome "to my old friend". Commander Wong, who was then the senior Chinese naval officer, came to pay an official as well as personal visit. The Japanese consul-general, to whom I turned over the shipwrecked Koreans, came on board and thanked me for their rescue.

Of my interview with General Oi regarding the shooting of Lieutenant Langdon, I will not write here, as it was made official in my dispatches to the secretary of the navy. The tragic affair was later settled by the state department. It is in keeping, however, to say that nothing was left undone or unsaid by the Japanese highest authorities at Vladivostok to show their regret. I think they realized that the limit had been reached.

From Captain Richardson I learned the details of the story:

Langdon, a young lieutenant in the *Albany*, had been onshore to a Russian New Year's party and was returning to his ship after midnight. When passing the headquarters of a Japanese regiment, he was challenged by a sentry who, disregarding Langdon's uniform and proper answer to the challenge, fired several shots with his rifle—one of which entered the officer's back. The wound was fatal and Langdon died the next morning.

Before my arrival General Oi had ordered a court-martial, which was in session when I arrived. As a matter of fact, the result of the court was not made public for many weeks, and I believe the final action of the Japanese in Tokyo was to pay $10,000 to the mother of the officer and to offer an apology to the United States. But the record of the general court-martial was kept in Tokyo 40 days.

On concluding my interview with General Oi, and considering it desirable not to remain longer in northern waters, I sailed in the afternoon of January 23 for Manila. The weather was clear and cold, the thermometer down to 9° above. The body of Langdon was transferred to the *New Orleans* for transportation to the United States. The casket was covered with floral offerings, including a metal wreath by General Oi and the Japanese high command.

I lunched at the consulate with the hospitable Macgowans and after luncheon, looking from the window across the Golden Horn, had my last view of the perimeter of the bay which was entirely frozen over from shore to shore. Many skaters were on the ice and on the north side the hills were covered with snow. I could see the Catholic church, a prominent landmark in the cleft of the hills across the water, where several American sailors who had died during the preceding two years were buried in its cemetary.

Admiral Chernilovsky-Sokol came on board to say good-bye. To this fine, outstanding looking officer, I am indebted for many courtesies during the vexatious days of our service together.

We passed Russian Island before dark and in the thickening twilight the little Russian church on the point and the bare trees looked drear and forlorn. *Vale, muy vale, Siberia.*

At Manila in January 1921 the carnival season was on and the city was gay. Coronation night is a great event, but as the rain was heavy and my box flooded, Senator Quezon took us all into his box. The coronation was a beautiful affair and showed fine organization and administration. The historical details of Magellan and Legaspi were excellent. The impersonation of the cardinal was fine, but I felt that part of the show would have been improved by the omission of the communion service and the mock religious features. The covenant between Legaspi and the first royal governor of the Philippines and Solomon, the defender of Manila, was well enacted. During the coronation ceremony the bands played the national airs of the United States, Spain and the Philippines.

On the second of February came my Ides of Quintilis. On the quarterdeck of the *Huron* there was presented to me, in the name of the officers and crew of the flagship, a silver service in the presence of the officers, their wives and the crew.

On February 4 1921 I hauled down my flag and ceased to be a seagoing officer of the navy, after 27 years of service in all classes of more than 40 ships, many of which I had commanded. The ceremony occured at 2:20 and as I went over the side and got into the motor barge waiting for me alongside, all hands cheered ship and the band played "Auld Lang Syne".

At 4 p.m. we went on baord the *Empress of Russia* with Lieutenant Holcombe who accompanied me to the United States. My staff came on board the *Empress* to bid us good-bye. At ten o'clock, as the ship left the harbor, the *Huron* siren blew her whistles and made all the noise possible. The destroyers blinked "good-bye" and the *Huron* signaled with her searchlights, "To Admiral Gleaves: Good luck, good health, good-bye."

The voyage home in the *Empress of Russia* from Manila to Vancouver was a fitting end to the cruise. A fine captain, a fine ship and fleeting glimpses and farewells to old friends in five ports of China and Japan. At Hong Kong we lunched on board the *Alacrity* with Admiral Duff. At Shanghai, Admiral Borrett sent his barge to Wusung to bring us directly to the city and to lunch with him and his charming family. Dr. Findley also entertained us at dinner. At Kobe the Japanese authorities gave us the courtesies of the port and at Nagasaki Mr. Mitamura of the famous Mitsu Busan Kaisa drove us to Mogi for tiffin. Two pretty geisha girls came with us to serve saki or Scotch whiskey.

At Yokohoma I saw for the last time the *fidus Achates* of Lafcadio Hearn, Mitchell MacDonald, an old shipmate in the *Texas*. He was then on the retired list of navy paymasters. A few weeks later he met a noble death in the earthquake in the vain attempt to save an unknown woman's life in the destruction of the Grand Hotel.

On March 1 the *Empress* arrived at Vancouver and my party

reached Seattle the next morning.

My last cruise was ended. For me the lights had twinkled on the rocks for the last time.

ADDENDUM

After duty on a board in Washington on safety at sea, I was appointed to command of the First Naval District and the Navy Yard at Boston. There on my birthday, 1 January 1922, at the inexorable age of 64, I hauled down my flag.

So ended my nearly 49 years in the navy and my continuous command, ashore or afloat, for over 20 years, beginning with the Dolphin on November 2, 1901.

Appendix I*

In a biography "background" usually means ancestry. Not in this. Albert Gleaves came of fine old pioneer and fighting stock-soldiers at Valley Forge and Kings Mountain, first settlers of western Tennessee, and after them many good citizens recognized as such in that state and others. That may seem important to believers in the effect of heredity.

If they are right, it is surely because of the upbringing of the child by the parents and of pride in keeping a name in honor, rather than because of any actual transmission of moral qualities in the blood. Every officer of the United States Navy, whatever their own antecedents, has the best of rearing at the most receptive age and the honor of the service to maintain. Their best ancestors are those who have gone before them in that service, whether or not they have in their veins the blood of any of them or of all the "caste of Vere de Vere".

It is not by the illustrious only that the background has been created. It has been formed also by those who have kept honor clear by risking and often giving their lives for others in the sea, or in blazing turrets, or wrecked submarines, or standing by dying comrades in obscure places of the earth, whether or not any other person will ever know or "long remember" it. Sometimes their deeds are told to the public, if the evoking tragedy seems of sufficient importance to the press. More often they are published, if at all, in a small "inside" paragraph, and even when blazoned on a front page, are soon forgotten outside of the service.

Those are the heroes, sung and unsung, to whom opportunity has come, and rarely in vain; but even those have formed only a part of the background of the navy. The greater mass of it has been made and maintained by the nonheroes who devote their whole lives to the steady, quiet performance of duty, the rigors of discipline, the training and welfare of those entrusted to their command, the tact and good breeding that keep an efficient and happy ship and a wardroom what a gentleman's club should be, and, above all, to the faithful discharge of responsibility.

On a battleship every captain at all times, and every watch officer from time to time daily, has in his charge several million dollars worth of ship and equipment, and more than a thousand lives; and every commander and line officer on every other man-of-war bears responsibility in a less but always great degree. All this on a salary of from 14 hundred to six thousand dollars a year, and every married officer has the assurance from a grateful country of a pension to his widow of $30 a month for the support of herself and then for each child she may have.

Nothing but love of the service and pride in it can keep anyone in such a profession, and nothing but love of her husband and pride in his career can make a woman stand by him and keep him in it. It is to be hoped that some day a great poet will write the epic of the wives of the army and navy.

Higher pay, anywhere nearly commensurate with the responsibility, might possibly deteriorate the service by attracting officers with less pure zeal—those

*Introduction written in 1934 by Admiral Gleaves' friend and editor.

working for money. Yet it does seem that protection should be assured to the families of those in the service in order to relieve anxiety. A widow's pension should be, at least, half that of her husband's pay at the time of his death and be continued after her death to any young children then living.

Where did the background begin? The fascination of the ocean and its perils goes back to the man, sung by Horace, "with oak and triple brass around his heart who first launched his fragil raft upon the savage sea". It grew through a long line of mariners and vikings of every race, and came to us directly through the great Elizabethan sailors who explored and colonized what is now Anglo-Saxon North America, and fought the Spaniard in the New World and smashed his Invincible Armada in the Old. Their deeds are an inheritance to us as much as to England—perhaps more, for without them we should never have had our country.

If someone should quarrel with an elder sibling, or rather with the steward of the family affairs, and leave the common establishment, keeping part of the farm for themself, they do not thereby abandon their family tree. Drake, Hawkins, Grenville, Raleigh and Frobisher are ours. John Hawkins was the first to fight Spain in the New World at San Juan d'Ulloa in 1568. Hamilton Hawkins led a division at San Juan Hill in 1898.

But apart from that inheritance of our navy, its own self-made traditions began, naturally, with our Revolution. Seamen were plenty and good in the 13 colonies—all on the seaboard—and many young men eager and capable to be officers. Long before Lexington, George Washington at the age of 14 actually received a warrant as midshipman in the Royal Navy, and returned it only because of his mother's tearful anxiety.

The sea-born infant was fortunate in its principal nurse—that extraordinary sailor, son of a Scotch gardener, who became the intimate and wise adviser of statesmen and diplomats, the favorite of courts and queens, and, above all, a ship fighter of the first rank, with an almost uncanny knowledge of navies and their needs in material and men.

The letter of John Paul Jones to Joseph Hewes, chairman of the Provisional Marine or Naval Committee of the Continental Congress, of September 14, 1775, has been a creed for the navy every since. As literature its style, clearness and force are well-nigh perfect—as are most of Paul Jones' other letters also—and create a wonder how the "son of obscure peasants" and skipper of merchantmen acquired his mastery of language.

No man is perfect, and many an officer has fallen short of that creed at times. The failings and eccentricities, as well as the triumphs, of many will appear in this book; but all have professed and followed it as best they could and never a one more closely than Albert Gleaves.

Imagine the struggle of the tiny Continental navy, with a maximum at any time of five 32-gun frigates and twelve sloops of 24 to 28 guns and eight of ten to 16, against its mighty parent! Of course, it had little or no far-reaching effect on the military operations of the enemy, but it did hamper them occasionally. Too, it did keep its opponents busy, contributing powerfully to bringing in France. But above all, by victories in single ship actions over equal or superior force and by gallant fights against overwhelming odds, the navy did set a mark for the aim of the next generation, and for all the rest in all of years to come.

After the Revolution the navy was dropped, being deemed too costly for the young nation—a very expensive economy as was soon found. Within 15 years thereafter began the depredations of our former allies in the Revolution, the French—or rather of their successors in government. Ships of war were built again. Besides capturing or sinking privateers and engaging in reprisals, the *Constellation* brought into port two French frigates. The depredations stopped.

Next came the Tripolitan War to save our merchant seamen from robbery and slavery. The sea fights with the corsairs were usually between small vessels, always victories for us and occasionally brilliant, though not important. In operations against fortified harbors and cutting out expeditions, the young officers and their men opened the eyes of older navies. Lord Nelson called the *Philadelphia* affair the most daring deed of the age.

Then came the War of 1812. The captains and commodores trained in the quasi war with France and on the Barbary Coast made good indeed. Sent to sea with 17 ships and 500 guns against more than a thousand with over 28,000 guns, they took 15 King's ships with 370 guns and lost 13 of their own with 317 guns. One of the 13, the *Essex,* was lost in a battle finer than any victory. Out of 14 duels between ships of nearly equal force they won twelve, counting as one the *Constitution's* capture of a frigate and a sloop of war, both at once. On the Lakes, starting with no vessels but building them, they swept Erie and Champlain clear, taking or destroying 20 vessels and 200 guns at a cost of eight small craft and 37 guns.

In the early days officers began as midshipmen at sea, sometimes as mere children. Farragut, when he went on the *Essex* with Porter, his father by adoption, was nine years old. They had to grow up rapidly. This same Farragut, the younger Porter and their famous predecessors of the War of 1812—besides hundreds of fine seamen and gentlemen of the old navy whose names are not written so large in history—were the ones who kept alive, in peace as well as war, the code of John Paul Jones.

Yet there must have been many promising youngsters who fell by the way because of trials and temptations beyond the strength of their years. The fate of each must have depended very much on the ship's company in which his service began. Furthermore, most of those who won through and measured up to the creed undoubtedly had received a good foundation at home.

In a growing and democratic country the navy could not forever be officered from such a restricted class. Any attempt at such restriction would have made it hateful. Every word of John Paul Jones' about the necessity of aristocracy on shipboard is true, but he did not mean gentle birth. That would have been absurd from the gardener's son. The problem was how to give equal opportunity to every boy in the nation, and yet mold every capable beginner into a good officer and a gentleman.

The army had solved the problem as early as 1804 with West Point. In 1845 the navy at last came to the same solution. Why it took so long was probably due to the prejudice that a sailor must be trained only on a ship and never in a college. In that year was founded the Naval Academy at Annapolis—a school that is unique except for its sister institution on the Hudson.

To both come youths from all over the nation and from every sort of parents—and a miracle is performed. Look over the plebes when they first arrive and then, four years later, look at those same boys who have stood the gaff and won their commissions. Their minds have been developed by gruelling study, their bodies by constant exercise and denial of indulgence, their carriage and manners under the merciless eyes not only of their officers but of the upper classmen as well. Hazing at its best teaches the virtues of modesty, unselfishness, consideration for others and tact. Such initiation fits one for command and life in a ward-room.

Less than 16 years after the establishment of the Naval Academy came the horror of 1861. Each man had to determine for himself where lay his allegiance. For Northern men the choice was easy—in fact there was none, for their states remained under the flag.

For Southerners it was terrible. The flag at the peak means more to sailors than to any other class of Americans. They were not lawyers to argue the constitutional rights of states. Their ordeal was coping with the dilemma, "Must we make war on our own homes and families, or shall we desert that flag in its hour of danger and even fire on it—for we cannot skulk?" Small wonder that so many stood by it.

Those who did resign and go with the South did marvels with the small navy they built up in spite of hopeless handicaps. Those who remained in the old service helped to shorten the hideous struggle by the greatest blockade in history, and by the exploits at New Orleans and Mobile and on every river and inlet in the field of war—alas, against their own countrymen and often against classmates, shipmates and even brothers.

McKean Buchanan, whose gallant son was killed in the *Bayou Teche,* was on the *Congress* when his brother Franklin smashed her with the broadsides of the *Merrimac*. After "Buck" was wounded, the command of the *Merrimac* devolved on Catesby Ap Roger Jones, of the famous old navy family of Virginia with the moveable Ap in its name. He had two brothers and a first cousin in the Union army or navy, and three brothers in the Confederate army or navy.

Some people nowadays refuse to call it a civil war! Yet through the bitterness of it all, the former brothers-in-arms, though fighting each other as long as either could fight, treated those who fell into their hands with unfailing kindness, courtesy and even affection—and thereby ran true and added again to the background of the navy.

Eight years after the end of that dreadful time, the wounds scarcely healed, there came to Annapolis from one of the states of the late Confederacy, Tennessee—the native state of Farragut as well—a little boy of 15. He was destined not only to maintain the background but to increase it splendidly and rise to the highest rank in the service. Not in the thunder of embattled fleets or in a sea duel—as no doubt he dreamed and as every Viking would wish—but as the head and heart of an exploit in performance of the "impossible", the like of which for seamanship, daring, ingenuity and perfect planning and execution had never been seen before in naval warfare.

In 1873, however, all that was 44 years below the boy's horizon. What loomed immediately above it with terrifying uncertainty was his entrance examination. He has spoken for himself.

—Waldron Kintzing Post

Appendix II*

Naval Historical Foundation Collection
ALBERT GLEAVES
A Register of His Papers in the Library of Congress

The bulk of the papers of Albert Gleaves (1858-1937), naval officer, author and historian, was deposited in the Library of Congress in 1950 by the Naval Historical Foundation. A second somewhat smaller installment was added in 1955.

Linear feet of shelf space occupied:	10
Approximate number of items:	6,000

Scope and Content

The papers of Albert Gleaves span the years from 1803 to 1946 with the bulk falling in the period from 1877 to 1937 [and] consist mainly of diaries, journals, correspondence, a speech, article and book file, scrapbooks, newspaper clippings and records of the Asiatic Fleet, supplemented by notebooks, photographs and a file of miscellaneous material.

Like all midshipmen of his time, Gleaves was required to maintain a professional journal of his duties and stations aboard ship. Unlike most other officers, however, Gleaves continued this practice all during his career. His personal diaries and journals, covering the years from 1902 to 1936, record his exceedingly varied interests and activities. This unbroken series, when taken as a unit, presents a picture of naval life in particular and the world in general during a half century of peace interrupted by two years of war.

Gleaves was an intensive reader and carried on extensive correspondence about his reading with friends and colleagues in and out of the navy. His four books, published between the years 1904 and 1925, testify to his gift for naval biographical research and historical authorship. In his diaries and journals are marginal annotations showing his reading habits formed during the long passages at sea which were common in the late 19th century and early 20th century navy. Likewise noted

*Excerpted from "Albert Gleaves—A Register of His Papers in the Library of Congress", Washington: Library of Congress, 1968.

are lists of reading material to be included in his personal stores before departing on a cruise or an anticipated tour of duty at an overseas station.

For the ten-year period after graduation from the Naval Academy Gleaves served at sea in both the Atlantic and the Pacific Fleets. The collection contains official and personal correspondence to document this period of his life. For the next decade he alternated between duties afloat and ordnance billets in various naval yards around the country. For the period from 1885 to 1897 there is only minimum documentation. Only a few diaries, a scrapbook and a file of correspondence with John Henry Gibbons cover his service for these years.

The beginning of the Spanish-American War in 1898 found Gleaves in command of the USS *Cushing*, carrying dispatches between Florida and Cuba. His ship was anchored close to the USS *Maine* the night before the latter was blown up in Havana harbor.

After the war and a brief tour of duty as navigator on board the USS *Alabama*, Gleaves commanded the USS *Dolphin* and then the USS *Mayflower*, both of which were used as presidential yachts by Theodore Roosevelt. During these two commands Gleaves won [Roosevelt's] friendship and respect and throughout Gleaves' later career there are occasional exchanges of correspondence between the two men on naval, professional or social matters.

Following the duty in the presidential yachts, Gleaves assumed command of the Naval Torpedo Station where his first reports to the secretary of the navy resulted in a high-level review of torpedo ordnance. After a trip to Europe in 1907 to inspect foreign ordnance installations Gleaves returned home to help persuade the navy department to establish its own facilities for manufacturing torpedoes independent of private or foreign sources. Typically, the details of his investigations in Europe and his part in the establishment of these facilities are incorporated in a small notebook label "Torpedoes, Mines and Nets"; his activities, observations and conclusions are recorded in a 1907 personal narrative-type diary. Ordnance, along with hydrography, captured Gleaves' interest throughout his entire naval career.

After a tour of duty in the office of the assistant secretary of the navy with collateral duty as a member of the General Board, Gleaves was again ordered to sea in 1910. From 1911 to 1914 he was stationed ashore as commander of the Second, then the Third, Naval District.

In 1916 Gleaves was promoted to flag rank and ordered to command the Torpedo Flotilla and later the entire Destroyer Force of the Atlantic Fleet. Material readiness reports from the squadrons, plus orders, dispatches and letters from his flagship, the USS *Birmingham*, bear out the observation that he was largely responsible for preparing the Destroyer Force for combat readiness. His foresight was vindicated when the ships were declared ready for instant convoy duty in 1917. After the convoy system got under way Gleaves was detached from the Destroyer Force and assigned as commander of the Cruiser and Transport Force for the duration of World War I.

The records indicate that he was responsible for the transport of almost one million troops to France, and for their return after the Armistice. The hectic war years and the postwar period are throughly documented by correspondence, diaries and journals, newspaper clippings and innumerable magazine articles in his several scrapbooks. He was promoted to vice admiral in 1918 and, less than one full year later, to admiral. He was showered with honors both at home and abroad for his wartime service, and in September 1919 he was assigned to be the commander of the Asiatic Fleet.

Once on the Asiatic Station Gleaves showed a talent for diplomacy in dealing with the representatives of the Russian, Chinese and Japanese governments. His correspondence shows that he kept the navy department fully and continuously informed of all intelligence activities associated with his command. There is a wealth of information concerning the Japanese Army in Russia after the war, the Communist takeover in Siberia, the evacuation of the Czechoslovakian troops from Russia and the general state of affairs in Russia at the time of revoluationary unrest.

The collection also includes firsthand observations which are notable for their frank, forthright opinions and some remarkable predictions as to the future status of the United States in the Far East based on valuable bits of intelligence gleaned from a wide variety of sources. His habit of exchanging protocol visits with other ranking European naval officers provided another source of information for the navy department. His diaries, typed each day aboard his flagship, contain rich source material on the conditions which eventually led to the epic events some 20 years later.

The period after his retirement from the navy, from 1922 to 1937, is poorly represented in the collection. Subjects of interest, such as naval arms limitation conferences and the air power controversy of the 1920s are given outline treatment.

Included are copies of almost all of his speeches, articles, radio broadcasts, lectures and pamphlets cover[ing] a variety of topics, usually naval, generally delivered or addressed to some civic, patriotic or service group. There is some correspondence concerning his publications, especially the book *James Lawrence.*

Of interest is a large number of typed pages of a manuscript which Gleaves intended to use as a basis for an autobiography includ[ing] a collection of stories, yarns and anecdotes gathered from old-time enlisted retirees. From the sample gathered one regrets that Gleaves did not manage to save more stories for posterity. Gleaves intended these firsthand memoirs and anecdotes for future use in his writings. They form an interesting part of his collected papers.

Almost all of the scrapbooks and newspaper clippings in the collection relate to some aspect of Gleaves' career or to notable incidents in naval history. A file of correspondence concerning his many decorations and awards, letters of congratulation concerning his various promotions to flag rank, a file of biographical material and a short but interesting poetry file round out the collection.

Index

Compiled by Albert Gleaves Cohen

Additional copies of this book may be obtained from your local bookstore or by sending $9.95 plus 75¢ handling and shipping to:
Hope Publishing House
P.O. Box 60008
Pasadena, California 91106